COURTING
DANGER

COURTING DANGER

ALICE MARBLE

WITH DALE LEATHERMAN

ST. MARTIN'S PRESS : NEW YORK

Design by Helene Berinsky

Library of Congress Cataloging-in-Publication Data

Marble, Alice, 1913–1990.
    Courting danger / Alice Marble with Dale Leatherman.
        p.   cm.
    ISBN 0-312-05839-X
    1. Marble, Alice, 1913–1990. 2. Tennis players—United States—
Biography. 3. Women tennis players—United States—Biography.
I. Leatherman, Dale. II. Title.
GV994.M3A3 1991
796.342′092—dc20   90-26945
[B]   CIP

First Edition: June 1991
10 9 8 7 6 5 4 3 2 1

To Jessie Wood Marble

CONTENTS

MY THANKS

To Alice Marble for being such a willing partner in this project and for allowing me to "get inside her skin" so that the story emerged with one voice—that of a great champion and courageous woman. It was a very personal and gratifying experience for me. I deeply regret that her death on December 12, 1990, robbed her of the chance to see her story in print.

To Rita Mae Brown for recommending me to write this book, and for her continuing support as my friend and mentor.

To Laurie Liss, my agent when I began this project, for being the best editor I've ever had. She and her red pen bent me without breaking me, and my work is much the better for it.

To my friends Donnelle Oxley and Sue Slick for making it possible for me to write. They took over the upkeep of my farm and remained faithful to me even when I couldn't come out to play.

To Major Anne Buhls for cheering me on from Saudi Arabia, where she was serving in the U.S. Army.

And to Alicia Byers of the Library of Congress for lighting all those candles for me. God noticed.

Thanks also to the writers whose work helped me to understand the world of tennis in Alice's day: Helen Hull Jacobs's *Gallery of Champions* (A. S. Barnes and Company, Inc. 1949), Ted Tinling's (with Rod Humphries) *Love and Faults: Personalities Who Have Changed the History of Tennis in My Lifetime* (Crown Publishers, 1979), Billie Jean King's *We Have Come a Long Way: The Story of Women's Tennis* (McGraw-Hill Book Company, 1988), and Larry Englemann's *The Goddess and the American Girl* (Oxford University Press, 1988).

—Dale Leatherman

PROLOGUE

When I won Wimbledon in 1939 and became world champion, it was the fulfillment of my lifelong dream, yet the moment was bittersweet. I knew I'd probably never play at the All England Tennis Club again. There might not even be an All England Tennis Club—or even a London. The world was preparing for war, and international tennis was about to go on hold.

If I hadn't been a tennis champion, I would have been a bystander throughout that terrible war, and never would have had a chance to strike back at those who took what was most precious to me. Tennis gave me the opportunity to serve my country, but it did not prepare me for what I was asked to do—be a spy.

Fifty years ago, the United States was a beginner in the spy business. That's hard to believe now, when the high-tech espionage we see on television is not far from the reality practiced by our agents in the dark corners of the world. But back then there was no CIA, no real intelligence service except small corps initiated by various branches of the armed forces.

Then World War II began, and it was obvious that discovering Germany's secrets could save thousands of lives and perhaps mean the difference between victory and the hideous alternative. The country needed spies, fast. From the ranks of those not already in uniform came a motley but brave bunch, most of whom went undercover with altered identities. Others who were public figures used their celebrity status to travel freely abroad and circulate under the very noses of the Nazis as artists, musicians, actors, and wealthy dilettantes. After all, who would suspect Cary Grant of being a spy? Or a tennis star named Alice Marble?

When I agreed to use tennis as a cover for an assignment that had little chance of succeeding, I felt I had nothing left to lose but my life, and at the time I didn't care about living. A few months later, on a dark mountain road, I found that I *did* care. When my life was in danger I did what I've always done; I fought. My mother didn't raise a quitter—my life story is proof of that!

Sometimes I wake with the memory of that night, and it's as if the years have lifted like a raised curtain. I'm in the car again, reaching for my gun. . . .

I had a gun I would use if I had to. Pushing the thought from my mind, I tried to concentrate on driving. It would be a miracle if I didn't die at my own hand. I had survived so many terrible auto accidents, my luck was probably all used up. God, how I hated being behind the wheel of a car! But it was my only chance.

I threw the car through turn after turn, one foot on the gas, the other on the brake. When the road straightened, I floored the gas, feeling the powerful surge of the stolen Mercedes. But the other car was still behind me, and I could feel myself perspiring despite the coolness of the night. My palms were wet on the steering wheel, and there was a cold trickle between my shoulder blades. I shivered, fighting off terror. Giving in to panic would only send me over the edge to certain death. Better the devil I *didn't* know, in the car behind me, than the one I did.

The mirrored headlights were blinding now, and I squinted to see the road ahead. My pursuer closed the gap, then moved into the other lane. My heart pounded faster. What would he do? Shoot me? Force me over the side of the mountain? I steeled myself against whatever was to come and pressed on the accelerator. The other car came alongside, and we rocketed in deadly tandem through another turn and into a brief straightaway.

Like a cornered animal facing its executioner, I turned to see who was in the car alongside.

—ALICE MARBLE

ALICE MARBLE'S
PERFORMANCE RECORD

National singles champion at Forest Hills (U.S. Open)—1936, 1938, 1939, 1940

National doubles champion (U.S. Open)—1936, 1938, 1939, 1940

National mixed doubles champion (U.S. Open)—1936, 1938, 1939, 1940

National clay court singles champion—1940

National clay court doubles champion—1940

World (Wimbledon) singles champion—1939

World (Wimbledon) doubles champion—1938, 1939

World (Wimbledon) mixed doubles champion—1937, 1938, 1939

United States Tennis Association Rankings
  No. 1—1936 through 1940
  No. 3—1933
  No. 7—1932

Wightman Cup team—1933, 1937, 1938, 1939

Woman Athlete of the Year—1939, 1940

Tennis Hall of Fame inductee—1964

International Sportsman Hall of Fame inductee—1967

1 : HARD LESSONS

I look back on my life and see a mosaic. From a distance, it's a striking picture—of becoming the best tennis player in the world; of being a part of the glamorous world of movie stars and the fabulously wealthy; of love and death; of victory and defeat; and of adventure and danger.

Up close, I can see the pieces, how people and events contributed to my life until it was whole and rich and colorful. I've lived many lives in my lifetime, and had so many scrapes with death a cat would envy my survival. The pieces of the mosaic are memories now, and as vivid to me as the day they happened.

I became friends with Clark Gable when I was twenty-three, and it would have been easy to like him even if he hadn't been handsome and fun and a famous movie star, because he reminded me of my father. Like my father, Clark had been a lumberjack in the Sierras of northern California before he started acting, a job he was more proud of than playing Rhett Butler, or being the idol of every female over eleven.

Harry Marble was proud too; handsome, rugged and so *alive*. I was only seven when he died, too young to understand the irony of his being injured in a car accident and later dying of pneumonia, when he'd topped two-hundred-foot trees every day and had never gotten hurt. He died on Christmas Eve, and the holiday ever after held bad memories for me.

I was old enough to know our lives had changed, and to feel the pinch of being poor. It was 1920. We had recently moved from the Sierra town of Beckwith to San Francisco, and my mother Jessie

1

was left with five children: Dan, thirteen; George, eleven; Hazel, ten; Tim, four; and me. Dan and George soon quit school to work six days a week laying hardwood floors.

I was glad I was too young to quit school and work. Once I learned to read, I discovered that I remembered everything I read, almost word for word. One of my teachers accused me of cheating, a humiliating incident because my family set great store by honesty, but I redeemed myself by reciting a textbook page verbatim. I was gifted with a photographic memory, the teacher said, and very, very lucky. I supposed she was right; I didn't have to study as hard as my classmates. But I was too young to imagine just how important this gift would be later in my life.

Uncle Woodie came to live with us, helping to support the family with his earnings as a cable-car brakeman; he became one of the first great influences in my life. A former semipro baseball player, he taught me how to play and took me to see the local professional team, the San Francisco Seals. I soon shared his passion for the sport. Uncle Woodie was also there for me at one of the most devastating moments in my life.

San Francisco was one big playground for a kid from the backwoods. My first pair of roller skates became my automobile, my locomotive, my sailing ship; I wheeled away on a new adventure with my friend Billy at every opportunity. One summer afternoon, darkness was almost upon us while we were still far from home.

"C'mon, I'll race you," I yelled to Billy. He nodded, and we spun away, our skates clattering across the pavement cracks. We reached a wide street and dashed into it without looking. We were on familiar turf now; I could see the hardware and candy stores. I would be on time for dinner.

I had just skipped over the streetcar tracks when I heard the car's warning bell, the screech of locked brakes on the metal tracks, and the startled cries of passengers thrown from their seats. Looking back, I saw Billy stumble on the tracks and fall screaming under the trolley's wheels. I will take that memory to my grave.

The news flew through the neighborhood, and Uncle Woodie came running, gasping for breath by the time he reached me. When he picked me up, I clutched at his shirt with its familiar smell of pipe tobacco and took a quick look back. A blood-soaked coat was draped over Billy's mangled body, and his mother's screams could be heard over the approaching sirens. I closed my eyes. Uncle Woodie carried me home, took off my skates, and tucked me under a blanket on the sofa.

It was months before I skated again, and I never attended another funeral after Billy's. I'd seen my father and my best friend put into the ground in less than a year.

At thirteen, baseball became the center of my universe. Every summer day, I was at Recreation Park, watching the Seals play. Joe DiMaggio, Lefty Gomez, Lefty O'Doul, Frank Corsetti and Smead Jolly all played for the Seals; most of them went to the Yankees later. Admission cost a dime, but I was resourceful and determined. I could earn a dollar a day stocking shelves for the grocer, and I could always win money pitching pennies.

My ten-year-old brother Tim and I went early with our gloves and a ball so we could play catch in the bleachers before the game. In the stadium atmosphere, we could pretend we were big-league players. We were doing just that one day when a player walked over to the fence.

"Say, boy," he called, "how'd you like to climb down and play with me?"

I glanced at Tim, then realized he was talking to me! My hair was cut short, and my skirt was obscured by the fence.

"I'm not a boy, but I'll play with you."

Before he could change his mind, I scaled the fence, ran onto the field, and began to play catch with him. How lucky could I be! The field was filling with players, and I kept expecting someone to tell me to leave. Instead, my hero, Lefty O'Doul, asked me to shag flies for him. Joe DiMaggio, beside me in center field, yelled encouragement.

When DiMaggio went in for batting practice, O'Doul joined me in the outfield, and kids began calling from the stands: "Hey Alice! Ask Lefty to throw us a ball!" O'Doul gave me a handful of balls, which I pitched into the stands, careful to throw them to my friends.

It was almost game time. I started toward the gate, but O'Doul stopped me. "Come on," he said, and led me to the dugout. We stepped down into the dark shade of the overhang, and O'Doul said, "Hey fellas, this is Alice . . . ?"

"Marble," I said, out of breath. All my idols were there! I didn't notice the reporter leaning against the dugout wall, jotting down notes.

"Alice Marble, a girl who's got a better arm than most of you jokers!" The players' laughter was loud and friendly. "Let's recruit her," called the catcher, and before the afternoon was over I was the official mascot of the Seals, with the privilege of warming up with the team every time they played.

The reporter from the San Francisco *Examiner* came to our house; in the next morning's paper was a picture of me winding up

3

to pitch and a write-up calling me the "Little Queen of Swat," saying I "performed like a veteran" and was "truly remarkable for a girl of thirteen." I carried the clipping in my pocket until it was barely legible. It was my first taste of fame.

As the mascot of the Seals, I was on the field when Babe Ruth himself came to San Francisco on his way to the Orient. There was to be a contest—about twenty women were to pitch for distance —with the Babe judging. When one of the contestants didn't show up, the promoter told me to take her place. Grabbing my glove, I ran out to center field, where the baseball great stood.

Ruth watched me warm up, then called me over. "Kid," he said (he could never remember names, so he called everybody kid), "throw it high."

I looked at him, puzzled. I had been taught to throw from center field so the ball would hit the pitcher's mound and be caught on the bounce by the catcher.

"Throw it high," Ruth repeated. "You get more distance."

When my turn came, I threw the ball into the stands behind home plate and won the competition.

Twenty-five years later, I was snowbound overnight on a New York train headed for Chicago with another Babe, my friend Babe Didrikson Zaharias.

"You know," she said to me, amusement dancing in her eyes, "I never told you, but I was one of the women you beat in that pitching contest in San Francisco. Boy, we felt like fools. Beaten by a thirteen-year-old!"

I told her about my tip from Ruth; we laughed together. We argued the merits of her favorite player, Ted Williams, and mine, Joe DiMaggio. Then Babe pulled a harmonica from her handbag and entertained our fellow passengers until long after midnight. Everyone loved Babe, and she could do anything. If she had taken up tennis earlier in her career, the history of the sport might have been different. With her remarkable athleticism and strength, she could have been the greatest tennis player of her time, perhaps all time. I wouldn't have wanted to face her in her prime.

There were very few women athletes like Babe to serve as role models when I was growing up, but I set my sights on being a professional baseball player nevertheless. If I was good enough, the sex barrier would fall.

During my first year in high school I grew seven inches, gained forty-five pounds, and became painfully self-conscious. At five foot seven and 150 pounds, I was built like a fireplug; only when I was playing sports did I feel confident. I lettered in softball, basketball, and track, and I was still mascot of the Seals.

My brother Dan, despite the demands on him as head of the family, was creating a brilliant sports record for me to emulate. At nineteen the best handball player in Northern California, he had earned shelves full of gleaming trophies. He also had a temper so violent that he often banged his head or rammed his fist through handball-court walls. His emotions caused him to lose matches he should have won, but he never managed to control them. I saw all of his matches and frequently imitated his fits of temper in my own sports. Dan was my idol.

I suppose it was my devotion Dan was counting on when he handed me a tennis racquet. "Allie, I bought this for you. You've got to stop being such a tomboy. Go out and play tennis."

I stared at him. "What will the Seals say? And the boys at school? I won't play that sissy game!"

He sighed and put his hands on my shoulders. "You can't keep hanging around the ballpark, and hitting balls through people's windows, and . . . and acting like a boy."

I shook off his hands contemptuously and started to argue, but he cut me off. "You can start tomorrow after school at the park."

I cried myself to sleep that night, beginning afresh each time I thought of how the Seals fans cheered when I was introduced with the team. My life was over, and my brother was the cruelest man on earth.

The day began even worse than I had imagined. "Marble's play-ing ten-nis, Marble's playing ten-nis," the boys teased when they saw me with the racquet. Humiliated, I stuffed it in my locker. After school, I walked to Golden Gate Park with Mary, the only girl I knew who played tennis. She couldn't play baseball or basketball, though, and I assumed I could beat her at her own game. It looked simple enough.

Mary taught me how to score and where to stand to serve, and we played until it was too dark to see the ball. I lost every game. In spite of myself, I was captivated. I loved the sound of the ball striking my racquet, and wanted very badly to be able to control where it went when I hit it.

I strolled home, hefting the racquet, twirling it, enjoying the feel of it in my hands. Before the week was out, I was hooked. Dan was delighted.

From the very beginning, I had a powerful serve, a natural pro-gression from the baseball pitch I had been working on since I was seven. Serve and volley quickly became my style. I could rely on my keen hand-eye coordination and quickness of foot to get a racquet on anything that came over the net.

My ground strokes were terrible. I tried to imitate other players, particularly "Little Bill" Johnston, California's champion, but there was a lot of the baseball slugger in my game. Nobody criticized me, because I was winning. I played hard, aggressively, yet with the joyous abandon of a child enjoying a game.

On Friday nights I washed and pressed the only tennis outfit I owned—a long white pleated skirt and a middy blouse—for the Saturday tournaments at Golden Gate Park. At six in the morning I was up, dressing for the mile-long walk from our house on Twelfth Avenue in the Sunset district to the park. Matches began at nine, but first the courts had to be dried. Along with the other players, I dragged old blankets across the asphalt surface to absorb the moisture.

There was such demand for the courts that I would play a set, then volley over a park bench, waiting for another turn on a court. It was a maddening process, but I did whatever I had to do to play.

I was at Golden Gate Park every day after school, and the entire weekend. It was a huge, delightful place, always astir with friendly people. I loved everything about the park: its baseball diamonds, bowling greens, handball courts, horseshoe pits, bridle paths, bright flower beds, museum, and the bandshell where my mother attended concerts. Near the tennis courts were a hot-dog stand, a carousel, and a smelly buffalo you could ride, two kids for a nickel.

When we had a few extra pennies, we played the games in the park's amusement center, throwing balls and bricks at milk bottles. My brothers taught me how to drive a long nail in three strokes. I won countless dolls and stuffed bears from the owner of that concession before he put out a closed sign whenever he saw me coming.

The park was my favorite place. I never dreamed that I could come to harm there.

One evening after school, the sun had faded to a red glow when I said good-bye to my friends and started home. The Stanyan Street entrance was in shadow, and the light from the street lamp failed to penetrate the darkness under the trees. In that darkness, someone was waiting for me. Suddenly strong arms grabbed me from behind, and a hand clamped over my mouth. I tried with all my strength to pull away, but I couldn't. I was being dragged deeper into the darkness.

Someone was playing a trick, but it wasn't very funny. I kicked back at his legs and tried to bite the fingers across my mouth. I tasted my own blood; my lip had split from the pressure of his grip.

He threw me to the ground and pinned me there, on my back. In the darkness, I could see nothing, but I could hear his ragged breathing and feel his hands on me. When I tried to scream, he slapped me, then stuffed a handkerchief in my mouth. Breathing through my nose was made more difficult by the warm flow of blood from both nostrils. He had slapped me hard. I was scared as I had never been before.

The fabric of my blouse ripped, and I felt his rough hands on my breasts. Holding me down with one hand on my throat and the weight of his body on my legs, he grabbed my skirt, pulling it up above my waist. In a panic, I tore at his arm, but he increased the pressure until I could barely breathe. I was groggy, on the edge of consciousness.

With his free hand, he grasped my underpants, jerked at them until they tore free, and spread my legs wide, kneeling between them. For a moment he fumbled with his belt and zipper. Roughly he shoved himself inside me, grunting like an animal, every thrust carrying him deeper. Pain shot through me, and screams rose in my throat, only to be blocked by his savage hold on my windpipe and the filthy cloth in my mouth. I thought I was going to die, and almost wished it, to stop the pain. Mercifully, I fainted.

When I opened my eyes, the woods were quiet except for the sound of sobbing, my own sobbing. The pain hit me when I pushed myself to a sitting position—pain so violent that I immediately turned my head and vomited.

Grabbing the trunk of a tree, I pulled myself to my feet and stood swaying, doubled over in agony, feeling the blood running down my legs. I staggered toward the house near the park entrance where my mother's sister Josephine lived.

At my knock, she opened the door and paled. Putting her arm around me, she helped me inside, calling to her maid to boil water and bring towels. Aunt Josephine spoke softly, distracting me from what she was doing while she cleaned me up.

She gathered my stained clothes and left the room. I could hear her on the phone, telling my mother I had the flu and could stay with her a few days to prevent the other children from catching it.

Her next call was to a doctor she knew well. He came immediately. Gently, he examined me, then asked, "Alice, do you know the person who raped you?" I shook my head.

"Can you describe him?" I shook my head again and he sighed.

"I'm going to give you a couple of shots and stitch you up. It's almost over now."

I closed my eyes, wanting it to be over, wanting to wake from the nightmare, but I knew it would never be over. I was fifteen, and I had been raped. Aunt Josephine and I agreed to keep the incident a secret from my mother; three days later I went back to school with a story of how I'd gotten the bruises on my face and throat falling down the steps.

The physical pain abated, but the psychological hurt was just beginning. What had been done to me was so intimate, so humiliating. I knew that virginity was something special, something you saved for the person you fell in love with. Mine had been stolen, and it made me angry, deeply angry, with the kind of helpless rage that comes when you want revenge and know it's impossible.

I was also ashamed. If I had lost my virginity in the backseat of a car with some young stud, I might have still felt that way, but at least it would have been my choice. I didn't mind being accountable for my own actions, but now I was to be accountable my whole life for what someone else did *to* me, not *with* me.

I walked the halls at school, certain that "it" showed, that people somehow knew. Was the guy who raped me one of those faces in the hall? Had he told his buddies about his "good time"? Were they all snickering about me, and telling my girlfriends I was a tramp? I was mortified, and repulsed by the very idea of sex.

Rape at any time in one's life is traumatic, but if I had had a loving sexual relationship before it, at least I would have known it could be that way, rather than the hideous thing that happened to me.

Aunt Jo encouraged me to forget the incident, to put this terrible thing behind me. Perhaps if I had talked about my feelings, like rape victims today who seek counseling, my life would have been very different. I never hated men in general, just the bastard who raped me, but it was ten years before I could bring myself to have a physical relationship.

The rape affected my life in a positive way, too; it made me tough, and made me turn all the more to tennis to counteract my low self-esteem. I didn't care so much about winning, just the good feeling that came from playing the game well. Later, tennis became a substitute for sex (though a poor one), the physical activity giving a measure of release.

*   *   *

8

Ignoring my progress in tennis those first two years would have been like turning one's back on a summer brushfire. I wasn't much to look at—a chubby teenager with acne, nice blue eyes, and blond hair pushed carelessly behind my ears—but I was beating players with much more experience, and the West Coast tennis world began to notice.

2 : EASTERN DEBUT

One spring evening, "Little Bill" Johnston, who had battled "Big Bill" Tilden for so many years, came to see me. Meeting him was such a thrill I could scarcely concentrate on what he had to say.

The Northern California Tennis Association wanted me to be its representative in the Northwest and Canadian championships, a tour of two and a half months. The association would contribute seventy-five dollars toward my expenses.

Seventy-five dollars sounded like a lot, but one look at Dan's face told me it wasn't enough. After Johnson left, he said, "It's just not possible. We can't afford it. You'll need new clothes and more travel money. Next year, Allie."

Next year! I devoted all my free time in the next few weeks to odd jobs and sold my glove and bat, but managed to raise only twenty dollars. Even if I managed to earn another ten dollars before the time we had to accept or reject the association's offer, it wasn't enough. When I was about to give up, three twenty-dollar bills arrived by mail in a plain envelope addressed to me. I looked at Dan, but he was as puzzled as I was.

My mother broke the silence. "Alice, the Lord is good to you. Now you can have your trip."

We never discovered who my benefactor was. I left on tour with thirty dollars' worth of new clothes, two new Kro Bat racquets donated by Spalding, and $97.50.

After rain delayed play for three days at Vancouver, we were scheduled for two or three matches a day. It was my first experience on clay courts, and sliding about in my new shoes quickly drew blisters on my heels. After several days, my heels were so

10

badly infected that a doctor advised me it was unsafe to continue playing.

I couldn't quit. Instead, with the heels cut out of my shoes and rubber bands holding them on my feet, I won my first tournament on foreign turf. I returned from the tour loaded with trophies, and with $6.37, which I immediately returned to the tennis association.

The following summer, I was Northern California's junior champion, and made my first trip to the Eastern tournaments. It had been only three years since Dan put that first racquet in my hands, but I was going to play in the under-eighteen championships in Philadelphia and in the national championships at Forest Hills, where greats like Molla Mallory, Suzanne Lenglen and Mary K. Browne had played!

I was lucky to be going at all, considering the strain that my clothing and incidentals put on the family budget. The tennis association paid for transportation and accommodations, but the rest was up to me—or Dan, who worked overtime to make it possible.

I traveled by train all the way to New York's Grand Central Station, got my bags, and walked through the tunnel to the Roosevelt Hotel. At the busy hotel desk, I signed the register, feeling at once very grown-up and very lonely. I was to share a room with Bonnie Miller and her mother, but they hadn't arrived. Bonnie, junior champion of Los Angeles, was my doubles partner for the tournaments ahead.

I felt out of place in the high-ceilinged, fancy suite where the bellhop placed my bag. I had tipped him a dime, as my mother instructed, but he smiled and handed it back to me, wishing me luck on the courts. From the window I looked down at the human beehive on the street below. And I thought San Francisco was a busy place!

The next day Bonnie and I moved to an inn at Forest Hills close enough for us to practice on the grass courts of the famous West Side Tennis Club, where all the national championships had been held since 1921.

The stadium ringed a large patch of green where three courts were marked off each day for the championship matches. Behind the stadium, clay courts fanned out like a giant collar of rust.

The moneyed atmosphere of the old club made me feel shabby, though my clothes were new and of good quality. I just didn't feel comfortable among the rich patrons and their offspring. They all spoke in boarding-school drawls, as if their teeth were wired together. I was glad when we left to play in our first grass-court tournament at Seabright, New Jersey.

11

My relief evaporated minutes into my first match, with Mrs. Agnes Lamme. I had walked onto the court as I always did, cocky and more excited than nervous. Having practiced only with Bonnie, I had no idea what the Eastern players were like, but I was sure I could handle them.

My first serve was good but bounced high, and my opponent met it squarely. I watched the ball leave her racquet, moved into forehand position, swung my racquet, and missed the ball by several inches. Mortified, I looked over my shoulder at the ball. Trying to block out the titters of the crowd, I served again, and again the ball came back to me, solidly hit, but manageable. I was ready, my racquet in full backswing. The ball bounced and flew at me, inches above the ground. I nearly went down on my knees to hit it, and, before I could recover, my opponent put it away.

The difference between grass and the hard asphalt courts of home was now brutally clear. I hardly felt I was playing the same game! If only the green grass would part, right down the chalk center line, and the earth swallow me. There was no other way to avoid humiliation.

Bonnie and I had practiced on grass, but we both had the same weaknesses, mostly because of our Western grip. My serve and forehand carried so much topspin, the ball bounced high, giving my opponent an easy shot.

I had never heard of Mrs. Lamme, but I quickly learned that she knew her surface. The match was over quickly—6–1, 6–0— but every minute seemed like an eternity. The only points I made were off my volleys. I felt such a fool it was hard to hold my head up leaving the court. I was the junior champion of Northern California, yet I had been made to look like a beginner.

It didn't get any better. I lost in the first rounds of tournaments leading up to the nationals at Forest Hills, and when the draw was posted for the nationals, my name wasn't on it. I was horrified. I had come all this way to play!

My application had apparently been lost in the mail. Under pressure from my California sponsors, the U.S. Lawn Tennis Association's executive committee called a special meeting and decided, for the first time in history, to make up a completely new draw.

The publicity over the whole mess, coupled with my poor showing so far, was debilitating. I had played my first opponent many times before on asphalt, and had never lost to her, but she polished me off in less than half an hour on the Forest Hills courts.

Of that match a New York *Sun* reporter wrote:

The little matter of a lost letter between California and New York caused more trouble for the USLTA than all the other 63 entries put together, and after watching Miss Marble, husky player from San Francisco, lose to Mary Greef Harris, this writer feels that the trouble caused by Alice Marble was for naught. We hear about so many "coming champions" from California that we are beginning to cry "Wolf, wolf."

After the match, I stayed in the locker room until my desire to watch the other matches became stronger than my shame. I found a seat in the stands far from the other players and sat, chin in hands, watching the action on court.

When a stocky, dark-haired woman took the seat beside me, I paid no attention until she spoke. "I can understand your disappointment, but you have a whole lifetime of tennis before you. I'm from California, too, and I lost in the first round three years in a row."

I looked at her, curious. She smiled. "You have worlds of natural ability but no strokes or strategy. Watch all the tennis you can and figure out what you need to learn."

With that she was gone. I hadn't a clue who she was, but she knew tennis if she'd made it to Forest Hills three times, and her interest was a balm to my pride. Later, I pointed her out to Bonnie.

"Alice! That's Mary K. Browne!"

"Mary K. Browne?" I stared at the woman who had been three times national champion before I was born. When we met again, I was a different person, listening reverently to everything she said. If a champion like her was interested in me, maybe there was hope.

I was a different person, too, when I stepped onto the court before the huge veranda of the Philadelphia Cricket Club. It was the first round of the National Junior Championships and my old confidence was back. Grass be damned. I couldn't go back to the family a loser.

For a while, it looked as if I would beat the odds. I made it to the final round of the singles by capitalizing on my net game. But in the final, before a capacity crowd on the shaded veranda, I was sorely outplayed by Ruby Bishop, winning only five games in two sets. I had beaten Ruby before, in California. The disappointment was too much for me. I shook hands, then ran from the court before anyone could see my tears.

I was sitting with my face buried in my hands when Mrs. Harrison Smith, the tournament chairwoman, entered the locker room with my runner-up medal.

"I don't want the damn thing." I took it from her and hurled it across the room.

"Alice, you have to learn to lose, too, difficult as it is," Mrs. Smith said, sitting down beside me. "One day you may be playing on center court at Wimbledon. You'll notice above the entrance the words of Kipling: 'If you can meet with Triumph and Disaster/And treat those two impostors just the same.' Try to remember that. Meanwhile, you have a doubles match with Bonnie in ten minutes. Better get changed."

I was still sulking when the doubles match started, and we handed our opponents the first set before I realized I was taking my anger out on Bonnie instead of the other team.

I caught my partner's eye. "Let's get 'em."

"You're on, Allie!" Her voice was full of relief. She smacked me on the behind with her racquet and trotted to our backline.

In that wonderful way spectators sometimes have of sensing a turn of events and then helping it along, the crowd began to cheer for the California underdogs, forgiving my bad behavior in the first set. They were rewarded with two hard-fought sets of good tennis, and Bonnie and I took the championship.

I found our opponents gracious in defeat. I needed to learn that skill, just as much as I needed ground strokes for grass. I hadn't won the trophy I wanted most, but I felt good about our doubles win, and I had learned some tough lessons.

The train ride back to the West Coast gave me plenty of time to think. By the time I arrived in San Francisco, I could reply with ease when questioned about my singles match in Philadelphia. "Ruby played too well for me. My game's okay on California's hard courts, but I need a coach who can teach me to play on grass."

I didn't say that I had a specific coach in mind. I wanted the best—Ruby Bishop's coach, Eleanor Tennant.

3 : TEACH TENNANT

The following year, I won the state singles title again, and again went east to the nationals. I arrived at Forest Hills two weeks early, threw myself into practice, and watched other players with their coaches, looking for things to incorporate into my game. I felt like a pauper grabbing crumbs from a rich man's table, and deeply resented the fact that I couldn't afford a coach.

My first singles opponent was the tournament's number five seed, Sarah Palfrey of Boston. Sarah was only a year older than I, but had had seven seasons in major tournaments on grass. When I upset her, I was almost as stunned as she was.

The last ball hadn't stopped bouncing when the flashbulbs began. I was news again—the "unknown" who had beaten the seeded player. I was so excited I wired Mother and Dan from the clubhouse and, the next morning, reveled in the headlines: "ALICE MARBLE UPSETS SARAH PALFREY IN BRILLIANT MATCH," and "FUTURE CHAMPION IN ALICE MARBLE." It was all so delightful—and short-lived.

In my next match, I won the first set against Englishwoman Joan Ridley, and was leading four games to one in the second when I served a ball that hit the white chalk line for an ace. One more point and I would lead 5–1. Victory was so close. One more game for the match.

Joan walked to the umpire's stand. "Sir, the linesman's view was blocked. That ball was out."

"The call stands, Miss Ridley." The umpire waved her back to her place on the court. She obeyed, but stood for several minutes, talking to herself and wiping her face. I bounced on the balls of my feet, tense, waiting. The crowd began to complain, and, by the time Joan decided to play, my concentration was gone. Before I knew

15

it, I had lost the set, and then the match. I held my temper, knowing I'd been outsmarted, not outplayed.

Marjorie "Midge" Morrill, a tall, likeable Bostonian, helped me get revenge that same afternoon in the doubles semifinals against Joan and her English partner, Elsie Pittman.

It was late, and normally the fans would have begun to trickle out of the stands, but they stayed, caught up in the fury of our match. For two and a half hours we played, straining to see balls in the lengthening shadows, fighting for every point.

The next day, Fred Hawthorne wrote in the New York *Herald-Tribune*:

> The most stirring play of the tournament was seen late last night, when the sun had set behind the top rim of the lofty stadium bowl, in a doubles match between Miss Morrill and Miss Marble and Mrs. Pittman and Miss Ridley. Consummate masters of the doubles game, the English pair were regarded as pretty sure to come through the match. But largely through the sheer speed and crushing power of the blonde and stalwart California girl, Alice Marble, well backed by Miss Morrill, the English pair were turned back. The Californian's service was a deadly weapon of attack and many times Miss Ridley was not even able to get her racquet on the ball. At times, in the manner in which she leaped clear off the ground to bring down a high lob, Miss Marble brought back to mind that famous master of the smash, Maurice McLoughlin.

Hawthorne's column was widely read, and the succeeding days brought me countless compliments from players, officials, and spectators. Forest Hills seemed a friendlier place, and I knew that, poor or not, I belonged there. I was good enough, and I knew I could be better.

Midge and I were defeated in the final by a better pair—Sarah Palfrey and Helen Jacobs. Helen was national champion that year, and both she and Sarah would be tough opponents throughout my career.

I left Forest Hills very proud of my runner-up doubles trophy, and went straight to Los Angeles for the Pacific Southwest Tournament, which was attended by the movie stars en masse. Some of my favorites were in the stands—Loretta Young, Errol Flynn, Marlene Dietrich, Charlie Chaplin, Bette Davis, Myrna Loy, Norma Shearer, Kay Francis, Claudette Colbert, Robert Taylor, Robert Montgomery . . .

Montgomery introduced my match with a charming speech.

God, he was handsome! They were all handsome. I had never seen so many beautiful people in my life. It's a wonder that I managed to play tennis at all, but I did, defeating Mrs. Florence Harper, 6–4, 7–5, for the trophy.

There was a social afterward, and I met most of the stars, but I was too shy to carry on lengthy conversations with people I had idolized all my life.

I left Los Angeles for San Francisco as the state's number one player and seventh in the nation, but I knew I had gone as far as I could on my own. Back home, I talked to Dan, who had been urging me to quit tennis and enter the University of California. I'd already passed the entrance exams, but I decided to postpone my education and get a job so that I could pay for lessons with Eleanor Tennant. More than anything, I wanted to study under her.

Before I had a chance to contact her, she came to me. A slim woman of about thirty-five, my height, with graying hair and a generous smile, she seemed to fill up the living room of our little house. She was witty and charming, her strong voice with its slight British accent conveying an easy confidence.

I could see that my mother and Dan both liked her, but they were reluctant to say yes to the sweeping plan she proposed—that I spend a month with her several times a year, earning my lessons by helping her with her other students and doing her secretarial work. Teach, as Eleanor Tennant would be nicknamed, taught at the posh Bishop School in La Jolla and at the Beverly Hills Hotel.

She had even found me a job in San Francisco as a forty-dollar-a-month typist and file clerk at Wilson Sporting Goods, the company that made her signature racquets. My schedule would leave the late-afternoon hours free for practice, and included a liberal leave policy for my visits to Teach in Los Angeles.

Everything I wanted was suddenly within my reach—everything I had dreamed about, everything I had worked for. With a coach like Teach, there was no telling what I could do. I looked at Dan and Mother. They had to say yes.

Dan's voice was gruff, but I knew he was happy for me. "If you're going to play tennis, you might as well be the best tennis player you can be. Miss Tennant, you won't be sorry you gave Alice this chance."

I went with Teach that evening to a party across the bay. Teach's friends had a lovely estate, and a string quartet was playing in one corner of the large living room. My mother would have loved the music, but Teach was indifferent to it. It was a party, and she obviously loved parties. She was immediately the center of attention,

17

and I later learned this was true whether she was with movie stars or millionaires or servants. Everybody loved Teach. She could tell stories—clean or raunchy, depending on the company—for as long as she had an audience.

I sat on the fringe of the group and watched her. "My coach": I savored the words. My whole life had changed the moment she walked into our house. I studied her, wanting to know everything about her.

When she stopped her car on the street below my house, I asked her, "How did you get started in tennis?"

She laughed. I didn't know how rarely she talked about her personal life. "I've never been shy about going after what I want," she began.

She was born in 1895 in San Francisco to English parents. At the age of eleven she stole a tennis racquet from a house guest. She was mystified as to what to do with the thing until she happened to see a woman carrying a racquet. She followed her. When the woman boarded a horse-drawn bus, Teach, incredible as it may sound, ran alongside the bus until her quarry got off at Golden Gate Park.

The racquet bearer turned out to be Mrs. Golda Meyer Gross, one of the Pacific Coast's top women players at that time. After watching Mrs. Gross play, Teach was convinced that she could do just as well. And so she began as I did, playing on the public courts with anyone she could, picking up pointers from better players.

Teach did all sorts of jobs to support her tennis habit. At a time when few women could drive a car, she learned so that she could become the Standard Oil Company's first female traveling sales representative.

Former national champion Maurice McLoughlin saw Teach play and urged her to leave Standard Oil for the position of hostess and tennis coach at the Beverly Hills Hotel. It was a giant step forward for Teach. Her quick wit and wonderful way of relating to people soon made her a favorite of the stars she taught. Douglas Fairbanks, Sr., Enid Storey, Norma Talmadge, and young Marion Davies soon were inviting their coach to give them lessons on their home courts, as much for the entertainment she provided as to improve their games.

After two years, Teach convinced the tennis association that her coaching had been done as an amateur. (How she accomplished this, no one knows, but the maneuver was typical of Teach.) She began competing in amateur tournaments, and in 1920 was ranked third in the country behind Molla Mallory and Marion Zinderstein—a very close third. In the last women's National Championship held in Philadelphia before the competition moved to Forest Hills, Teach forced Mallory to three sets in what many thought was the best match of the tournament.

"I was at the peak of my career when I fell in love and got married," Teach said quietly. In the dim light of the gas street lamp, I could see her jaw tighten. She stopped.

I found out later that Teach discovered her husband was unfaithful, and left him for a brief relationship with "Madame Helene," a well-known lesbian of the time. Long on memory and short on forgiveness, Teach never had another man in her life. She divorced him, and continued to teach tennis.

When the "talking movies" came out, Teach had added the new stars to her retinue—Carole Lombard, Joan Crawford, Clifton Webb, and Jean Harlow—and her reputation grew. She sailed through the Great Depression without a hitch in her career.

I said good night to Teach and fairly floated up the stairs to my house, amazed that such a person was interested in teaching me. Within a month, she summoned me to La Jolla.

I could feel my heart hammering when the taxi from the bus station dropped me in front of the small apartment Teach shared with her sister, Gwen. Teach opened the door at my knock. "Alice! Come on in."

I put down my bag, draped my coat over the back of a nearby chair, and started to speak.

"Hang it up," Teach said, pointing to the closet. "You'll have to do it eventually."

Her tone was pleasant enough, but firm. It was my first lesson in discipline—and discipline, I soon learned, was everything with Teach. Everything in her house had its place; she herself was always immaculate, with her hair stylishly cut, her nails perfect. She had wonderful taste in clothes and looked beautifully groomed even in tennis clothes.

Teach's instruction didn't end on the tennis court. I dressed as she told me; I even learned to hold my fork in my left hand in the English manner, as she did. I wasn't allowed to cook or drive or make decisions. She convinced me I was good at nothing *but* tennis, and I focused entirely on my sport, just as she intended.

Ours was a strange relationship. I've heard it said that Teach was a "second mother" to me, but that was far from the truth. She treated me like a child, but without the warmth of a mother. It was difficult for her to show affection, and I understood why when Gwen told me of their childhood. Their parents had a disagreement, about

19

what no one ever knew, and though they continued to live together, they did not speak to each other for *fifteen years*. They communicated, when they had to, through the children. There were six of them, but I only knew Teach's brother, Litton, who later committed suicide, and Gwen, who had a weak heart and was supported by Teach all her life.

Shortly after I started working with Teach, one of my contemporaries said to me, "You can't be with her. She's a lesbian."

"What difference does that make?" I bluffed, not wanting to admit I didn't know what a lesbian was. At the first opportunity I looked up the word in the dictionary. "Woman from the island of Lesbos," I read, and was more puzzled than before. I knew Teach's parents were English. She had to be English or American. Lesbian? Finally, an old friend enlightened me.

It didn't matter then, or later, when I was aware of Teach's occasional, very discreet affairs. She never asked me to be her bedmate, though some of the other players no doubt thought I was.

Now that I had the coach I had coveted, I expected miracles, but they didn't happen. Every day I saw her techniques working for others, but no matter how hard I worked, my game didn't get better. I was frustrated, and so was Teach, but the woman who had stolen her first racquet, who had talked her way from professional to amateur status, wasn't about to give up on me.

4 : BEESE'S GAME

One day Teach drove me to an elegant mountaintop estate in Montecito, near Santa Barbara. When I asked where we were going, she just said that there was someone she wanted to watch me play.

We followed a winding road up into the mountains, each switch-back presenting a wider panorama of the Pacific. Under a canopy of pale, cloudless blue, the dark ocean was flecked with bright colors where sailboats danced in the wind. I couldn't enjoy the view, though. I was curious and a little excited about meeting someone whose opinion was valued by my headstrong, independent coach.

That someone was Harwood "Beese" White. A lanky, balding man, he towered over me. His gray eyes sharply assessed me when Teach introduced us. His smile revealed tiny white teeth, which gave him a slightly carnivorous look, but his expression was friendly enough.

Harwood White. This was the man who had helped Teach with several of her top students, including Ruby Bishop, who defeated me in the 1931 National Junior Championships. I had heard a little about him—that he was a multimillionaire from a Michigan furniture family, that he became interested in tennis after a broken back ended his career as a gymnast, and that he was considered a somewhat eccentric, if brilliant, teacher. So the mountain comes to Mohammed, I thought, glancing at Teach. White led us to his tennis court.

"Show me what you can do," he said, settling his long frame into a lawn chair.

Teach and I hit for about ten minutes before White stood and walked onto the court, his eyes on Teach. She stopped and looked at him, my return bouncing past her unheeded.

He shook his head and spoke as if I wasn't there. "That's the worst tennis game I've ever seen."

I stood motionless for a moment, then began to quiver with anger. How could he say that? I was number seven in the country! I heaved my racquet the length of the court and watched it sail over the fence and land in the citrus grove. I glared at Teach.

"I know what you have in mind, but I'm *not* taking lessons from *him*!"

"You will, if you want to be a champion!"

I had learned to recognize that tone of voice. There was no appeal.

I turned to White. His face was unreadable. I sighed, knowing when to back down. "I'll get my racquet."

I was cocky, but I wasn't stupid. If Teach thought White could make me a better player, then I was willing to listen, much as I disliked him at that moment. If I challenged her, she would write me off; my coach didn't suffer fools.

When I had retrieved my racquet, I stood in front of White. "Where do we start?"

"We throw out everything you know and start over."

He swiveled the racquet handle a quarter turn in my hand, to the Eastern grip. "Now, hold the racquet loosely around the end with two fingers and your thumb."

Teach stood at the net in the far court, hitting balls to me while White directed me from the side. "Step into the ball. Full swing, full follow-through. Don't *hit* the ball; *meet* it. This is not a game of strength."

I did as he said, and began to realize he knew what he was talking about. I couldn't control the ball while holding the racquet so loosely, but I was generating just as much power with a fraction of the effort. When White called a halt, I turned to him, puzzled.

"It shouldn't work, but it does," I said. "I thought I had to grip hard and hit hard."

"What do you think now?"

"I was wrong." Confusion and shame churned inside me. He was being very gracious. If I had been in his place, I would have told Teach to take her brat elsewhere.

"It's a start." He smiled and I felt better.

It was the beginning of the most intense learning experience I ever had. Beese (I was soon calling him by his nickname or, affectionately, "Papa") drilled me in the dynamics of tennis—the theory and execution of strokes—while Teach taught me strategy and honed my competitive edge, determined to develop what she called the killer instinct.

The only thing I had going for me was "ball sense," the hand-eye coordination and sense of distance and timing that help an outfielder know where to put his glove to catch a fly ball—or a tennis player to know where a volley is going the instant it leaves an opponent's racquet. Beese began to build a new set of strokes around that innate ability, starting with a change to the Eastern grip, which was vital for play on grass. My situation was worse than that of a beginner, because I had to unlearn the skills I had come to depend on.

From the beginning, everything he told me differed from what I had learned on my own. In fact, his methods contradicted those of *most* pros. His was a scholarly approach. He had *studied* tennis, breaking it down into a science of movement. What he learned he passed on to a fortunate few, free of charge, and I quickly realized how lucky I was. I was also grateful for my photographic memory, because working with Beese involved much reading and note-taking. Beese gave me stacks of instructional manuals, insisting that I study the methods of other tennis teachers. I didn't like any of them.

"Why?" Beese would inquire, and I would try to explain how I found each system lacking in flow, in naturalness, compared to what he taught. Hearing what he had hoped to hear, Beese would grant me one of his rare smiles; I was beginning to share his convictions. I took notes as I watched him at work, so that I could duplicate his methods with the young children whom he assigned me to teach.

Teach, who had always played and taught by instinct, was learning too, incorporating many of White's techniques into her teaching regimen.

My strokes became more powerful and more controlled every day. There was a beautiful bang in the middle of the racquet when I hit the ball, and the feeling it gave me was sheer bliss. This was pure tennis—the sort of tennis I wanted to play.

Beese made sure I was always overmatched by making me practice with his male students, a lesson in humility as well as a stroke-builder. I soon preferred practicing with men, and later arranged to have male hitting partners at all my tournaments.

Beese White's mountaintop home was to become my winter training center for the next ten years. It was a grand place, isolated by fifty acres of citrus groves and woods, and with a wonderful guest house for Teach and me.

My new game went on display for the first time in the Southern California Championships. I had never really played a traditional women's game, but now I was even more aggressive, and the press reacted with headlines saying "MARBLE'S PLAYING A MAN'S GAME!" They made it sound like an insult. No woman before me had really played the serve-and-volley game, but I knew I was doing the right thing. The tennis world is easily shocked, and change comes slowly.

My style of play wasn't the only thing causing comment. I could abide skirts no longer, and began to wear culotte-type shorts that ended at mid-thigh. They were in good taste, revealing far less than today's outfits, but I had *dared* to wear something different.

In this change, there was a precedent. In the 1920s the great Suzanne Lenglen rebelled against those awful long skirts, petticoats, and high-necked blouses, showing up on the court in a one-piece sleeveless dress that stopped at mid-calf, with no petticoats, and a bandanna rather than a hat. Once the other players got over the shock, they quickly followed her example; later, I suppose they followed mine. After Gertrude ("Gorgeous Gussy") Moran played Wimbledon in the forties with lace-trimmed panties peeking from under a short ballerina skirt, "proper attire" became a matter of choice.

My clothing was not an issue at the Southern California Championships. As the highest-ranking player, I was expected to win, but the debut of my new game turned out to be a disaster when I lost in the semifinals to an unranked player. I had defeated myself, falling back on my old style but without the confidence that had carried those inferior skills.

I never did that again; it was the new game or nothing. I won a few minor confidence-builders, and then breezed through the California State Championship at Berkeley. I was champion of California again, and with an entirely new game.

Within a week I got word that I was to represent Northern California in several eastern tournaments, building up to the qualifiers for the international Wightman Cup team and the national championships at Forest Hills.

I was delighted—and scared. My game was still far from dependable, and the thought of putting it to the test on grass made my knees weak.

I spent a few days in Boston as the guest of Mrs. George W. Wightman, the "Queen Mother of American Tennis" since 1923, the year she started the Wightman Cup matches between women's teams from the United States and Great Britain.

"Mrs. Wighty" was housemother to more than two generations

of young women players, and no matter who our coaches were, we listened to Mrs. Wighty's advice. The former Hazel Hotchkiss won forty-four national championships—more than any other player in the history of the sport—including four singles titles at Forest Hills, and mixed doubles in the 1924 Olympics.

After a few days' practice on her fine grass courts, I won the Longwood Country Club and Essex tournaments in Massachusetts, then was stopped in the Seabright semifinals by Sarah Palfrey, whom I had defeated in the early rounds of the nationals the year before. I wondered if I would always be jinxed at Seabright.

There was a final qualifying tournament for the Wightman Cup team, a three-day invitational in East Hampton, New York. Because of my standing as California champion and my recent performances everyone said I was a shoo-in to make the team, but I was still worried.

I arrived hot and tired at the Maidstone Club in East Hampton to find that I was slated to play both singles and doubles in three days. It had to be a mistake.

I sought out Julian Myrick, chairman of the tournament committee and the man who, in one USLTA position or another, controlled tennis for twenty years. I disliked Myrick at first sight. I found him talking to some other players, his voice an irritating staccato, commanding like a dictator whose decisions were above question.

I introduced myself to him, noticing that I was almost as tall as he was, and asked, "How can you expect me to play singles and doubles in three days?"

"Mrs. Moody [national champion Helen Wills Moody]," he replied, "has afforded you the honor of playing with her in the doubles." God, the little man was pompous!

"Then suppose I only play in the doubles?" That way, I could save myself for the Wightman Cup singles the following week.

Myrick, who also chaired the Wightman Cup matches, sniffed, the nostrils of his pointed nose quivering at my impudence. "My dear, you have to prove your worth by making a good showing here. Then *perhaps* you'll qualify for the Wightman Cup team."

I tried to stay calm. "But I've won two tournaments to Sarah Palfrey's one, and neither she nor Carolin Babcock is scheduled to play both."

"I'll be the judge of who's to play, not you." He walked away, leaving me seething.

I should have wired Teach right away; she would have known what to do. Instead, I had a bitch session in the locker room with some of the other California players, and ultimately decided to do as Myrick said. I was afraid he'd keep me off the team if I didn't.

I had no problems the first two days of competition, but on the third day, I faced the semifinals of both singles and doubles, starting with a ten A.M. match against Midge Van Ryn. Midge was tough and experienced and I was drained by the time I passed her down the line to end the third set, 6–4, 4–6, 7–5.

"You almost had me, Midge." My cockiness had long since evaporated, baked out of me by a relentless sun that was nearing its zenith and growing hotter by the minute. How did New Yorkers stand this humidity? The pounding in my temples reverberated through my body, echoing painfully in my joints and turning my stomach into a queasy knot.

"Mrs. Moody is ready to play doubles," urged an anxious official. I changed clothes and dashed back to the court. *Mustn't keep royalty waiting*, I thought, less than reverently. I respected my partner's achievements on the court—from 1927 to 1933 she didn't lose a set in singles play—but I resented her haughtiness.

When I was eighteen, I looked up to her just as all the young players did, and wanted to be a champion just like her. Then Helen's coach, old Pop Fuller, invited me to a luncheon in Helen's honor. He presented me to the champion, and said something meant to flatter Helen: "Now that you've won everything in sight, wouldn't you like to help a young hopeful like Alice get her start so she can do what you've done?"

Helen looked at Fuller, genuine surprise on her face. Then she looked at me. "No, I wouldn't," she said, and walked away. It was an embarrassing moment for Fuller and for me. I never again wanted to be like her. We played together many times, but we were never friends. Helen didn't have friends on the tennis court.

She did have a classic kind of beauty—fans of both sexes pinned her picture on their walls and fought for a glimpse of her. She was my height and weighed about 135 pounds, but she seemed bigger because her legs were heavier than mine. She whacked the hell out of the ball, especially on her forehand (like Steffi Graf), but her footwork was terrible. Only her remarkable sense of anticipation got her where she needed to be on the court.

Sportswriters called her the American Girl, but the players knew her as "Poker Face" because she was expressionless on the court and unapproachable off it. Bill Tilden called her "the coldest, most self-centered, most ruthless champion known to tennis."

In an English locker room, I once heard a player wondering

aloud why Helen had a private dressing room while twenty-five of us shared a common dressing room and bath.

"Would Garbo bathe with chorus girls?" someone answered.

While Helen and I warmed up against our opponents in the doubles semifinal, buxom Betty Nuthall and the diminutive Mary Heeley. They were an incongruous couple on the court, but two of England's top players and pure hell to face if you weren't in top form. We weren't.

"My back's been bothering me, Alice," Helen said. "I'd rather not aggravate it." I nodded, understanding that she wanted me to cover for her. Through three tough sets, I took every overhead shot, compounding the match's toll on me.

When we squeaked to a narrow victory, Helen strolled off the court, flashing a smile at the cameras, and I trailed behind her, trembling from heat and fatigue. I was scheduled to play the singles final in an hour.

In the locker room, the scales showed that I'd lost five pounds in three hours of play. One of the attendants put cold towels on my neck and face, and the California girls hovered about me.

"I'm fine, really," I told them. Damn that Myrick! He would surely dump me as a Wightman candidate if I quit now. I felt my throat tighten in a wave of loneliness for Teach.

Every move was becoming an effort. My feet were on fire, my knees and elbows ached. Ignoring the lunch set up for us, I drank several cups of tea loaded with sugar, and ate some toast.

When I met former national champion Betty Nuthall in the singles final, the on-court temperature had reached 104 degrees and the humidity made every breath an effort. The court rippled and blurred before my eyes, and I knew I was moving like an automaton. I shook my head and tried to focus on Betty.

"Are you all right?" She walked to the net to look at me. I nodded. At least I was still on my feet. I couldn't quit; what would my family think?

The first set was a bitter battle; I won it 7–5, but it took everything I had. Betty ran the second set out easily. I was beyond pain, but my body simply would not do what I asked. My whole world had become the searing sun and the blur of a speeding tennis ball; sometimes I couldn't separate the two.

Sweat stung my eyes and my clothes were plastered to me. Brushing wet strings of hair from my face, I walked to the locker room for the ten-minute rest between the second and third sets. Slowly, I sank onto a bench and leaned against the wall, grateful for the shade and relative quiet.

It was time to go. When I stood up, I caught my breath in pain. My leg muscles had cramped, and I had trouble walking to the court. Betty polished me off in less than ten minutes.

I tried not to think about the doubles final. The pounding in my head had reached such a crescendo that it hurt to think. When a USLTA official urged me to quit, I shook my head, too weak to talk. I later learned that she and several others had appealed to Myrick, who replied that the crowds had come to see Mrs. Moody, and he could not disappoint them.

I peeled off my wet clothes, put on my fourth outfit of the day, and, hardly aware of how I got there, stood on the court beside Helen Moody. She could see the shape I was in, but said nothing. We were defeated in straight sets, and she left the court without a word to me.

Dazed as I was, I heard people calling out to me from the stands, applauding my effort, and someone put a steadying arm around my waist. My legs didn't seem to belong to me anymore.

I was startled when I saw myself in the mirror—the hollow eyes, the clothes that hung from my body. I had lost fourteen pounds in nine hours, playing four matches totaling eleven sets (108 games) between ten twenty A.M. and seven P.M. on what the sports writers vowed was the hottest day of the year. No one's been crazy enough to try it since.

That evening, at the home of my hostess, I fainted dead away. The doctor diagnosed sunstroke and mild anemia, and prescribed a few days of rest.

The New York sportswriters made much of my "feat of strength," with headlines saying "ALICE MARBLE GETS BAD DEAL" and "TENNIS ASSOCIATION FORCES ALICE MARBLE TO PLAY 108 GAMES."

Myrick was outraged. He protested the newspaper accounts, and the press kept the story alive for days. Everyone blasted him, including Teach, who phoned from California. Mother wired me to see if I was all right, and I assured her that I was, refusing to admit even to myself how rotten I felt. Despite my losses in the finals, I had made the Wightman Cup team. That was all that mattered. The weakness and dizziness would surely go away.

On the day before the Wightman Cup competition, the team doctor forbade me to play in the singles. I begged him to let me play in the doubles on the final day of competition, and he reluctantly consented. But my strength gave out during the first set, and we were soundly defeated. I took it hard; if I'd let someone else play, the team might have won.

A few days later, I lost to Betty Nuthall in the quarterfinals of the nationals, after leading five games to one in the final set. It was a bitter blow to be out so soon. I was playing well, but I had no endurance.

I fainted again during practice at the West Side Tennis Club, and several USLTA members cautioned me to get more rest. I was already spending most of my off-court time in the sleep of total exhaustion.

When the final of the nationals came, I watched the match of the year between Helen Wills Moody and Helen Jacobs, the world's top-ranked players. The press said the two Helens were bitter rivals. It made a good story, but it wasn't true.

Moody treated all her opponents with the same cool detachment. Jacobs, a fierce competitor, had never beaten Moody and badly wanted to retain the championship title she had won the previous year, in Moody's absence.

During the first two sets, Moody remained impassive while Jacobs whittled away at her. Jacobs smiled slightly when she won the first set, 8–6. It was the first set she had *ever* won from Moody. She moved to the net often in the second set, hoping to take advantage of her slower opponent, but Moody's deep drives and sudden cross-court shots earned her the set, 6–3.

Jacobs went to the locker room for the ten-minute rest period, while Helen Wills Moody inexplicably remained on court, sitting on a chair at the umpire's stand.

When play resumed, Jacobs won the first three games, and excitement hung in the air like the smell of blood at a cockfight. When Moody walked to the umpire's stand and reached for her sweater, Jacobs rushed over to her.

"My leg is bothering me. I can't go on," Moody said.

"Would you like to rest for a while?" asked Jacobs.

"No, I can't go on."

Moody pulled on her sweater, walked off the court, and all the way to her apartment in the Forest Hills Inn two blocks away. Bedlam broke out on the court, and a low rumble rose from the stands as disbelief turned into outrage. If Mrs. Moody had the strength to walk two blocks, she could have stayed on the court for twelve more points. The New York crowd growled its disapproval at the display of bad sportsmanship.

Jacobs accepted the forfeit with quiet grace, though she knew, as we all did, that she had probably been robbed of a legitimate victory. I was disgusted.

The confusion redoubled when Mrs. Moody telephoned from

her apartment to say she would play her doubles match. Fearing that the New York crowd would pelt the court with debris, the tennis association refused to allow her to reappear. Instead, they hastily arranged an exhibition. I teamed up with Elizabeth Ryan, Moody's partner, to play Betty Nuthall and Freda James, who had just become doubles champions due to Moody's "indisposition."

Unfortunately, the public was cheated of even that consolation match when Betty's return ricocheted off the top of the net and hit me squarely in my right eye. I was led off the court, temporarily unable to open *either* eye.

My eye was blackened and bloodshot, but a doctor applied salve and put a patch on it. The patch was quite a conversation piece, and my eye was fine in a couple of days.

When I got back to the West Coast, Beese and Teach were still furious at Myrick, but pleased that I'd played consistently well before I was overtaxed. Their pride in me was worth more than any trophy.

The dry California air did not make me feel better, as I had hoped, but it was such an exciting time for me I refused to admit I was sick. In a year, I had risen from seventh to third in the national standings. My career was taking off.

In a few weeks, I played England's top-ranked Dorothy Round in the Northern California Championships. Happy to be back on hard courts, I won in two easy sets before a crowd that was decidedly in my corner, but the best thing about winning was seeing my brother Dan, resplendent in his new policeman's uniform, smiling from the stands.

Afterward, I was swamped with party invitations but I turned them all down and went off to the movies with Dan. We sat in our favorite seats and ate chocolate creams the way we used to.

5: HEARST CASTLE

The movies. When I was a child, ten cents let me into that magic world. I saw every movie that came to town, and—thanks to my photographic memory—had a wealth of knowledge about all the actors and actresses, even the bit ones. Movie stars were a breed apart to me, untouchable and wonderful.

Teach Tennant drew me into the Hollywood crowd as naturally as if she were introducing me to a group of ragtag players in the city park. The stars I had idolized she made a part of my everyday life, as they were of hers. It began when I returned to Beese White's place after two months at home.

I had wanted to go directly to Los Angeles with Teach after the Northern California Championships, but it was obvious to her that I hadn't recovered from the sunstroke back East. A doctor verified that I was anemic, and started me on a course of crude iron injections that were so painful I was sure I would never sit comfortably again.

"Listen to the doctor, and *no* tennis," Teach had commanded. "Don't even pick up a racquet until I see you again."

Obediently I rested, drawing strength from my mother's cooking and long walks in the parks. I arrived at White's place in Santa Barbara feeling stronger, and prepared myself for the laborious practice routine, but after a few days Teach had a surprise for me.

"You and I have been invited to Mr. Hearst's ranch in San Simeon," she said. William Randolph Hearst, his mistress Marion Davies, and many of their guests at Hearst Castle took tennis lessons from Teach.

"No!" I couldn't believe it. I had heard of the newspaper magnate's lavish place—who hadn't?—but it was as far from my reach as Buckingham Palace.

"Yes!" she said. I bounded over the net and hugged her. She laughed, and added, "That is, if your mother says okay."

My mother, who did not share my fondness for movie stars, took some convincing.

"I really can't turn down Mr. Hearst's offer," Teach explained, "but I don't want Alice to miss her lessons."

I would be under her supervision, Teach went on, reminding my mother what a stickler she was for diet and training. Hearst's place was beginning to sound like a convent.

Mother gave in.

"Teach, you're amazing," I told her later, much to her delight. "You can convince anyone of *anything*." I soon realized that her persuasiveness was not only charming, it helped her make winners of her students. She made them believe in themselves. It worked on me.

The sun was dropping into the sea when we turned off Coast Highway between San Luis Obispo and Monterey onto a mountain road leading to the Hearst Ranch. At an iron gate, a guard let us through with a touch of his cap and an "Evening, Miss Tennant, Miss Marble."

My excitement grew with every turn up the narrow dirt road as llamas, camels, kangaroos, zebras, giraffes—and animals I couldn't identify—peered at us, curious and unafraid.

"Teach, tell me I'm dreaming!"

Teach was enjoying herself. "You haven't seen anything yet." Hearst owned the world's largest privately owned collection of wild animals—more than a hundred species. They roamed at will over two thousand acres of hillside and canyon, protected by ten miles of eight-foot-high wire fence. And that was just a corner of the forty-thousand-acre ranch. All told, the multimillionaire owned 240,000 acres of land stretching from the mountains to the sea.

"La Cuesta Encantada," Teach said softly, her eyes aglow in the fading light.

"Meaning . . . ?"

"The Enchanted Hill. Can you see why?" We crested a steep hill, crossed a drawbridge over a moat, and pulled into a cobblestoned courtyard. I stared up at the castle, its Mediterranean facade tinted a warm rose by the last rays of the sun. From the twin towers, a Belgian carillon filled the air with music.

"My God, it's incredible!" I swiveled in place, taking in the panorama of mountains, sea, and an architectural opulence I never knew existed. Laughing, Teach took my arm and led me toward the massive front entrance.

32

A butler opened the door; we walked into the Assembly Room, the largest room I had ever seen. A tennis court would fit in it, with space to spare. I craned my neck to look at the ornate ceiling twenty-four feet above us, then let my eyes sweep over the Renaissance tapestries decorating the walls above massive wooden chairs (four-hundred-year-old walnut choir stalls from Italian monasteries, I learned later). I was stunned and, for once in my life, very nearly speechless.

"So *this* is Alice!" I felt a hand on my arm and tried to gather my wits. I turned to look into the pair of eyes that had stared back at me from the movie screen so many times.

"Miss Davies, I'm delighted to meet you!" I said, trying not to sound breathless, though I felt as if I had stepped into an atmosphere lacking the oxygen I needed to fuel my pounding heart. Marion Davies spoke with a slight stutter, but she was so completely at ease that I soon stopped noticing it. She was shorter and a bit heavier than I, with short blond hair nearly the shade of mine. Her smile was friendly, and I smiled back, my nervousness easing.

Teach and Marion hugged and began chattering away like the old friends they were. I gave little thought to the fact that Marion was probably the first mistress I'd ever met. She was a *star*, and she looked just like she did in her movies.

Mr. Hearst came up beside Marion and said, "Welcome to San Simeon." He was tall and heavyset; when his words came out in that famous high, squeaky voice of his, I was so surprised that I just grinned, shaking the hand he offered. I was somewhat frightened, remembering the stories that he had killed a man, but they were just rumors. His face was kind.

"Thank you for having me," I managed. "Your house is . . . it looks like something from the movies!"

He laughed, pleased. "Doesn't it, though?"

Then we were surrounded by about thirty people introducing themselves and saying they had seen me play. I found myself gulping for air again. The people saying they had seen *me*, as if that were a big deal, were stars like Jackie Cooper, Jean Harlow, Charlie Chaplin, Gene Raymond, Paulette Goddard, Bing Crosby, Constance Talmadge, Bebe Daniels, and Hollywood director Raoul Walsh. There were other faces I didn't know, those of newspapermen who worked for Hearst and of Marion's old Follies girlfriends.

As soon as I could, I began exploring the room. With my weakness for sweets, it took me no time to discover the open boxes of fine candies—not the one-pound boxes you buy for Mother's Day, but ten- and twenty-pound containers! Teach caught me in the midst of a glorious dilemma over chocolate creams and caramels, and settled it by removing me from temptation's way.

A waiter offered me a drink, which I refused, but I noticed that most of the guests were holding glasses. Later I learned that, in deference to Marion's alcoholism, this was the only place Mr. Hearst allowed liquor, aside from wine at dinner. He was usually very amenable to his guests' wishes, but not on this point. Guests drinking in their rooms found their bags packed and waiting for them at the front door. (I marveled at how Albert the butler always seemed to know when someone was sneaking a drink.)

I was in a delightful daze at nine P.M., when Marion announced dinner by ringing a cowbell. The guests began filing into the Refectory—the main dining room—which was dominated by an ancient monastery table. On standards along the side walls hung richly colored Italian silk banners ("The laundry's hanging out," an irreverent guest once remarked). Candles flickered in ornate three-foot-high silver candlesticks on the table and on sideboards that ranged along both long walls. I exhaled in a rush, realizing I had been holding my breath since I stepped into the room.

Fifty-two guests were at dinner that night. There were never fewer than twenty-five any time I visited the castle. Mr. Hearst and Marion always sat across from each other at the center of the table. Teach and I sat on opposite sides of the table, flanking our host and hostess. (For some reason, Hearst liked me, and I was often seated next to him.) There were no place cards to guide us; Marion directed us as we entered the room and, after a mild melee, we all found our chairs.

When we were settled and Albert had signaled the staff to begin serving, the man on my other side introduced himself as Hearst's representative in London and told me that many of the dining room's trappings had been part of an old Italian church. The large red-velvet chairs in which we sat had been choir stalls.

"This room, like the rest of the castle," he said, "is filled with treasures, priceless works of art from all over the world. Some say they would have been lost to war and time if Mr. Hearst had not collected them."

"It's all so overwhelming!" I said. I turned to see Mr. Hearst smiling benignly at me. I was an Alice in a Wonderland far beyond Lewis Carroll's imagining.

More than anything that night, I was intrigued by the table at which we sat. Narrow, but about fifty feet long, it ran almost the length of the room. The center was laden with cheeses of all shapes and sizes, and bottles of sauces from all over the world. I felt oddly reassured by the paper napkin on my lap and the common catsup and mustard bottles scattered among the exotic ones.

Dining at the castle was like eating aboard ship. Everything was elegant—French-style, more or less—and there were always delicacies. It was there I first tasted real turtle soup, escargots, and truffles.

After dinner we saw a movie in the fifty-seat theater. Marion Davies played a feisty Irish girl in a stuffy English manor, a remake of *Peg o' My Heart*. Relenting on her training rules, Teach let me stay up with the others until almost three A.M. Sprawled on priceless rugs in one of the castle's fourteen sitting rooms, we talked about the movie we had just seen, and others.

On one of my later visits to the castle, Bing Crosby was there for the premiere of a movie in which he starred with Marion. The former Follies girl had a marvelous knack for comedy, but when Hearst pushed her into movies where she played the femme fatale in fancy hats and dresses, she was terrible. He wanted her to be his dream star, but I don't think she was comfortable in that role, on screen or off. She was honest and unpretentious, and I came to be very fond of her.

Mr. Hearst doted on Marion, lavishing her with gifts. When I admired a ring she was wearing, she said, "Here, take it," pulling it from her finger. "I have dozens more."

"I can't!" I was at once touched by her offer and awed by the great wealth she enjoyed. I had been poor all my life, would probably always be poor, but I seldom envied the rich. Too many of them were unhappy. I had everything I wanted: a chance to play tennis.

The wonder of the place did not end when Teach and I retired to our bedroom. (There were thirty-eight bedrooms in the castle, each with an adjoining bathroom, at a time when indoor plumbing was not all that common.) Looking at the tapestries and rare paintings on the walls, I moved carefully lest I bump into one of the vases or statues about the room.

"Teach?" The room was so big I had to raise my voice so that she could hear me on the other end. "I think this is the most exciting night of my whole life!" I flopped down on my bed. "I actually sat on the floor with *Charlie Chaplin*! And Jackie Cooper is such a doll! I can't believe it. Pinch me!"

"I'm going to do more than that if you don't settle down and get to sleep," she replied, but I could tell that she was pleased to see me enjoying myself. Teach thrived on repartee with the "jet set" of our day.

Everyone at the ranch was keen on tennis and the two courts

atop the indoor Roman pool were always full. On my first day, Mr. Hearst was my partner. Teach played opposite us with Charlie Chaplin, and all the guests turned out to watch. At sixty, Mr. Hearst seemed ancient to me, but he played beautifully.

I quickly discovered that Chaplin cheated, calling balls out when they were in. My anger flared, and I started trying to hit him with the ball. I probably would have succeeded in making a fool of myself if Teach hadn't caught my eye. I settled down, but I was disturbed.

When the score went to 5–all, Marion whispered to me, "Let them win."

I shook my head. "We're going to win." It wasn't until later I realized her concern was Hearst's health, not diplomacy.

We won, 10–8. Perspiring, the big man gave me a bear hug and said, "Alice, you're the best partner I've ever had!"

True or not, his words made me feel wonderful, as he intended. Sensing my anger at Chaplin, Mr. Hearst made sure I never again played against Charlie, always with him—and I made the calls. That night, Chaplin entertained us by playing his left-handed violin, and I forgave him. Whatever his hangup was about cheating, he was clever and fun to be with.

6 : HEARST CASTLE

1933

Days at La Cuesta Encantada slipped easily by, and I never stopped marveling at the beauty and extravagance of the place—the army of servants, the zoo animals, the guest houses, the gardens, the pools . . .

I soon discovered the indoor pool beneath the tennis courts. The large room was designed like a Roman bath, with alabaster lamps glowing on hand-set blue and gold mosaic tiles, many of which were eighteen-karat gold fused in glass. Naked statues stood guard, their reflections eerily lifelike in the pool's surface. The indoor pool would have been a wonder anyplace in the world, but it was the outdoor pool, the 104-foot-long Neptune Pool of sky-blue marble, that was the centerpiece of La Casa Grande. Hearst told me he'd enlarged it twice before he was satisfied with its size and shape. It took 345,000 gallons of spring water to fill it.

Sometimes I'd slip away from the other guests after dinner and sit watching the lamplight play on the smooth surface of the pool, casting ethereal reflections on the Greco-Roman statuary, colonnades, and temple. I felt as if I had left my center-row seat in the theater and stepped right into the silver screen, and in a sense I had: In the sixties, scenes in the movie *Spartacus* were filmed around the pool.

During the rare moments when I wasn't playing tennis, I explored. Equipped with a map of the castle's interior and the grounds, I climbed marble stairways to formal gardens with ancient urns, statuary, and sundials set among beds of flowers. The air was filled with fragrance, the tinkling music of fountains, and the sounds of construction. Hearst was always building, adding, changing, making

room for new treasures he'd found abroad. "If he ever stops building, I think he will die," I wrote in a letter to my mother.

"Pleasure is worth what you can afford to pay for it," Mr. Hearst
always said, and I'm sure he enjoyed every dollar he spent turning
that stretch of California into a paradise to share with his lover and
his friends.

Cary Grant, a frequent partaker of Hearst's hospitality, once
called San Simeon "a great place to spend the Depression," and
there were many who would agree with him.

Most of my day at the castle was filled with tennis. Teach
wouldn't let me swim (it makes the muscles too loose for tennis),
but I occasionally sunbathed with other guests by the Neptune Pool.
Morning and afternoon I'd have two-hour lessons with Teach; other
times I played with the guests. Some of them were good; most
weren't.

"It's good practice for you," Teach said when I complained
about the poorer players. "If you hit the ball too hard, the others
can't play with you. If you hit it too soft, they'll clobber you. You'll
have to set your pace."

Teach was right. It was good practice. Being able to change your
pace is critical in tournament play. You can't keep hitting the ball
hard unless you're as strong as Martina Navratilova or Steffi Graf.
Otherwise, your opponent adjusts to your speed and turns it back
on you. I used change-ups to great advantage throughout my career.

My visits to the castle—there were many over the course of
several years—would last about a month. On one occasion, just
after I got my driver's license, Teach traveled to the ranch with
someone else, and asked me to drive her car up.

I felt fine, even a bit cocky, driving all by myself, until I reached
the five-mile private road through the game preserve. I was driving
slowly, watching for animals, when several sets of bony knees came
into my field of vision. I stopped the car, rolled down the window,
and peered up into the curious faces of a herd of giraffes. They
surrounded the car, and I sat helplessly in their midst until one of
the groundkeepers rescued me.

"Would you drive me on up to the castle?" I asked, sliding over
into the passenger seat.

"Sure," he said, laughing and getting behind the wheel.

"I had visions of Teach's car being trampled. She would kill me
if I survived the stampede!"

He laughed again. "You're not the first one. Winston Churchill
was stranded for more than an hour by those lazy giraffes."

On another occasion, Teach called me as I was preparing to

leave San Francisco. "Meet Roscoe Turner at the airport as soon as you can. You're going to fly to the ranch."

I did as she said, not breathing a word to my mother. No one we knew had ever been in an airplane, and I doubt that she would have shared my enthusiasm. In 1933 air travel was not commonplace.

Turner fit the stereotype of the dauntless World War I ace (which he was), with his calm, rugged face and carefully curled mustache. The plane was an open-cockpit type. I swallowed hard. Then I saw Turner's other passenger: a lion cub.

"Don't worry." Turner laughed at the expression on my face. "This little guy is safe as a kitten. He's going up to join Mr. Hearst's zoo."

My heart fluttered at about the same pace as the propeller on our little craft as we flew up into the mountains; I was decidedly weak in the knees when we drifted to a gentle landing on the ranch's grass strip. The castle from the air had been breathtaking, but I was distracted from the view by the lion cub, who insisted on slapping me with his big paws in an effort to play.

The guests had a good laugh at dinner when I recounted my adventure. Several leading actors—Robert Taylor and George Brent, for instance—had their own planes and often flew to the ranch, but doing so wasn't entirely safe. The mountains were high and the wind currents could be dangerous. Two newspapermen had been killed when their plane crashed at the ranch during a storm.

The guest list was ever-changing. Robert Taylor, Barbara Stanwyck, Marlene Dietrich, and George Bancroft were there during one of my stays. Louella Parsons, the gossip columnist, was often there. Carole Lombard and Clark Gable spent their honeymoon at La Cuesta Encantada.

One evening Marion told me a very special guest was arriving at the cocktail hour. I wondered who could be special to this group.

I had evening clothes with me, but Marion insisted on dressing me for the occasion. We were miles from any clothing stores, but Marion's various dressing rooms were like branches of Bullock's and I. Magnin's department stores, containing dresses, sports clothes, and shoes of all sizes. If I wanted to ride, Marion could have me turned out properly in a flash. If I chose to play golf, she was ready with all the latest fashions for the links—in my size.

Dressing me became a group effort. Marion chose a dress the blue of my eyes, with a low back. While she did my hair, Jean Harlow applied my makeup.

Harlow was a truly beautiful woman, with eyes that mesmerized, and a warm, sexy smile. "Alice, you're going to make the men wild," she told me, dabbing rouge on my tanned cheekbones. I blushed. Laughing, she hugged me, and turned to the mirror to put the finishing touches on her own face. Silent-film star Bebe Daniels (a contemporary of Rudolph Valentino) did my nails.

Someone made sure I had the right accessories, and I took the elevator down to the Assembly Room. I moved through the room, looking for the special guest who had everyone in a stir. David Niven arrived. Was he the surprise?

"Young lady, I admire the moles on your back," said a voice behind me. I turned to face a tall, bearded man. A dirty old man, at that. Before I could say as much, Marion was at my elbow.

"A-A-Alice, this is your dinner partner, George Bernard Shaw. Mr. Shaw, tennis star Alice Marble."

"Mr. Shaw, what a pleasure," I said, recovering quickly. The great playwright bent to kiss my hand. I realized then why I would be sitting next to the honored guest. Hearst knew I had done a thesis on Shaw as part of my entrance exam to the University of California. Fortunately, Hearst's pairing worked. I made a tremendous hit with both guest and host by keeping Mr. Shaw entertained all evening. He was on a brief trip, and that was the only night of his life he spent in the United States—at Hearst Castle, with a kid from a middle-class family as his dinner partner.

"What did you talk about?" Teach asked later.

"Him." I kicked off the high heels and sat down to rub my feet. "I knew the names and characters of every one of his plays, so I talked about his work and he talked about himself. He was a delightful old coot, but so egotistical!"

Teach laughed. "That memory of yours comes in handy."

It served me well on other occasions. Mr. Hearst had novel ideas about dinnertime entertainment. Sometimes he would ask me to sing, or Chaplin to play the violin, or other guests to perform. Our host's contribution was yodeling, which he did very well. (I tried it once and sounded like a turkey on the chopping block.)

Other times, we'd play "Who Am I?" Someone gave the initials of a silent-movie star, and the others were to guess the actor's name. One night, Mr. Hearst asked me to start off.

"Okay. H. B."

An hour later, no one had guessed the identity of H. B., not even Jackie Cooper, who also had a great store of movie trivia in his head.

"We're not leaving the table until someone gets it," Hearst said, but at last he gave in. "We have a movie to see. Okay, Alice, who's H. B.?"

"Holbrook Blinn, the villain who tied girls to the railroad tracks."

Hearst roared with laughter, leaning back until his chair creaked. I was sure that it had never been so tested in its three hundred years of choirboys.

One evening after dinner, a group of the "girls" retired to Marion's dressing room, called the Loo. There was a tap on the door, and Albert, the omniscient butler, appeared with bottles of champagne and glasses on a silver tray. He put the tray down and backed out as if his pants were on fire I suspected that these lapses in the no-drinking policy were a secret Albert shared with no one but the mistress of the house.

Marion popped a cork, and Teach handed me a full glass. "Try it. See if you like it."

I didn't like it, but my attention was riveted on the conversation and I sipped the drink absentmindedly, not realizing the glass was being refilled each time I put it down.

The former chorus girls were letting down their hair. They talked of their abortions and of how they had dieted by eating and then vomiting. They reminisced about their times as starving extras waiting to make it in New York, their voices rich with the same passion old army buddies reserve for talk of wars gone by. There was a unique intimacy to the gathering of women, and I felt special to be included.

I was getting an education, and I was getting drunk. "Bedtime," Teach said, standing up to a chorus of groans. She had contributed a number of raunchy stories to the conversation, and no one wanted her to leave.

"I'm not going." My words were slurred. "I'm having fun." I tossed my head in a show of defiance, and the move was just enough to upset my balance. I toppled from the table where I'd been perched, right into Teach's arms.

"Tomorrow morning is going to be even more fun," Teach said, winking at our companions and aiming me toward the door.

It was a beaut of a hangover, enough to put me off champagne for life. I only drink it now with orange juice or with a sugar cube in it, just to be sociable.

Not all of Mr. Hearst's guests were movie personalities. His business colleagues from around the world frequently met at the ranch, headquarters for his vast media network when he was there.

There was even a wire machine, and a bulletin board where you could read the next day's news.

One morning I came down to breakfast and someone passing by said, "Hello, Venus." Puzzled, I looked after him, then shrugged and helped myself to eggs from the buffet. Then one of Hearst's foreign correspondents grinned at me and said, "Good morning, Venus."

"Why on earth are you calling me Venus?"

"Check out the Yellow Sheet on the bulletin board. Brisbane's written a column on you."

The previous day, the famous columnist Arthur Brisbane had arrived. He seemed very interested in my tennis, and asked me a lot of questions. I hadn't realized I was being interviewed! His story, which ran in all the Hearst papers, read:

> What a girl Alice Marble is, with everything the Venus de Milo has, plus two muscular, bare, sunburned arms marvelously efficient. Her legs are like two columns of polished mahogany, bare to the knees, her figure perfect. Frederick MacMonnies should do a statue of her. And she should marry the most intelligent young man in America, and be the perfect mother with twelve children, not merely the world's best tennis player, which she probably will be.

I was immediately the brunt of good-natured jokes, but my mother was not pleased when she read what she said were "suggestive" remarks about her daughter. She wrote a terse note telling me to come home right away. The night before I left, everyone drank to my success and I went feeling that I could do anything in the world. Venus de Milo, indeed!

Mother soon forgave Brisbane. I think she was secretly proud that the columnist had thought so highly of me. When he came to our house and asked my mother if I could spend Christmas in Miami with his family, she agreed. The poor man had lost his youngest son to illness, and his wife had become a recluse.

Brisbane paid all my expenses, including the forty dollars a month I would be missing from my intermittent job at Wilson's. I traveled from California to Florida by train, and spent two weeks with the Brisbanes. I think Arthur and his two sons were happier with me there, though Mrs. Brisbane never came out of her room.

Several weeks later, Arthur Brisbane and I met back at San Simeon. He was playing poker, and I stopped to watch.

"Alice, do you play poker?" Brisbane asked.

"Yes, sir, I do." My brothers had taught me.

"I'm tired. Would you take my hand? In the morning, we'll either split your winnings or I'll cover your losses."

I agreed. I had good cards and, of course, remembered every card that was turned up. The evening went quickly. When we threw in our last hands, the men pulled out their checkbooks and started writing me checks. I had won $1,200, an enormous sum in those days.

"I can't take your money," I said. "I didn't know what we were playing for. My mother would kill me for gambling!"

"But you won it," they insisted. Teach was going to give me hell for being late. I left the checks on the card table and hurried to our room.

The next morning, Mr. Hearst pulled me aside. "Alice, I understand you're as good at cards as you are on the courts. Why didn't you take the money you won?"

I repeated what I had said the night before, and he nodded his big head thoughtfully. "I understand, my dear. Think no more of it." He walked away chuckling to himself. In 1936, when I came home after winning the National Championship, there was a new green Chevrolet in front of my house, a gift from Marion and Mr. Hearst. It was my first car, and I kept it for many years.

Marion and Mr. Hearst were lifelong fans of mine. No matter where I played, there was always a telegram from them, wishing me luck or congratulating me on a win. My favorite one said simply, "To Alice, who will be champion whenever she wants to be."

7 : FRANCE

"Beese! Teach! I'm going to France!" Waving the telegram like a flag, I burst through the door onto the patio and did a quick dance in front of them. Beese's wife, Alex, served cocktails on the patio every evening, just when the sun was putting on its final light show of the day.

"You mean England, don't you?" Teach looked puzzled.

"France first, then England!" I smoothed the telegram and handed it to her.

It was traditional for the Wightman Cup team, America's top women players, to play in England, but this year the USLTA had arranged for us to play a series of matches in France first, then go on to Wimbledon in June for the Wightman Cup competition. We were to sail from New York the first of May.

I pleaded with Teach to go with me, and this time Beese agreed. "I have a bad feeling about this trip," he told Teach. "I'm afraid something will happen to Alice if you're not there."

Beese and Teach were both deeply involved in astrology, and Beese had seen something in my horoscope he didn't like. Beese, who had studied under the great Evangeline Adams and had written books on the Beyond with his brother Stewart Edward White, was always poring over my "signs." His predictions often came true, but I tried to dismiss them as lucky. My mother had taught me that God was the only one who knew our destinies.

Teach *did* believe in Beese's predictions, which made it even harder for her to refuse me, but when she explained that she could not afford to take two months off from teaching, I stopped nagging her. I was being selfish. Teach supported me with her teaching income.

"I promise, no marathons like East Hampton," I told my two coaches. "I won't do anything stupid."

I arrived at New York's Waldorf-Astoria Hotel without incident. But the night before we were to sail I was dressing for a big farewell party when I realized the good-luck pin Teach had given me was missing. It was a tiny gold raccuet with a pearl head, studded with diamonds and rubies (she had given an identical one to Carole Lombard), and I never played without it.

The pin was very expensive, but that wasn't what upset me. Its loss seemed like another bad sign. I was already feeling insecure about the trip because of my health. Suppose I had started playing again too soon? I had been plagued with colds all winter and hadn't regained the stamina I had before East Hampton the previous summer. Everyone expected me to do well, but I wasn't sure. I wasn't sure at all.

I picked up the hotel phone and called Teach. Yes, she had seen me put the pin in my jewelry case. "Relax," she told me. "It'll turn up. Go enjoy the party—and make me proud in Europe."

Our team captain, Helen Jacobs, was already in France, but Sarah Palfrey, Dorothy Bundy, and Josephine Cruickshank were there, their excitement as obvious as my own. Across the room I saw Carolin Babcock and her mother, Mrs. Babcock, who was traveling with us. They smiled and waved. Everywhere I looked in the big ballroom, I saw Eastern players I hadn't seen in months, along with tennis officials and sponsors. I waded into the crowd.

The New York reporters soon found me. Many of them were the ones who had written of my "feat of strength" during the Wightman Cup qualifier the previous year.

"I feel great," I lied to them. "I'm a California girl. I just needed to get back to the sun and my mother's cooking!" They laughed and wished me luck. "Bring us home a success story," one of them said.

I greeted Julian Myrick with civility—an effort, considering I hated the man's guts, but I respected the power he held over the country's tennis players.

"I trust your health has improved?" he asked. I stared at his beaky nose, said what he wanted to hear, and excused myself as soon as I could.

Then, caught up in the gaiety of the moment, I forgot about everything. The ballroom was beautifully decorated and the band was playing all the popular songs of the day—"Blue Moon," "The Continental," "Stars Fell on Alabama," and one of my favorites, "All Through the Night." I love to dance, and there were many willing men.

45

When the band took a break, my partner led me over to a cluster of people around an older woman I had never seen before.

"She's a mind reader," Carolin Babcock whispered. "She's predicting everyone's future." Aloud she said, "Do Alice next!" and pushed me to the front of the group.

I felt foolish, but everyone insisted, so I stepped up to the psychic. She was beautiful in a disturbing way. She was almost an albino, with waxen skin, white-blond hair, and eyes of the palest blue.

Grasping my hands in hers, she commanded, "Look at me." I gazed into her eyes. The pupils were large in the dim light, the irises a thin rim of blue. I tried to pull away and laugh the whole thing off, but she held my hands tightly.

In a moment, she released her grip, but her eyes still held mine. "You will rise like a skyrocket and then fall to earth," she said quietly. I stared at her. Around me I heard a collective intake of breath. This wasn't funny. I shook off the goose bumps and forced a smile.

"I'll watch my step," I said, reaching for my partner's arm. The band was playing again, and we spun off across the dance floor in a waltz. My thoughts were on Beese's words. Was something bad going to happen to me?

All ill omens were forgotten the next morning when I walked up the gangplank of the German ship *Bremen* for my first trip to Europe.

"Miss Marble, look here," the photographers called. I turned and waved, smiling for all I was worth. The flashes dazzled me, as did the cheering crowd. I felt tears on my cheeks, tears of excitement and a little homesickness. Europe was a long way from California.

The morning papers were tucked under my arm. Reporters had written of my future with the optimism that comes so easily to journalists. I was indeed rising like a rocket.

"God," I prayed silently, looking down at the sea of faces on the dock, "please don't let me fail."

I shared a cabin with Josephine Cruickshank, a big, gawky girl with great energy and enthusiasm. Together we hit balls against the wall in the gymnasium and walked the deck, trying to stay fit. At night, we put on evening dresses for dinner and dancing. The trip would have been such a lark if I had felt better! I tried, but every night was the same. I fell into bed exhausted while Josephine was still out dancing.

The morning of the sixth day, we docked in Le Havre and boarded the train to Paris. Helen Jacobs met us at the station and helped us count our bags as they were loaded into taxis. During the drive to the Ritz Hotel, she turned to me. "Was the trip rough?"

"No, not at all. It was wonderful."

She was watching me. I knew I was pale, and there were dark circles under my eyes. I thought Helen would question me further, but Carolin squealed at her first glimpse of the Louvre, and we were all caught up in the sights of Paris. My mother would have loved it. I blinked back the sudden tears. This was no time to be homesick. The taxi sped along the bank of the Seine, and I focused on my surroundings.

The next morning we had a team practice at Stade Roland Garros. It was hot, unusually hot for Paris in the spring, and the stadium was airless as a shoebox. Helen and I played two sets, which she won easily. When we got back to the hotel, she followed me into my room and sat down.

"What's wrong?" she asked.

"What do you mean?"

"Your game is off and you look terrible, for starters."

"You were good today."

"Not *that* good. C'mon, Alice. Are you ill?"

"I guess I'm a little homesick. Everything's so different here." I was hedging and Helen knew it. "I'm tired and my muscles ache, but I can't sleep," I admitted. "I thought everything would be okay when I got back on the court again."

Helen nodded. "I think you should see a doctor." She stood and walked to the door. She turned back to me. "We're all a little homesick. It's frightening, not knowing how tough the French will be. But we'll do okay. I'm sure of it."

I gave her a smile of confidence I didn't really feel. A year earlier, cocky as I usually was, Helen would have been warning me not to be too bold.

The next day, the physician who attended the French team examined me. A blood test showed my hemoglobin count was 50. "Isn't that low?" I asked. I had learned a little about anemia by that time.

"It's nothing to worry about," the doctor said. "You're slightly anemic, but it shouldn't keep you from playing. Try to get plenty of rest."

At least he didn't tell me I couldn't play. And he didn't give me any of those dreadful iron shots. I was relieved at the French doctor's conclusions, but I would have been happier if he had discovered I had the flu and given me medicine for it. If I was okay, why did I feel so bad? Could I make a decent showing on the courts?

Things got worse. I hated the French courts, the French players, and, most of all, the French language. I had always assumed that wherever I went, *someone* would speak English. Aside from my teammates, everyone—even the visiting Europeans, it seemed—spoke French. A day of deciphering the score—*quarante–quinze* instead of forty–fifteen—left me so morose that I skipped dinner and stayed in my room, writing letters home.

I also felt insignificant around champions like Hilda Sperling of Germany and England's Dorothy Round. My California championships were nothing compared to the victories of these European legends. They didn't *look* like champions, though. The way they played was strange, so lacking in athleticism. But their game was perfect for the slow courts. Mine was not. My teammates were adjusting to the clay surface, but I played worse every day.

The weather grew even hotter, and I realized Long Island had no corner on humidity. It was sweltering when I faced France's number two, Sylvia Henrotin, for my first match of the series.

Stade Roland Garros, built in 1927 in honor of a World War I aviator, has high retaining walls at both ends and is notoriously airless at court level. Warming up, I understood why Don Budge had once fainted there during a tournament. My racquet kept slipping in my hand, and no amount of sawdust from the box at courtside would help.

Play began. Sylvia was clever—and knew her turf. She treated me to a round of sharply angled drives, chops, and volleys that ran me all over the court. The woman was playing *my* game, and beating me at it! I lost the first game, then took the second on service.

I shook my head to clear the dizziness. Every breath I took was painful, yet seemed to draw no air into my lungs. When we changed ends, Sylvia looked at me strangely. My distress must have showed.

"Four games to one, Miss Henrotin," said the umpire, in French. I didn't care. The match was important—Sarah Palfrey and Carolin Babcock had lost, and Jo Cruickshank was working on split sets; only Helen Jacobs had won. But I was more concerned with trying to get my breath. The air was thick, the stadium damp and hot as a steam bath. I was gasping; I could hear the sound, but it seemed to be coming from somewhere outside my body.

Sylvia served. I struggled. Then the score was 5–1, my service. My first serve was long. I dumped the second into the net, and moved to the other service court, blinking to bring my opponent into focus. It was hopeless. I felt my knees buckling, the racquet slipping from my hand, then the hard clay against my knees, my arms, my cheek.

I was dimly aware of being carried off the court, then nothing until I came to in the American Hospital at Neuilly. Mrs. Babcock smiled with relief when I opened my eyes. When I collapsed, the other players still had doubles matches to play, so Carolin's mother accompanied me to the hospital.

"My dear, you gave us such a scare!" she said. "You fainted from the heat. How do you feel?"

"Tired." The word came out in a weak croak. I looked around at the small room, its sterile walls relieved by one obligatory print of a famous still life. "How long do I have to stay here?"

"The doctor says it's probably sunstroke, but he wants to keep you a couple days for tests."

"A couple days?" I was letting the team down. Suppose the doctors wouldn't let me play?

That evening, all the players—even the French ones—crowded into my little room. The air was fragrant from the flowers they brought, and everybody was so encouraging that my spirits rose.

"I thought I'd killed you," said Sylvia Henrotin in her best English.

"So did I," I replied. That drew such a burst of laughter from the group that Dr. Dax insisted everyone leave. The jowly, gray-haired physician had the bedside manners of a stone.

"Tomorrow, Alice." Helen waved from the door.

The next morning, a nurse brought me a Paris newspaper. There was a big article about my collapse, and a photo of two men carrying me off the court, but no clue as to what was wrong with me. Sunstroke again, I decided, but that didn't explain the pain in my back and chest. I felt as if I'd been speared.

Dr. Dax finally enlightened me with his first diagnosis: anemia and pleurisy. He explained that pleurisy was an inflammation of the lining around the lungs, and very painful.

"You're right about that," I said. "How long does it last? When can I play again?"

He shook his head, the loose skin of his cheeks quivering. "Not in this tournament, I'm afraid. We'll try to have you ready for the trip to England."

I spent two days indulging in self-pity. It went well with the pain, which eased just slightly with medication. I drifted in and out of sleep, scarcely aware of visitors. My temperature rose to a dangerous level, and stayed there. Dr. Dax suspected gallbladder trouble, then ruled that out.

I got the impression no one knew what was wrong with me, except for one nurse, who told me I was going to die. I never saw her again after I repeated her words to the doctor, but I suspected she was right. I felt as if I was going to die. I had no appetite, and cried for hours at a time. Not even Helen, who had been through the misery of pleurisy, could cheer me up.

She didn't tell me that her illness had put such a strain on her heart that she missed the 1930 American season, and was afraid she might never play again. She was concerned that playing in England would jeopardize my health and my tennis future. She told Dr. Dax as much. He agreed, without telling her the full extent of his findings.

Ten days after my collapse, Helen cabled Teach to come for me. Her response was immediate: "Unable to come to Paris. Will meet Alice in New York."

Helen arranged for the American Embassy to take care of the travel details when I was able to leave the hospital.

It was a despondent group of players who gathered in my room to say good-bye. They were leaving me in Paris, which weighed much more heavily on their minds than their defeat by the French. But the team was due in London, and couldn't delay any longer.

I tried to put a good face on it. "You all just needed a chance to adjust to European conditions. The British won't stand a chance. Some of us," I gestured to my prone body, "adjust slower than others." That drew a laugh.

After tearful hugs, they were gone. Helen left me half a dozen beautiful peaches that must have cost a fortune. The French nurse served them to me with sour cream, and for the first time in ten days, I showed a bit of my old spirit. I threw dish, spoon, and all in the wastebasket, sobbing all the while. I had never felt so alone.

Then came a visit from Dr. Dax, who said he had my complete diagnosis. Finally. He was quite matter-of-fact. "You have tuberculosis. I'm sorry, but you will never be strong enough to play tennis again."

"You're a sadistic S.O.B.," I said after a moment. I turned my face to the wall and prayed that I might die before morning. But the next day came, and the next, and the next.

Six weeks after my collapse, I persuaded the doctor to let me go home. The pain from the pleurisy was nearly gone, and I was more homesick than I'd ever been in my life. My mother wrote me every day, and Teach had driven to New York and was waiting for me there.

I was bundled into a taxi and taken to the train bound for Le

50

Havre. A special berth had been prepared for me on the train, and one of the nurses from the hospital traveled with me. I had taught her to play solitaire during my stay at the hospital. The train had scarcely left the station when she pulled a deck of cards from her bag.

I was quite willing to be distracted; we played double solitaire until we reached Le Havre. There, in order to catch the return train to Paris, she left me sitting in a wheelchair at the dock.

I shivered in the breeze from the ocean. I was beaten, and my life was over. Tennis was my life. I had never thought beyond it. What was to happen to me now?

8: GOING HOME

1934

Two crew members of the *Aquitania* wheeled my chair up the gangplank and took me to a small private cabin, where the ship's nurse helped me to bed. After she left, I stared at the oval of blue sky visible through the porthole, feeling the ship tremble slightly as we got under way.

How different from my New York departure! "You will rise like a skyrocket . . ." I was an athlete then, on my way to represent my country. What was I now? Nothing. Less than nothing. A liability.

"Useless," I told the wheelchair the nurse had left at the foot of the bed. A sob rose from deep in my throat, followed by a rush of tears. I pounded the bed with my fist. It was so unfair! Just when I was getting someplace with my tennis.

The ship's doctor made me spend the first three days of the voyage in bed. The pleurisy had subsided to an occasional twinge, and I felt well enough to complain. I was sick of reading, I told the doctor. I was even sicker of being trapped in that room with my dismal thoughts. "Please, can't I get out of here for a few hours a day?"

"We'll see," was his reply, part of the universal language of doctors. At mid-morning the next day, he introduced me to Paul Fuller, an American lawyer.

"The American consulate in Paris asked me to look after you," Fuller said, "but I was afraid the doctor here wasn't going to let me be a proper escort."

"A few hours in the sun and a good lunch," the doctor cautioned. "*No* dancing!" We all laughed (I thought I'd forgotten how), and Paul Fuller wheeled me to the upper deck. I tilted my head back to feel the sun on my face, breathed deeply of the tangy sea air, and thought of days at the beach with my brothers.

"This is absolutely glorious," I said, my eyes closed. "Thank you for rescuing me."

I liked Paul Fuller from the start. He looked a lot like my father, with his strong face and quiet brown eyes. He made me feel secure, and most important of all, he made me laugh. I couldn't have had a better traveling companion.

Lunch became the focus of my day. Mr. Fuller ordered, and every day it was a surprise, something strange and wonderful. At least, he made it seem so. We dined on marrow bones one day, snails the next, frog's legs another, and always finished off with delectable desserts like baked Alaska and cherries jubilee. He was so kind and made such an effort to lift my spirits. It worked. He gave me courage. At night, in my cabin, I thought about the alternatives he had suggested to my tennis life-style. It beat self-pity.

We were a day out of New York when I saw Mr. Fuller staring at the wake of the ship, tears in his eyes.

"Why are you sad?" I had seen the look on his face before, at unguarded moments.

"I'm going home to bury my son. He was killed in an accident. He was twenty-one."

I felt the tears in my eyes. "All this time, you've treated my problem like it was such a tragedy. It's nothing compared to your grief. I *am* alive."

"Yes, you are, and that's why you've been so good for me. Don't worry about your mother and Dan and Teach. They love you. Your only concern right now is getting well."

I don't know what I would have done without Paul Fuller. When the gangplank was in place, he wheeled me down to the busy New York dock. For the first time, I saw Teach Tennant cry, a devastating sight. She was always so strong.

"I'm so sorry. . . ." She bent down to hug me. "If I'd gone with you . . . Beese said I should go. . . ."

"It's not your fault," I said. "I guess I just overdid it." I introduced her to Mr. Fuller, then said my good-byes to him. We were waiting for the purser to clear my bags through customs when Mr. Edward B. Moss, secretary of the USLTA, found us.

"I'm here to take you to the USLTA offices," he said. "You have to make an accounting of your expenses abroad."

For a moment, Teach looked as if she were going to hit him. "You stupid damn fool! Can't you see this girl is ill? If the tennis association wants to see us, we'll be at the Roosevelt Hotel."

Moss retreated without a word, and it was several days before Teach allowed him and Julian Myrick to see me. They brought along a doctor, who examined me and studied the X rays that had been taken in Paris.

"This girl will never play tennis again," he said.

"Myrick, this is all your fault," Teach said. "That stunt you pulled in East Hampton—"

"She could have defaulted if she wasn't up to it."

"With all your crap about Moody, and not disappointing the spectators? You put pressure on her. You're responsible for her being like this! The association should pay all her medical bills until she's well. That's the least you can do, now that you've ruined her career, her life—"

"Out of the question. Her passage to France and back, the hospital, the doctors' bills, cost us a fortune! And she never finished a match! She's been a bad investment, and now that she'll never play again, there will be no gate receipts to make up for the expenses."

They continued to hammer away at each other, their voices rising. I went into the bathroom and shut the door.

"Get the hell out of here," Teach screamed. "And you leave her alone, you understand?" She slammed the door behind them.

We stayed at the hotel for a week so I could rest. Teach came as close to being motherly as she ever had, but she couldn't improve my spirits. How could I believe her when she said she didn't care that my tennis career was over? The disappointment was there every time she looked at me. I avoided her eyes. I had failed her, and Dan, and everybody who believed in me. Yes, it was an illness, but if I'd taken better care of myself . . . I could never make it up to any of them.

"They've written my obituary," I said when I saw the newspapers. I wadded up one sports page and threw it across the room. Teach kept the papers from me after that.

It would be easier on me to travel by train, Teach decided, so she arranged for a sleeper and someone to drive her car back to California. The journey cross-country seemed endless, and my anxiety increased as we drew near San Francisco. How would Dan pay my medical expenses? I hated putting a financial strain on my family. That's all I'd ever given them. Bills. First tennis bills, now doctors' bills.

Dan and George carried me up the long flight of steps to our little house in the Sunset district—the steps I'd raced up as a child. They cried, I cried, my mother threw her arms around me and cried.

54

"Enough," Teach said finally. "This looks like a wake. She's going to be all right."

My mother agreed, and everyone calmed down. I was settled into the upstairs bedroom, the room where my father died. Our family doctor examined me, and prescribed rest and quiet. What a surprise, I thought. I welcomed the rest nonetheless, weak and ill as I felt. Although it was the middle of summer, the house seemed drafty and cold to me, so I stayed in bed all the time.

Dan was so heartbroken it hurt me to look at him. Our conversations were broken by uncomfortable silences. He had made so many sacrifices for my tennis career; now it was gone. What could he say to me, or I to him?

George, on the other hand, was a delight, sitting on the end of my bed and talking about everything but my illness. He had grown into a pragmatic sort of guy, but with a wry humor I enjoyed.

Tim, a lanky teenager, was bored with everything, including my illness. He never got over feeling abandoned when the "Marble Battery" of Marble pitching and Marble catching was dissolved overnight in favor of tennis.

Hazel, who had left her worthless husband, worked for the telephone company during the day and helped with the housework at night.

Mother was wonderful, smoothing the wrinkles out of my bed, bringing me books, cooking special meals for me. But I felt terrible every time she had to climb the stairs. All my life she'd been short and stocky, but now I noticed she had lost a lot of weight and looked tired. She didn't tell me, but she had cancer. I did realize that she wasn't able to take care of an invalid, so I wrote to Teach, asking her advice. I couldn't let my mother continue this way.

Teach came to see me, bringing with her a specialist who said I would improve more rapidly in a warm climate and a quieter atmosphere. When I agreed to go with Teach to Beverly Hills, Mother and Dan were annoyed, but they yielded to Teach's pressure. Mother resented my going to an outsider. "She can get all the care she needs right here, in her own home," she said.

"Mom, it's too much work for you," I said. "Please, I'd rather do it this way." The day I left, she kissed me on the cheek without a word.

"I've had about as much upheaval in my life as I can take," I said to Teach when we were in the car. All my things were in the back seat, even my tennis racquets, though God knows why Teach insisted on bringing them.

"I know," she answered. "I'm taking you someplace where you can have six weeks of absolute rest and quiet."

I hid my surprise. I thought I was going to Teach's house in Beverly Hills, as she had told my family. Instead, she drove me to Pottinger's Sanatorium in Monrovia, twenty-five miles from where she lived.

"You'll be able to rest here, and the doctors can look after you," Teach said, looking around the bungalow. It was a lovely little place, screened on three sides and surrounded by flower beds and well-tended lawns. I hated it on sight.

Teach had doubled her teaching load to pay for the sanatorium, but she still drove fifty miles to see me every day. Her sister Gwen came often, bringing the letters Mother had mailed to Teach's house in Beverly Hills. When I was away from home, no matter where I was, Mother wrote to me every day. Something else arrived by mail—my lucky pin, which had been stolen by a hotel maid and later recovered. I cried at the sight of it, at the thought of all the times I'd worn it. I'd probably never wear it again.

Gwen arrived one day and announced, "I'm going to teach you to embroider. It'll give you something to do." Ignoring my protests—and insults—she pulled a set of linen towels and several skeins of colored thread from her bag, and drew her chair close to my bed. I didn't want to hurt her feelings, so I gave in, cursing to myself when I stabbed my fingers.

I put the work aside when she left, but soon picked it up again. I couldn't ignore the challenge, tame as it was. From tennis championships to tea towels: How my goals had shifted! Still, embroidery did pass the time, and when I sent the finished towels to Mother, she responded with a long, warm letter. I think she treasured those towels more than any of the trophies I brought home, and I knew she had forgiven me for leaving.

I was under orders to stay in bed except to go to the bathroom. The nurses (guards, I called them) came by the cottage frequently to make sure I complied. One day they found me gone. After a search, two white-clad Amazons came panting up to where I sat, on the bank of the lake. I was puffing calmly on a cigarette.

One of them snatched it from my lips. "You're not supposed to smoke!"

"I don't." I stood up and walked back to the cabin, pleased in a perverse way that I had created a stir. The place was deadly dull, filled with people like me, vegetating.

Dr. Pottinger examined me once a week, always with the same comment. "Hm, yes, you're doing nicely."

"But am I getting well?" I growled. "How's my blood count? How do my lungs look?" I wanted to know specifics, but his replies, always placating, said nothing. I was no longer in pain, but the inactivity was making me weak. I watched the muscles in my arms go slack and my thighs turn to flab. I was watching my body die.

Six weeks—an eternity—passed. When Teach arrived, I was packed and dressed. "Let's get out of here," I said, then noticed that Dr. Pottinger had followed her through the door.

"The doctor says you're doing fine, but you need another six weeks of rest," Teach said. I glared at Pottinger, who nodded. How could I act like an ingrate when Teach was working so hard to pay my expenses?

"Whatever you say." I turned and began to unpack. I lost hope then. I thought of the man who had stopped outside my cottage a few days earlier and stood talking through the screen. He laughed when I told him my stay was a short one.

"They tell everybody they'll be here six weeks. I've been here two years. You'll never get out." There were dozens of patients with similar stories. What could I do? Every letter from my mother encouraged me to come home, but I couldn't burden her. And Teach obviously thought I was better off here than at her house.

Every day was a slice of hell, and the nights were worse— sleepless, desolate hours of staring into the darkness. I had stacks of books and magazines, but found myself reading the same sentence over and over, with no comprehension. I've always loved to sing, but the words of my favorite songs just wouldn't come.

I begged Pottinger to let me walk in the gardens, but he forbade any physical exertion. Exertion! I had never been bedridden before, never been sick really, until that fiasco in New York. Now I lay in bed, listening to the radio. Soap operas, mysteries, talk shows and news droned in my ear all day long. And I cried for hours at a time.

Teach brought me presents—lounging suits and bright socks to keep my feet warm. The cottage changed when she was there. It was bright with her laughter, her energy, her tanned, healthy body. She spun story after story about her famous pupils, tales that should have lifted my spirits. Instead, they made me that much sadder. I would never again be a part of the life she described.

The second six-week period ended. "Please, God, get me out of here," I prayed. I was coming along nicely, Pottinger said, but I must stay another six weeks. I hadn't bothered to pack. Or dress. My clothes were all too small now, anyway. I hadn't lost my appetite, and the prescribed diet of rich food had added inches and pounds everywhere.

Gwen visited once a week. Her weak heart had made her a lifelong semi-invalid, and I quietly shared the puzzles and games this gentle soul brought to distract me. I knew she was trying to help me adjust to a different life-style. When she arrived with a three-foot piece of needlework for a fireside bench, I didn't protest. Instead, we spent the whole afternoon planning the colors of the flowers. I worked on it every day so I could show her my progress the next time she came.

"Dammit," I swore, sticking a pricked thumb in my mouth. I'd been trying to work while listening to a tennis match on the radio, but hearing the familiar names, the excitement in the announcer's voice on the close points, was agonizing. I put the needlework aside. Commentator Ted Husing was talking about Ethel Burkhardt Arnold: ". . . she's the best California player I've seen this year. . . ."

He had used the same words the year before, when he was talking about me. I snapped the radio off, interrupting Husing in mid-sentence. Bastard! Everyone in tennis had forgotten me. My old rage stirred, but faintly. What was the use?

One dull day tripped over another, until one morning a letter arrived with breakfast. Opening it, I read:

Dear Alice,

You don't know me, but your tennis teacher is also my teacher, and she has told me all about you. Once I thought I had a great career in front of me, just like you thought you had. Then one day I was in a terrible automobile accident. For six months I lay on a hospital bed, just like you are today. Doctors told me I was through, but then I began to think I had nothing to lose by fighting, so I began to fight. Well, I proved the doctors wrong. I made my career come true, just as you can—if you'll fight. If I can do it, so can you.

It was signed "Carole Lombard." I knew Teach coached the famous movie star, but I had never met her. I recalled reading about her accident and the plastic surgery requiring more than a hundred stitches in her face. Carole Lombard cared enough to write to me! I kept the letter in front of me, reading it over and over. But how could I fight?

On September 28, 1934, I celebrated my twenty-first birthday in Pottinger's Sanatorium. Just as I was wondering where my dinner tray was, I heard the sound of Mexican music. The sound came closer until three musicians were standing in my doorway. Behind them came Teach and Gwen with all the makings of a party—a cake blazing with candles, presents, and several of their friends who had become my friends, too.

I cried until I had everyone near tears. Then Teach said, "Dry up, for God's sake. This is a party!"

We all laughed, cut the cake, and opened the presents. The "guards" were nowhere in sight, and I wondered how Teach had arranged that. It was a bittersweet moment. The circumstances made my coming of age one of the most miserable birthdays of my life, yet the people who helped me celebrate it were special.

One of them gave me a small book, *The Message of a Master*. Several nights later, when I couldn't sleep, I reached for the book and read a few lines over and over until they remained in my mind. I did the same every night, just after the nurses' final rounds and before lights out. The story caught and held my attention.

The Message of a Master is the story of a failure—a man who had hit bottom mentally, physically, and financially. By right thinking, he turned his life into a success. The parallels were obvious. I started thinking too, examining the doubts and fears that imprisoned me as surely as the sanatorium did. If I didn't try, if I didn't fight back as Carole Lombard had, how would I know what I could do?

I was tired of people telling me what I *couldn't* do. My six-week stay had turned into eight months at great expense to Teach. The doctor had finally given me permission to spend fifteen minutes a day outside, and to walk to the pond seventy-five feet away. This wasn't living! It wasn't me! When Teach came to visit, my bags were packed.

"I'm never going to get well here," I told her. "If I stay much longer, I'll never get out of here alive. I've got to do it now."

She looked at me, gauging the determination in my eyes. "If you can make it to the car, we'll leave right now."

"I'll make it to the car." None of my clothes fit, so I threw a coat over my pajamas and picked up my bag.

"Give me that," Teach said, grabbing the bag in one hand and supporting me under the elbow with the other. We walked quickly, expecting someone to challenge us, but no one did. I was ready to faint when we reached Teach's car.

"No, you don't!" Teach said, catching me in her arms and leaning me against the car while she opened the door. Bundling me into the front seat, she ran around the car and slid behind the wheel. "I'm not breaking any laws," she said, starting the engine. "So why do I feel like I'm making a getaway?"

9: NEW HOPE

Teach wheeled her old black Ford out of the parking lot and onto the driveway. Turning to look out the back window, I watched the gates of the sanatorium disappear from view.

"Thank God—and thank you." I looked at Teach. She kept her eyes on the road, but reached over to squeeze my hand.

"That son of a bitch Pottinger," she said. "He's been stringing me along, taking my money, and doing nothing to make you better. *I* could have kept you in bed and stuffed you with food!"

We had driven a short distance when she pulled to the side of the road and stopped. There was a pay phone on the corner. Teach jumped out of the car and walked toward it, anger in every long stride.

In a few moments she returned, her lips a tight line. In answer to the question on my face she said, "Just tying up some loose ends."

She smiled then, eyeing my rotund figure. "God, what a mess you are! We've got work to do!"

Later I found out Teach had called Dr. Pottinger and confessed that she had snatched his patient.

"Your actions were dastardly," he told her. "If anything happens to that girl, you're responsible."

"You're damn right I am!" Teach shot back. "And I can certainly do more for her than you have. You made her an invalid. I'll make her well."

Pottinger folded pretty quickly in the face of Teach's wrath. He withdrew his threat to contact my family, and prudently decided to forget the whole thing. Teach would have ruined him if he hadn't. She was not a woman to trifle with.

Teach took me home with her. For reasons known only to her, she had taken charge of my future, Professor Higgins to my Eliza Doolittle.

How many coaches would go so far to help a student? The bond between us was to become stronger, but Teach always held back something of herself. Like a cat, she gave affection when she chose, *allowed* others to draw near only when she chose, and then ever so briefly. She'd withdraw in an instant, and leave you wondering what you had done. I stopped being hurt by it. Teach had her own secret agenda, and the strongest will I've ever known. She *willed* people to do what she wanted.

When I left the sanatorium and moved into her house, I subjected myself to that will, and gladly I was ready to accept her help on any terms. My family couldn't do anything for me, and who else was there? Teach was my *only* hope. With her, perhaps I could recover enough to lead a useful life, whatever that was. My mother had always put great store in being "useful." My immediate goal was to stay out of that sanatorium—or anyplace resembling a hospital.

Gwen created a homey atmosphere for me, settling me into my own room and waiting on me as if I were a child. My body had become an obscene thing, bloated and slack, and all my cockiness was gone. Carole Lombard's note was inspiring: I read it and felt encouraged, but to do what? Where was I to begin? If I exerted myself and became sicker, it would mean more medical bills for Teach. How much would she take before she gave up on me? Unsure of everything, I lay in bed, doing nothing.

My coach tolerated that for almost a week before she acted. If I lacked direction, she had more than enough for both of us.

"You are on a diet," she said quietly, relieving me of a dish of ice cream Gwen had given me, "and tomorrow you will walk around the block. Just one block. Stop and rest if you need to, but do it!"

I obeyed. The next morning, dressed in a tentlike shift, I waved to Gwen and set off. I was panting when I reached the corner. I leaned against a light pole until I saw some children watching me, then pushed off and concentrated on making the next corner. Two more corners to go. My thighs were rubbing together and I was beginning to sweat. This couldn't be. I used to go three sets and not feel like this.

A mother with a stroller passed me between the third and fourth corners. I plodded on. When I finally regained the sanctuary of the house, I passed Gwen without a word and walked out the patio door. Stripping off my clothes, I dropped them on the cement deck and slid into the small pool until the water lapped at my chin.

"Alice?" Gwen called at last. She had kept watch to see that I didn't drown.

"Yes?" I studied the way the water skewed my already distorted shape. I had gone from 140 to 185 pounds in the sanatorium.

"Lunch."

"What is it?"

"You know. Rare steak and steamed carrots."

"I'll be right there." Rare steak *again*. It'll build you up, Teach said. I dragged myself from the pool.

The walk before lunch became routine, gradually lengthening as I grew stronger. I got to know the workmen repairing the streets, the children going to school, and the neighbors picking up their milk and morning papers. They got used to seeing me walking, jogging, and skipping rope.

I mourned the desserts—and the chocolates. When you're ill, people ply you with candy as if it were medicine. If you eat it, it's a sign you're getting well. I had enjoyed *that* part of being sick.

"If we coddle you, you'll *think* you're sick," Teach said. "I want you to think about *not* being sick."

Teach's expenses grew. She took me to doctors, therapists, and quacks who, like her, set great store in astrology. I watched their faces while they studied my records, or while I answered their questions, always the same. I loathed them, all those strange men who saw me naked. Their minds were made up before they examined me. They were thinking *All those other doctors can't be wrong*. I could see it in their faces. This was "cover your ass" time—a fat examination fee and no responsibility.

I also hated their pity, their remarks about there being "other things besides tennis." What did they know about *almost* being a champion, almost realizing one's dreams? I endured the doctors for Teach's sake. But what was the use?

Four months after my "escape" from the sanatorium, Carole Lombard insisted that we see Dr. Commons, a Los Angeles physician. Carole and I still hadn't met, but she called me every day, and I knew she had been a great encouragement to Teach.

"Hi, Allie," she'd say on the phone, as breezily as if she were talking to an old friend. She always had a funny story, something that happened on the set or in one of her public appearances. She was such a regular person, a chum who treated me like an equal. I already adored her. Teach and her sister were my world now—

they and a famous movie star who, for some reason, cared what happened to me.

I stood in front of a fluoroscope for a long time while Dr. Commons pulled the slide up and down, his bright eyes studying the screen. At last he said, "Alice, I can't tell for sure, but I don't believe you have tuberculosis. You *had* severe pleurisy and secondary anemia—I can believe that—but tuberculosis . . . Let's get some X rays."

When the plates were developed, the doctor called me into his office and took both my hands in his. "My dear, tell me what you want most in the world."

"To play tennis." I wondered what *he* would offer as a consolation.

"Alice, you *can* play tennis again," he said, "but only if you obey my instructions. Your lungs are scarred—it *may have* been tuberculosis—but I see no reason why you can't play tennis."

"Oh my God," I whispered. "Oh my God!" I whirled in my chair to look at Teach.

"I knew it!" She jumped up to pump the doctor's hand. "I knew this girl wasn't finished! She'll do—we'll do—whatever you say, whatever it takes! Thank you!"

On the drive home, we chattered for a while, then fell silent, lost in our own thoughts. When we walked in the house, Gwen had the hopeful look she always wore when I had a doctor's appointment. Without a word, I flew into her arms, sobbing with joy.

"We'd better get out Alice's racquets," Teach said, laughing as Gwen gathered us both in her embrace.

I did my laps around the block with determination now, not resignation. Hope is a wonder drug. Now that I knew I had a chance, it was hard to go slowly.

Dr. Commons and I made a bargain. On the day my hemoglobin reached 75 and I had lost fourteen pounds, I could play my first game of tennis. He put me on liquids for two weeks and then a strict diet (one I was to follow for two years). I ate moderate portions of two vegetables and two fruits daily, and fruit juice. No coffee, no meats, no desserts. Would I ever again have a piece of chocolate? The very scent of it tormented me, so Teach and Gwen gave up chocolate, too.

Since I'd left the sanatorium, I had refused to go with Teach to Marion Davies's tennis court—I didn't think I could stand to sit and watch, and I wasn't anxious to be seen looking like a whale. Then Teach arranged a special evening that caused me to change my mind.

My coach came home one afternoon looking mischievous. "Get dressed," she said. "We're going to Carole's house for dinner."

At last I was going to meet the star! I was thrilled, but nervous, hating the way I looked—the weight, the acne . . . What would she think of me?

Teach rang the bell of the small house where Carole lived with her mother and brothers. The door opened, and there she stood, absolutely gorgeous in white slacks and a pale-blue sweater. The next moment, her arms were around me, her perfume light and pleasant like the smell of far-off honeysuckle carried on the wind.

"I'm so happy for you!" she said, holding me at arm's length. "It's like a dream, isn't it, having another chance at what you want to do?"

"Yes," I managed to say, lost in the blue of her eyes. It was also a dream to be embraced by Carole Lombard.

Teach kissed Carole on the cheek and we followed her into the house.

I soon got over being star-struck. Carole was so guileless, so completely unaffected, that being with her was as natural as if we'd been friends for years. Her mother, Petey, bossed her and her teenaged brothers, Frederick and Stewart, as if they were wayward five-year-olds, and I found myself laughing the way I used to at home, with my sister and brothers.

I had expected a glamorous house, but the only sign of Carole's success was the cook/housekeeper who served us a delightful dinner (the cook had prepared my "usual" for me). We talked about everything but tennis, and it was obvious Carole didn't need a movie script to be witty. She entertained us through dinner with stories of her days as a department-store clerk.

As she talked, I studied her face, looking for signs of the terrible injuries that had almost spelled the end of her career. There was a tiny scar on her upper lip, but, like Elizabeth Taylor's mole, it only accentuated her beauty. And she was beautiful, even without makeup. Her face was nicely shaped, her complexion perfect, her expression pleasant, relaxed.

Teach and Petey had known each other for many years, and shared a passionate interest in astrology and numerology. Carole, too, was deeply involved in the occult. She always had seers around her whose predictions, Carole said, came true much too often for mere coincidence or luck.

"It's too spooky for me," I told her. "I've had some unpleasant surprises in my life, but if I had known they were coming, I might have quit ages ago."

After dinner, we spent the evening playing parlor games and talking. Carole walked us to the car.

"Alice, promise me you'll come out to watch my lesson tomorrow," she said.

"Okay." I assented so quickly Teach smothered a laugh. Smitten as I was, if she had asked me to fly, I would have tried.

The next day, and every day thereafter, I was ready when Teach left for Marion Davies's tennis court. Carole, I discovered, had lovely tennis form, but when the photographers turned up, as they so often did, she always posed, one leg up in the air like a misguided ballerina. Teach and I teased her about it, but Carole knew what her public wanted.

At first I sat on the sidelines, then after a few days I started pushing balls into a corner and picking them up. This was no small task because Teach used at least five hundred balls for a lesson, but I had help. Carole had given me a dog, a dachshund/scottie cross so tiny I could carry him in my pocket. Jackie quickly learned to push balls with his nose and seemed as tireless as Teach. What a delight he was!

Teach coached a group of about twenty-five women on Marion's court, all connected to the motion-picture industry—Leila Hyams, an actress with MGM; Pauline Gallagher, wife of comedian Skeets Gallagher; Diana Fitzmaurice, wife of George Fitzmaurice, the director; Al Newman's wife, Beth; Frances Mayer, wife of Edwin Justus Mayer, the scenario writer; Dorothy Fields, the famous lyricist; actresses Enid Storey, Norma Talmadge, and, of course, Carole Lombard. It became my job to keep matches going among them on a dozen private courts scattered about Beverly Hills, and to keep records of the results for Teach.

Every day at noon, I served sandwiches in Marion's greenhouse, then sat on the sidelines when play resumed for the afternoon. Several beautiful old trees cast their shade on the edge of the court, and it was there I sat watching Teach drill her students, studying how she adjusted and tuned each one's game without ever making the process seem like work.

The tennis gang got together for a buffet supper once a week, usually at Dorothy Fields's house. They were delightful evenings, filled with talk of scripts, sets, costumes, and people. I hadn't even been on a movie set (though I was to go many times later with Carole), but I held my own in conversation, drawing on my memory of the movies.

It all seemed so unreal. When I talked, famous directors actually listened, nodding, laughing, sipping their drinks, their eyes on *me*.

It made me feel so sophisticated, so worldly. Worldly enough, I decided one evening, that I should have a drink in my hand, like everyone else.

"What do you have that tastes good?" I asked the bartender.

In a moment he handed me a frosty glass. "My special lemonade," he said.

Whatever it was, it did taste like lemonade, and I went back for many refills before the evening was over. Teach almost carried me to the car, and stopped patiently for me every time I had to vomit. After that, I decided I didn't need sophistication—or drinks. Everyone seemed to like me just as I was. And I was going to be even better.

10: COMEBACK

1935

I took a deep breath, trying to stop the trembling in my hands. I glanced at the other three people on the court. Louise Macy and I were about to play Teach and Carole, and I was more nervous than I had been during the Nationals at Forest Hills.

Earlier in the day, Dr. Commons had given me the okay to start playing again. It was a moment I had looked forward to for so very long, but now that it was at hand, I was afraid, desperately afraid. I struggled with the cover of my racquet. *Suppose it's too soon? What if I have a relapse? How many times can a person start over?*

"Here, I'll do that." Carole took the racquet from me. "You'll be okay, Allie," she whispered. "We all love you. If it's too much for you, we'll stop. You don't have to prove anything."

I gave her my best imitation of a smile. I had everything to prove. If I was going to get back to tournament form, I had to start competing.

Teach put the ball into play with a serve so soft even the rankest beginner could have handled it. I smacked a sizzler down the line between her and Carole, and tried not to laugh. Teach must have been nervous, too, to serve me such a plum, but that was the only point Louise and I didn't have to work for.

I was immediately swept up in the game I loved, illness forgotten. Nothing mattered more than hitting the ball, and hitting it well. I tossed the ball up and leaned into my service, grunting with the effort. Skimming two inches over the net, the ball landed just inside the service court, then bounced high and to the outside, catching Teach flatfooted. My coach gave a delighted whoop.

"My God, Alice's American twist hasn't suffered," she yelled. "That was one sweet serve!"

Applause came from the shade of the trees. I noticed for the first time that a crowd had turned out to watch, even some women who weren't scheduled to play that day. Everyone was rooting for me.

It was over too soon. "That's it," Teach called, trotting up to the net. "Three games is your limit today."

Then Carole was hugging me, and Louise, and the others from the sidelines were crowding in to congratulate me. I felt tears on my cheeks, and saw that Carole was crying too. Teach was smiling, her face radiant, her eyes lustrous.

"Looks like your strokes are still there," she said. "All you need is stamina."

As my blood count increased, so did the amount of tennis Dr. Commons allowed. Soon I was playing two sets of doubles a day. Teach and I had long days—glorious, rich days of sunshine, exercise, and companionship at Marion's court. Hour after hour my coach gave lessons while I filled in and shagged balls. Then I had my lesson, the others watching and applauding my good shots. Everyone was praying for my comeback almost as hard as I was.

On the days Carole had her lesson, I played with her afterward, or we played doubles with Teach and another student. It was during one of those matches that Eleanor Tennant got the nickname she was to carry the rest of her life.

It started with her habit of coaching the opposition while she was playing. Carole and I were beating Teach and her partner, but still she nagged us: "Alice, you were out of position on that shot." "Carole, watch the ball all the way to your racquet."

"Yes, *teacher* dear," Carole called sweetly in response to each bit of advice. By the end of our match, the name had been shortened to "Teach"—and had stuck. From that time on, Eleanor Tennant was "Teach" to everyone, even those who had never met the legendary coach.

Even now, I have to marvel at Teach's patience and her tenacious belief in me at that stage. I waddled about the court, short of breath, short of speed, short of everything it took to make a champion. There were no guarantees that I would ever be anything but a social player. No athlete of that time had ever come back from tuberculosis. I don't suppose they do, even today. I still wonder what kept Teach going. What did she see in me that no one else saw? She believed in me more than I believed in myself.

It had been that way from the start. Teach told Ted Tinling (the famous designer of women's tennis clothes) her impressions of me after my first lesson: "Alice was fat and heavy. Her stroke production was eccentric; worst of all, she had no control over her temper.

68

When she didn't get the play she thought she should have, she would sock the ball right over the chicken coop a block from where we were playing. But something happened to my solar plexus. This thing came to me which said, 'Alice can be a world champion.' "

Now here I was, even fatter and never further from world-champion material, yet Teach never wavered. She *never* stopped telling me I was going to be the world's best woman tennis player. I wanted to believe it; God, I wanted to believe it!

There was no time for an outside job in the tennis schedule Teach had set for me. I had never had much money, and it mattered little that I had none now. I handled Teach's books, correspondence, and schedules; in return, she gave me everything I needed, supplemented only by what little money Dan could send.

I was also deeply indebted to Carole, who was like a big sister to me. Only five years my senior, she picked up where Teach left off in rebuilding my confidence

"Let's go shopping," Carole would say, waving to Teach and pushing me toward her car. "Shopping" meant buying clothes for me. In and out of dressing rooms I went, parading outfits Carole selected. What she liked, she bought, ignoring my protests.

"If I ever make any money, I'll pay you back," I promised.

"Oh, shit," was her usual reply.

Carole's language, like Bette Davis's, was heavily spiced with profanity. That seemed so incongruous coming from such a beautiful woman. I got used to it when we were alone, but was always shocked to hear her talk like that in public.

I asked Petey why her daughter talked like a stevedore. "You don't swear like that. Why does Carole?"

"To keep men away," she said. "She's a pretty girl. When she first started acting, men were always after her, so she learned how to tell them off, but good! She thought that kind of language coming from her would make them leave her alone."

From what I could see, it didn't work. Men constantly sought her attention, and women enjoyed her company, though few of them could match her looks. Her language never improved, and I accepted it as a part of her. She was my best friend, my confidante. Our backgrounds and our lives were very different (though mine became more like hers when I, too, had a public following), but we had such fun together, and shared so much emotionally.

Carole's financial help also eased the burden on Teach, and brought me opportunities I could never have had otherwise. Realizing that acne was making me as self-conscious as being overweight did, she took me to a dermatologist and paid for the treatments.

And when Teach mentioned that singing might help my wind, Carole arranged for me to take lessons from Nina Koschetz, a Russian concert star.

"Any voice teacher would have done," I demurred, but I was ecstatic at the prospect of learning from Miss Koschetz. Singing did increase my breath control, and led to an interesting sideline later in my career.

In 1935, Teach accepted a teaching job at the Racquet Club, a resort in Palm Springs owned by actors Charlie Farrell and Ralph Bellamy. I went with her. I had been living with Teach a year, and both my health and my tennis had improved. My career, my very life, was tied up in my coach. She was forty, I was twenty-two.

While Teach gave lessons at the club, I ran the pro shop and played "social" tennis with members like Paul Lukas, Frank Morgan, Gilbert Roland, and Errol Flynn. They were the sexiest male stars of the day, and a mischievous bunch who loved to tease me. One day, several of them came into the shop, pretending to look at the merchandise.

Flynn called across the shop to me, "Alice. I need an athletic supporter—a jockstrap."

I blushed. "What size?"

"The largest you have, of course!"

The group howled with laughter. Embarrassed as I was, I laughed, too, and chased them out of the shop. Having grown up in a house full of boys, I was comfortable with men on this level. Their playful pranks showed me they considered me one of the boys, just as the Seals baseball team had. That was the way I wanted it. Seven years had passed since the rape, but I still had nightmares about it.

Palm Springs was a resort town of about thirty thousand people, with one theater, two hotels, and two little gambling houses (one where you could play for a dime and the owner served you chili, the other more like a Las Vegas casino). There was no real night life, but the stars who came there generated their own excitement. On days when it was too windy to play, and evenings (if we had the energy after a day on the courts), Teach and I had our choice of Hollywood parties.

At the club, Teach was swamped with actors. Tennis was the "in" sport, and she was the in coach. I added George Brent, Marlene Dietrich, and Robert Taylor to her schedule book in one day. Despite her famous clientele, Teach wasn't a movie fan, and hadn't the slightest notion who was famous for what.

One day I walked onto the court just as Teach said to Jeanette

70

MacDonald, "Miss MacDonald, your face is familiar. Where have I seen you before?"

Jeanette saw the expression on my face at Teach's remark, and burst out laughing.

Teach looked at me. "I've done it again, haven't I?"

I nodded. "Miss MacDonald is one of MGM's biggest singing stars."

When I wasn't rallying with the actors during their lessons, I often watched and applauded good shots. Most of them were pleased that I was interested, and no one had ever objected. That's why Teach's first lesson with Joan Crawford was such a shock.

They had just begun when Joan startled me by shouting in my direction. I looked behind me, certain that she was yelling at someone else.

"Get the hell out of here!" she called again, looking right at me. "Go on, I don't want you around. I don't want you watching me."

I left quickly, hurt at the dismissal, but I shouldn't have been surprised. Crawford liked control, having had little of it in her childhood. She grew up in terrible poverty; her father deserted her; and her mother had the morals of an alley cat. When Joan stepped on a broken bottle as a child and cut the tendons in her foot, the doctors said she would never walk again. Yet her entrée into Hollywood had come through her work as a dancer in New York.

I respected her for what she had made of her life, but I was glad that her interest in tennis was short-lived.

One day a little girl with a headful of curls walked onto the court where I was practicing my serve. "I'll bet you can't play tennis and ride a bicycle at the same time," she said without preamble. I laughed. What a little cherub she was!

"You're on!" I said. My challenger ran off to get a bike, and I found someone to hit balls to me. I returned enough hits to win the bet, and to amuse the people who gathered to watch. The club photographer popped off a dozen shots, and the next day's newspapers ran a photo of six-year-old Shirley Temple and me. We met many years later at the United Nations building in New York, and had a good laugh at the memory of our first meeting.

Periodically, Teach took me away from the Hollywood atmosphere of Palm Springs. I was beginning to like it *too* much, she said, and it was distracting me from my tennis.

On those occasions, we drove to an estate in the desert near Indio. The huge Spanish hacienda, La Finca de Esperanza, and thousands of acres of date groves belonged to Jim and Claire Beechnut Arkell.

Claire's family had once made a living selling homemade jams and jellies in upstate New York. Then one of her brothers went to South America, where he became intrigued by chicle, a tree sap that the natives liked to chew. He sent some of the stuff home to his family, who came up with a formula for chewing gum (in fact, Chiclets) and built it into the Beechnut empire.

For all their wealth, Jimmie and Claire were simple, low-key people. We played tennis with them, swam in their big pool, walked in the fruit groves, and lingered, caught up in pleasant conversation, over steaks cooked on the outdoor grill.

We returned from a visit to the Arkells as the Racquet Club was preparing for the big end-of-season tournament. Teach, I realized, had taken me away to relax before the event she hoped would mark my comeback. Carole urged me to enter, Teach said I was ready, and Dr. Commons added his blessing.

With some trepidation, I added my name to a list of entrants that included Southern California's best women players—Dorothy Bundy, Carolin Babcock, Dorothy Workman, and Gracyn Wheeler.

I had little trouble making it to the final, where I met Carolin Babcock, my Wightman Cup teammate on that fateful trip to France.

"Alice, you look great!" Carolin had said to me on the first day of the tournament. From the surprise on her face, I supposed that I *did* look good. My weight was down to 150 pounds, my acne had disappeared, and, with the help of Carole and Teach, I had more poise than before my illness.

Carolin and I faced each other across the net, and I wondered how I looked to her then. Having seen me dispatch several good players in the preliminary rounds, she wasn't smiling. During my two-year hiatus, Carolin had replaced me as third-ranking player in the country, and she knew I was hungry to regain that status.

I checked my brimmed cap, adjusting the cabbage leaf inside it, and fitted it snugly on my head. Laborers in the desert always put cabbage leaves under their hats to prevent sunstroke, and Dr. Commons had suggested I try it. I never played in the heat without one when I discovered that my head stayed cool, though the top of the cabbage leaf was hot. Despite my bad health history, I was never again dizzy after a match. Occasionally my hat would fall off, and people would ask, "What do you do with the cabbage, eat it?"

"Only if there's corned beef handy," I would reply. My hair smelled like cabbage, but that was a small price to pay.

Cabbage leaf in place, I beat Carolin Babcock, 6–2, 6–2, in the Racquet Club tournament, my first in nearly two years. The day was terribly windy, which was to my advantage since I was more accustomed to Palm Springs' weather than Carolin was, but it was a victory nevertheless. The club members in the stands rose to their feet, and I could hear my name being shouted over and over. Carole, her golden hair tossed by the wind, was bobbing up and down next to Teach, who stood grinning, her eyes fixed on me.

A subdued Carolin and I shook hands, and the party began. Teach was mobbed by well-wishers bearing martinis for her. Wes the bartender had done a land-office business before the match, fortifying members against the possibility of my losing; now he fueled a thirsty victory celebration.

Even my little dog Jackie was in the bar. People had been giving him cherries out of their cocktails, and he was none too steady on his feet when I made them stop.

I was probably the only person in the club who *didn't* drink that night. I didn't need to; I was high on the realization that I had done what only a handful of people believed I could do. I had beaten a devastating disease, I was on my way back, and nothing was going to stop me.

11 : PROOF

"I'm ready. I know I am," I told Dr. Commons. "*Please* tell me I can go east this season." I had grown to love this wonderful old man, but his caution now made me impatient.

He rested his hand on the thick folder containing my medical records and shook his head.

"The Racquet Club tournament took a lot out of you—more than you'll admit," he said. "I don't think you're strong enough for an entire season; it's too much stress. Can't you wait another year, just to be sure?"

"Please," I said again. We had been over this before. The tournament had tired me, but I was certain that it was conditioning, not rest, that I needed. At twenty-two, if I wanted a career in tennis, I couldn't afford to wait. I had to go east, and I had to do it now.

"Play a couple more tournaments, then we'll decide."

I sighed. It wasn't a total victory, but it wasn't a total loss either. I could visit my family in San Francisco and play in the state championships there, if Teach agreed. She did, sending me off on the train with a promise to join me later.

Home. I stood for a moment, looking up at the white frame house atop the hill. It had been less than two years, but it seemed a lifetime since I had been carried down those steps to Teach's car on my way to the sanatorium. I started climbing the worn cement steps two at a time, as I did when I was a child, counting "Two, four, six . . ."

When I reached "thirty," my mother saw me and ran down to meet me, throwing her arms about me with such enthusiasm that I thought for a moment we'd both topple down the stairway. I hugged her, loving the familiar smell of her, but something was wrong. All my life she had been plump; now I could feel her bones

74

through her cotton dress. Before I could ask her about it, she was hurrying me up to the house, both of us laughing and crying and trying to talk at once.

We were a family again. The house seemed smaller, Dan was heavier, and George's hair was thinner, but there was a sameness, a familiarity about it all that was comforting. I felt the warmth of their love, and realized how much I had missed them. Dan gave me a play-by-play account of the national handball tournament, in which he had finished second. Always second. My brother had the misfortune to be in the same generation with a handball star so good no one ever beat him.

Mother started to fill me in on the neighborhood gossip, but I interrupted her. "You've lost so much weight. Are you ill? Have you seen a doctor?"

"I'm not fat anymore. Is that any reason to complain?" She dismissed the subject with a wave of her hand, and returned to her recital of neighborhood births, deaths, and indiscretions. She had sworn the others to silence about her cancer, saying that I had my own health to worry about. I should have suspected something, but I was too thrilled at being home.

Hazel and I discovered that we were both grown women now, and had much to talk about—her disastrous marriage, my career as an athlete, and, of course, Carole Lombard and the other stars who lent a touch of glamour to my life. Sitting in the bedroom we had shared for so many years, we talked well past the curfew Dr. Commons had sworn me to.

My homecoming at the Berkeley Tennis Club wasn't as warm. Old friends like Helen Wills's coach, Pop Fuller, and champion Billy Johnston, after whom I had patterned my grip when I first started to play, were happy to see me. But some of the players still resented me for "defecting" from San Francisco to Los Angeles. How silly. Wherever Teach Tennant was, that's where I would be.

Other players were *too* friendly. I hadn't seen any letters from them while I was ill, so I assumed their interest was because of my Hollywood friends, or because my tennis career was on the upswing. I had become wise to the ebb and flow of popularity. In any case, it was easy to turn down social invitations. Dr. Commons's restrictions and Teach's insistence that I stay in training precluded anything but rest and tennis. I spent as much time as I could with my mother, not knowing her time was running out.

My comeback attempt was starting to make the news, but still the sportswriters were critical of my style. More than ever, I wanted to show what I could do.

Hazel went with me to the Berkeley Tennis Club while I worked my way through the preliminaries of the California State Championships to the final round. I was glad she was there. I needed a real friend to counter the vague hostility at the club. On the day of the final, Carole and Teach joined her in the stands. Carole gave interviews to a mob of reporters, and in every one she talked about me.

"Alice Marble has done what few people would have the guts to do," I heard her say. "She has come back from a terrible illness to play tennis again, and she *will* be champion."

If only I could live up to that boast! I had two things going for me besides Carole's and Teach's support. My earlier training with Teach and Beese had been curiously reinforced by all those lessons I watched during my recovery, and I had been practicing hard since the Racquet Club tournament. I knew I was ready. But that didn't keep me from feeling weak-kneed when I walked onto the court before an unfriendly audience.

Fans had packed the stands to see the final (and Carole Lombard), but only a handful clapped when I was introduced. My opponent was Margaret Osborne, the best player in Northern California and the darling of the San Francisco crowd. We were old friends, having grown up together on the courts in Golden Gate Park, and we were alike in many respects—strong, quick, and willing to take chances. I expected a tough match.

Margaret acknowledged the cheers with a wave of her racquet, and I felt dejected. This was my hometown too. But the hurt only lasted a moment. I had come to play tennis, and I settled to it with determination.

It took me less than half an hour to dispatch Northern California's best, 6–1, 6–1, and I was sorry it was over, despite the fact that I had not had the crowd with me. The gray asphalt court felt good beneath my feet, and the ball was fast and lively on the hard surface. My strokes were working, and I was relaxed and confident.

Early in the match I realized that although Margaret and I had started in the same way, she had only played in California and still used the Western grip. She would go on to win Wimbledon in 1947 and the U.S. championship in 1948, and would be a member of one of the best women's doubles teams ever, but in 1936 she still had a lot to learn.

Margaret's forehand carried so much topspin it bounced high and fat, and her backhand was weakened by an extreme underspin. Her strength lay in her net game, but I never let her use it. My ground strokes were low and fast, and though Margaret was quick, she had to work hard to get to the ball, and her returns were setups for my net game.

A radiant Carole Lombard handed me the championship trophy and hugged me. Her words rang out over a crowd subdued by the favorite's defeat.

"Congratulations, champ. The next trophy will be for winning the national championship!"

I sat in the stands with Carole, Teach, and Hazel the rest of the afternoon. The actress presented trophies for all the other matches, even the juniors. Everyone loved her, and she was enjoying herself. After my partner and I won the doubles, I turned down all the party invitations, and started home with Hazel.

Dan and Mother saw us coming up the hill with the big silver trophy and cheered. Mother prepared a special dinner of my favorite foods and everyone toasted me—with iced tea. It was a wonderful victory celebration, and when I left for Los Angeles the next day, there were no tears, just prayers and good wishes.

Dr. Commons brought me down to earth. "Going east is out. Your blood count has dropped fifteen points. I'm not going to bring you this far and let you destroy yourself."

There was no use arguing, so I prayed for a miracle, and did the only thing I could to make it happen—I stuck to my diet and training routine. Every morning, I ran and jumped rope. After breakfast, I worked on Teach's books, then joined her at the courts for my lesson. All afternoon I practiced with various men at the Los Angeles Tennis Club, where I was scheduled to play in the Southern California championships. Teach and I were staying with friends, but I saw little of them, excusing myself soon after dinner each night.

I was a model student and patient, and it paid off on both counts. I easily won the tournament to become number one in California again, and Dr. Commons decided I was strong enough, after all, to go east. Things were going so well—almost too well.

In June, Teach and I put our bags in her new Buick convertible and set out. "I won't let you go alone this time," she had assured me, "but I have to earn some money on the way."

Teach had arranged to do a tour of talks, clinics, and demonstrations for Wilson Sporting Goods, promoting the racquets that bore her name. Ours was a circuitous route—Chicago, Detroit, Cleveland, and points in between—but it would eventually get me to Forest Hills with my coach.

Teach had an incredible knack for teaching. She gave clinics in department stores, schools, public parks—sometimes addressing as many as five thousand people in a group. Singling out a few students, she used them to demonstrate her points, and the rest followed suit. She could make the laziest student run and the clumsiest hit the ball time after time. It was wonderful to watch.

At night, she dictated articles for the Hearst papers, which I typed and sent in for the next day's sports pages. After a few days, we loaded the car, drove to our next stop, and repeated the routine.

Teach seemed tireless, but I knew she was relieved when we neared Willoughby, Ohio. So was I. It was our last stop before New York, and promised to be our best. I folded the maps and stretched when Teach turned into the long lane leading to Field Day Farm, the little farmhouse where Mary K. Browne lived.

The former champion was on the porch when we pulled up. She looked up from her easel, grinned, and waved her paintbrush. Setting down her palette, she came to meet us smelling of turpentine, with a smudge of ochre on her chin. She was painting an Irish setter from a photo, one of the many dog and horse portraits she was commissioned to do.

As she and Teach embraced, I suddenly felt shy. This was the woman who had witnessed my dismal performances—and temper tantrums—on my first trip to Forest Hills.

"Alice," she said, turning to me. "I knew we would meet again."

She smiled, crinkling squint lines earned from years in the sun. It was a wide-open, honest expression, filled with compassion. I suddenly felt at home, and sensed that I always would be so with Brownie.

Each morning, the three of us played tennis on Brownie's cement court. And talked tennis. And tennis theory. A delighted guinea pig, I hit hundreds of balls while the two of them studied and experimented with my strokes, my stance, my footwork.

Afternoons, while Teach was conducting clinics in Cleveland, I played with the top local men on Brownie's court or at Lake Erie College, where Brownie taught tennis.

At night after dinner, we sat in darkness on the farmhouse porch, watching the stars and talking tennis. Brownie told us about the greats she had played with, players like Bill Tilden, Bill Johnston, Helen Wills Moody, and Suzanne Lenglen.

I had seen Brownie play Suzanne in San Francisco when I was about twelve; at least, I had seen a few minutes of the match. Dan had taken me to see them play, but it was hot and stuffy in the gymnasium, and I had fallen asleep.

"Suzanne was always angry," Brownie said, propping her feet on the porch railing. "She was so good that I used to earn bonuses on the pro tour whenever I won three games from her. But she was miserable. I remember her taking a swing at a photographer who

78

crossed her. The rest of us on the tour stayed clear of her. She dined alone with her mother, and complained incessantly that she wanted to go home. She was one hell of a player, though."

I adored Brownie. She was a gentle person, but it was no fluke that she was a champion. A flinty willfulness flashed in her big brown eyes whenever she was challenged.

"You can do anything you want, if you care enough," she told me.

I believed her, and was ready to twist the tail of New York tennis when the unthinkable happened. A telegram came from California, informing me that the U.S. Lawn Tennis Association had refused me entry to *all* of the Eastern tournaments.

"They think you're not well enough," Teach said, staring at the message. "That you'll collapse again. They don't want to be responsible. Myrick did this, that little weasel!"

She crushed the paper into a ball and threw it. She had her hand on the phone when Brownie stopped her.

"Teach, if you and Myrick start fighting again, it'll only make things worse. Let me see what I can find out."

Teach walked to the window and stared into the dark countryside. Her jaw was rigid and her eyes glistened, as if she might cry. Two long years of work, all her savings, and a lot of emotion had gone into my comeback.

Everybody in tennis liked Brownie, and it was her intercession that kept the door open, but just a crack. After a series of phone calls the next day, she walked out to the court where Teach was hammering balls to my backhand. The lesson had been a disaster, we were both so upset.

"Myrick is willing to give you a chance to prove that you're well," Brownie said. A telegram from Dr. Commons vouching for my health hadn't been enough to convince the tennis czar.

I looked at Teach, ready to rejoice.

"How?" Teach asked.

"By playing against men."

"That son of a bitch," Teach exploded. "He's determined to kill her!"

"I'll do it," I said, grabbing her arm. She stared at me. "I can do it." I looked at Brownie, who grinned back at me.

"There's no other way?" Teach asked, cursing under her breath when Brownie shook her head. "At least I'll be there to stop it if it's too much for her."

"So will I," said Brownie. I was glad she was coming with us. She was fun and supportive—and would be a buffer between Teach and Myrick.

12 : NUMBER ONE

1936

Four days in a row—days so hot the birds stopped flying and sought the shade—I faced male players on the Forest Hills courts. I tried not to think about what was at stake. Thinking only made the tension worse.

Thank God the players Myrick found weren't very good. (The Riggs-King match aside, I think it has been proven that it doesn't take a top male player to beat the best of the women.) And since I always practiced against men, I wasn't intimidated by them.

My last opponent quit when he was down 5–2 in the first set. "If she's sick, I'm at death's door," he said to Myrick and his committee. "It's too hot for me, but Alice is hardly sweating."

My nemesis watched the fellow walk away, then turned to me, his expression unreadable. I had him.

Incredibly, the committee's vote allowing me to play was only 3–2, much too close. I suspect the vote had less to do with my soundness than with the relative hazards of crossing Myrick or Teach. Brownie had no doubt helped swing the vote in my favor. I still shudder at how close I came to being barred from national competition.

I caught cold twice during the tournaments leading up to the nationals, and nearly panicked at the thought of being ill. I took aspirin, guzzled orange juice, and rested.

At Seabright, I beat Carolin Babcock, 6–0, 6–3. Moving on to the Longwood Cricket Club near Boston, I took the women's invitational singles. Then Gene Mako and I scored a terrific upset, wresting the national mixed doubles championship (played at Longwood prior to the singles at Forest Hills) from the favored team of Sarah Palfrey and Don Budge.

At Rye, I fell apart in the final against Sylvia Henrotin, my opponent the day I collapsed in Paris. I kept thinking of how the Frenchwoman's face had swum before my eyes, how I had tried to concentrate, to bring her into focus, to breathe, to move . . . In my distraction, I lost the Eastern championship to Sylvia in straight sets.

"You'll have to get rid of your ghosts," Teach said wryly. "Play *today's* match today. Yesterday's matches are history."

At the Essex Country Club Invitational in Manchester, Massachusetts, I advanced to the finals, as did my former Wightman Team captain, Helen Jacobs.

It was a real test for me to meet Helen. She would be trying for her fifth national championship in a few weeks, and I hoped to challenge her for it. The Essex match was a dress rehearsal.

I began the match with a bad case of stage fright. Every match I played, I felt as if I were on trial, even though I had passed Myrick's "test."

Helen took the first set, 6–3, before I pulled myself together. I bore down in the second set. My drives started to sizzle, their low, flat trajectory making them hard to return. I threw in chops and slices to keep my old teammate guessing, and soon the set was mine, 6–0.

During the ten-minute break, I cursed myself for dropping the first set, giving it away, really. Helen would toughen up for the third set. I had seen her pull herself back from the edge too many times.

When play resumed, I attacked, taking Helen to 3–1 before she really turned on, showing the stuff that made her a champion. In the closing three games, I could only manage two points. Unlike most players who favor their forehand, my opponent had a deadly backhand. She pounced on my returns to her strong side, made me eat them, and won, 6–3, to take the match.

I didn't like losing, but I felt that I was playing better than ever before and that I had learned a lesson. If I wanted to take the champion's crown from her, I couldn't ease into the game. I would have to play one hundred percent from the first service, and never let up. *And* avoid that backhand.

Teach had accepted an invitation from millionaire Gilbert Kahn and his wife to stay at their estate in Cold Spring Harbor, Long Island, for the two-week duration of the nationals. We had met the Kahns at the Palm Springs Racquet Club and, like most people, the couple had been charmed by Teach. At the time, Gil's father, Otto Kahn, was one of the most powerful bankers in the world.

I hid my annoyance. Teach and I *never* played singles. She played well, but she was nearly twenty years my senior. What was she trying to prove?

Teach had her way. Piping Rock was a beautiful country club, with acres of green lawn and big boxwoods. We watched part of a polo match, then headed for the courts, which were deserted. I quickly saw why; the grass had not been cut. At the sight of the long grass, I hooted.

"This should be interesting!"

"My thoughts exactly," said Teach, pulling out her racquet.

We played for about an hour, chasing balls that bounced crazily in the long grass. Watching Teach try to scoop up the low balls, I became helpless with laughter.

"You look like you're playing polo—or shoveling manure," I shouted. That set Teach off, and we both laughed until we were too weak to continue, then flopped down on a bench.

"Who won?" I asked between gasps.

"Who knows?" Teach wiped the tears from her eyes.

"Who cares?" I said, and we began to giggle again. It was the first real fun I had had on a tennis court in months of serious tournament play, months of proving that I still *could* play. I suppose I had become pretty grim about it all. Teach had known exactly what she was doing, bringing me here.

The next day, all my apprehension had lifted, and it was as much fun playing on center court as at Piping Rock. I won my semifinal match in twenty minutes, advancing to the finals. Helen Jacobs defeated Kay Stammers, and would play me to defend her title.

The once-divided Kahn household was now on my side, with Kay as my biggest rooter. But I knew that none of them had any real hopes of my beating the champion. Even Teach seemed more relieved about what I *had* done than excited about my prospects. I had certainly done well enough. My comeback had been erratic, but nothing to be ashamed of. I was the only one who thought I still had something to prove.

A little before noon on September twelfth, Teach and I left for the match, bolstered by everyone's good wishes. Charles—he of the cabbage leaves—made a little speech expressing the sentiments of the servants. Just as I was getting in the car, Mary, a Scottish maid, ran forward.

"Miss Marble," she said, her voice lilting and musical with the accent of her country. "Here's a bit o' heather. It'll bring you luck, ma'am." Touched, I gave her a quick hug. Teach and I said little on the ride to Forest Hills. I stretched out in the deep plush seat and tried to relax.

Jack McDermott, my favorite practice partner, was waiting to warm up with me. A crowd gathered to watch us, but I thought only about hitting the ball and running, running hard, stretching and jumping, making the blood pump into my legs and arms. If I thought about what was coming, my knees would turn to jelly.

Changing clothes, putting on makeup, and adjusting my cap with the cabbage leaf kept me from thinking about the match ahead. I had just put the sprig of heather in my shoe and was lacing up when the locker attendant said, "It's time for you to go, and I hope you win!"

"Thanks. I hope so, too." I breathed deeply a couple of times and went to join Helen Jacobs on the steps to the court.

Over the loudspeaker came the words: "This match will be between Miss Helen Jacobs, four times national champion and winner of the Wimbledon championship, and Miss Alice Marble of San Francisco."

We walked down onto the grass toward a wall of photographers. I won the toss for the serve. Rallying with Helen, I felt my assurance evaporating. My legs started to feel heavy, my throat dry. She looked so good!

The champion exuded confidence, moving easily in her tailored flannel shorts and English-made knit blouse. She looked strong, with her stocky legs and wide shoulders, and her green eyes flashed determination above the firm line of her mouth. Her right hand and thumb were wrapped in an elastic bandage, but that didn't seem to affect her hitting. Before the quarterfinals, Helen had slipped on wet grass and sprained her thumb, but her convincing defeat of Kay Stammers had dispelled any thought that she might be hampered by the injury.

The first set was a blur. I was so nervous, I'm sure I played like a robot, but I made some of the right moves. I broke Helen's service and went to 3–1 before lapsing into a string of errors. Helen won, 6–4.

I looked at the scoreboard, relieved that the score wasn't worse. I was going to be all right. Better than all right. Teach looked calm. Behind her in the stands were thirteen thousand fans, and they were cheering for me. It was because I was the underdog, but I loved their support all the same. Having the crowd behind you is a tremendous psychological advantage: It has caused many a player to take heart and come back from what seems to be certain defeat.

Buoyed by the fans, I won the second set easily. Helen and I went to the locker room for our break, closing the door on a stadium rumbling with excitement. Teach helped me peel off my sweaty clothes, her hands trembling as much as mine. There was a kind of awkwardness between us—a shyness, almost—as if we both wanted to say, "Look how far we've come," but were afraid of killing the magic of the moment. I ran cold water on my wrists while she poured tea.

"Hit to her forehand and work the net," Teach said automatically. We had analyzed Helen's game ad infinitum; I didn't need to be told. I nodded anyway.

"Mix it up. Make her hurry her shots."

I sipped the strong, hot tea. Teach was still talking, but I had stopped listening.

"Teach," I interrupted.

"Yes?"

"Two years ago, they told me I would never play tennis again. Now here I am in the final set of the final round of the national championship. I want to win—God, I want to win—but if I don't, I haven't lost."

"No, you haven't." Teach's eyes were bright, her voice husky with emotion. "Go on, go have fun."

I pulled on my favorite top, fastened the lucky pin on the lapel, and went out to play the final set.

The roar from the stands was deafening as we took our positions. Umpire Louis Shaw called for quiet, then said, "Play."

I won the first four games so quickly it surprised me. I kept Helen running with long drives deep to the baseline, cross-court chops, and drop shots. I had been avoiding her backhand, usually her strong side, but now I pressured it, too. The tactic surprised her. She didn't know what to expect from me.

The crowd's sympathies were swinging back to the champion, now the underdog at 4–0, but I was fueling my own fire. Hearing the cheers, Helen rallied to win two games; I took the next. The score stood at 5–2 when we changed courts.

I wiped my face, dried my hands on the loose sawdust in the big green box, and walked to the west court. Helen stood six feet back of the baseline, bobbing lightly on her toes, composed, ready for me. What did I have to use against her?

The American twist, with as much guts as I could put into it. I took a deep breath and served, feeling the muscles of my back bunch and stretch, grunting with the effort. The ball whined away from my racquet, threatening to spin out of its fuzzy skin.

"Fifteen–love, Miss Marble."

86

Helen met my next serve, and forced me into an error to tie the score. I served again. She lunged for the ball, but came up short. Thirty–fifteen.

I put everything I had into a high bouncing service, and ran to the net. Helen tried a down-the-line backhand, but I cut it off for a winner.

Forty–fifteen. We were at match point. I stood, bouncing the ball, reminded of a match three years earlier. I had had Betty Nuthall in the same spot, victory in my hands, and had lost. I decided to go to the net again, to go for broke. I served and sprinted forward, only to see Helen set up a high lob. I reversed and raced for the backline, legs pumping, gasping aloud with the effort.

I was going to be short; it was going to drop beyond me, but in bounds. At the last moment, I turned, leaped, and smashed the ball. It bounced in Helen's backcourt, and was caught by one of the ball boys against the back wall. Was it in? I saw his grin, and, above the roar of the crowd heard, "Game, set and match, Miss Marble. Four–six, six–three, six–two."

I stood for a moment, trying to absorb what had happened. It was over. Helen was walking toward the net, smiling at me. My racquet slipped from my hand, and I ran to meet her.

"Well played, Alice."

"I never thought I could do it, right up to the last point!" I shook my head in disbelief.

I felt an arm around my shoulders and looked into the smiling face of umpire Louis Shaw.

"Is it true, Louie? Have I really won?"

"You really won! You're champion of the United States!"

I saw Teach making her way toward me and ran into her embrace, nearly bowling her over.

"I'm so proud of you," I heard her say over the din. Later, when I had changed clothes and settled into the courtside box to watch Don Budge play Fred Perry of Great Britain, Teach leaned over and whispered, "Was Myrick's face red!" I returned her grin.

Budge played one of the most ferocious matches I've ever seen in tennis, bringing the champion to the guillotine time after time, only to have him slip away before the telling blow. In the eighteenth game, Perry scored on two passing shots against the tiring Budge, and finished him off with an ace. I almost forgot my own victory in the excitement of the game, but the reality of it rushed back when we were called onto the court for the trophy presentation.

I accepted the big silver bowl, shut my eyes in a quick prayer, then kissed the trophy. The photographers loved it. Their flashes melded into one bright blur of light. It was one of the happiest moments in my life, and much more than a tennis victory. I had been counted down and out, but I didn't stay down, and I surely wasn't out.

We were greeted by sheer bedlam at the Kahn estate. Most of the guests had been at the match, and the servants had heard it on the radio. Gil's mother, matriarch of the house, had invited fifty-nine people for a sit-down dinner; there were five hundred more on the grounds, dining at a lavish garden buffet and dancing to the Emil Coleman orchestra in the ballroom. When asked, I sang "Pennies from Heaven" and a couple of other songs with the orchestra before taking to the dance floor.

It was after midnight when Teach collared me and sent me to bed. The next morning, she allowed me to sleep in. At ten o'clock, a delightful breakfast tray arrived with flowers and a stack of telegrams. I tore open the top envelope, sipping orange juice as I read.

"You're the best! Love, Carole." I chuckled to myself, thinking of her speech at the Berkeley Tennis Club predicting my win. There were telegrams from my family, Beese, Marion Davies and Mr. Hearst, even Dr. Commons. I felt fulfilled, complete.

"Champion of the United States," I whispered, staring at my reflection in a silver plate. I had made it to the top. Could I stay there?

13 : HERO

Teach and I stayed in New York for a week after the championship, our days a whirl of public appearances, exhibitions, and dinners, all arranged by the USLTA.

"Funny, isn't it?" I asked Teach one night. "A month ago, the tennis association didn't want to know me. Now they act as if they own me."

"You're their champion now," she said, "their underdog, California-beauty, against-all-odds champion. The press loves you. Even Myrick loves you!"

We giggled at that. The tennis czar *had* to love me. The story of my comeback had transcended the sports pages and become an inspiration for everyone who had a debilitating illness. People who had never seen a tennis match were suddenly interested in the new champion, because I was a sort of Everyman's champion. Myrick, despite the villainous role he played in my story, was proud of me, and said so. It was good for tennis, and a refreshing change, for me, from the criticism of my game.

Returning to the West Coast, we were welcomed in grand fashion. The tennis associations arranged a full schedule of appearances to show off their champion, the poor kid who learned to play on public parks, and her famous coach. Teach thrived on the attention, and talked about me at every opportunity.

"Alice has worked very hard. I taught her the skills and the aggressiveness a champion must have, but it was her courage and determination that took her to the top."

She said this to countless groups of young players, admiration and envy in their eyes; to wealthy patrons of the sport at fifty-dollar-a-plate luncheons; and to women's groups, their combined perfumes as odoriferous as a flower show.

I told my story of illness, despair, and comeback so many times, I began to feel as if I were talking about someone else, some fictional character. But at last I had the chance to give credit to all those who had helped me, and to justify my style of play.

My winning the championship also showed that wealthy club players didn't have a lock on success. I walked over to Golden Gate Park one day, needing to get out of the house where I had grown up, to gather my thoughts, to reestablish contact with my beginnings. I stopped at a distance to watch the activity on the courts— some kids playing, others fidgeting on benches, awaiting their turn on a court.

If I could do it, so could they. I hoped I was an inspiration to them, along with Louise Brough, Helen Jacobs, and Margaret Osborne, all of whom were from middle-class families.

Winning the U.S. Open today guarantees a champion instant wealth through the endorsement of racquets, shoes, clothes, cars, and so on, as well as fat fees for playing in tournaments. That wasn't the case in 1936, when I became national champion. I moved in the wealthiest of circles, at home in the glamorous environs of the country's upper class, but I didn't have enough money to open a checking account.

We were no more true "amateurs" than players today are. Spalding and Wilson Sporting Goods supplied racquets and funded clinics, and the tennis associations did their best by providing travel, lodging, and a little pocket money, but there were always clothes to buy for tennis, for public appearances, for evening wear, and for our stays among the wealthy.

Only rich players could afford not to accept the help of patrons like Gil Kahn, banker Freddy Warburg, movie magnate Arthur Loew, Will du Pont, Jr., of the Delaware explosives family, and the department-store Bloomingdales. They opened their fabulous estates to us, providing rooms, meals, tennis courts, and a brief respite from money worries.

When Teach and I arrived at the San Francisco train station, the mayor, Mr. Rossi, who also owned the city's biggest florist shop chain, met us with an open limo laden with flowers. We were given a big parade through the town, with wailing fire engines, blaring bands, and baton-twirling majorettes. My family was in an open car behind the one carrying Teach and me, and my brother Dan, a newly commissioned motorcycle cop, rode at the head of the procession.

Spotting familiar faces, I waved and shouted their names above the noise. All the neighbors and many of my old classmates and tennis partners had turned out to welcome us, and I was moved as I had not been in the company of strangers in New York. This was real!

"Nothing like this has ever happened to me!" I said, turning to Teach, who was waving and smiling to the parade watchers on her side of the car. "Thank you."

"You've never been champion before!" Her expression was playful but her eyes were serious. "And thank *you*. I'm enjoying it, too."

There was another surprise waiting for me at home. Parked on the street in front of my mother's house was a new green Chevrolet coupe. I admired it on my way to the steps, but Dan stopped me.

"It's yours." He was grinning, and a set of keys dangled from his finger.

"What do you mean?"

"It's a present from Mr. Hearst and Miss Davies!"

There was a note on the front seat: "To the winner go the spoils!" and I was reminded of the card-game winnings I had refused. Mr. Hearst knew I wouldn't refuse this time.

There was a sobering aspect to my homecoming. When I saw that my mother weighed less than a hundred pounds, I knew something was wrong, and forced her into telling me she had cancer.

"Don't cry," she said, brushing the tears from my cheeks. "This is a happy time! Besides, when I can't be useful anymore, I don't want to be around."

"I'll stay here instead of going back to Palm Springs with Teach," I said.

"No, you won't. You will go live your own life—a wonderful life, too, now that you're well."

The time I spent with her seemed all too short, but she insisted that I stick to my schedule of engagements rather than "hang around the house underfoot." I always felt like a child with her, even though I was an adult now and my world was so much bigger than hers had ever been.

One day Mom agreed to abandon her kitchen and meet me downtown for dinner. Arriving early at the restaurant, I walked to the theater down the block, pushed fifteen cents through the ticket window, and went inside.

Just as I found a seat, the newsreels began, and the faces of Mussolini and Hitler flashed on the screen in grainy black-and-white. The Germans had elected Hitler their leader by a 99 percent margin, and the strange little man was meeting with the stout Italian to form the Rome-Berlin Axis.

The film switched quickly to Bruno Richard Hauptmann, charged with kidnaping and killing the Lindbergh baby. Teach and I had shared the country's outrage and sorrow at the crime, and, unaware of the doubts about Hauptmann's guilt, I was glad to see him brought to justice.

The sports news was next, leading off with the incredible Jesse Owens, winner of four gold medals at the Summer Olympics in Berlin. Then suddenly there was a tennis court on the screen.

"That's me!" I shouted involuntarily, leaping to my feet and pointing at the screen. There were good-natured titters and clapping from the audience, and I sank back into my seat, my face hot with embarrassment. But it *was* me, winning the national championship! It was the first time I had seen myself on film, and I carefully watched the darting figure with the white brimmed cap.

I was satisfied with my strokes; they looked much as I expected, but when I saw myself striding to the net to shake hands with Helen, I groaned and slid deeper in my seat. Now I was really embarrassed. The girl on the screen walked like a stevedore, or a farm girl following a plow. Why hadn't Teach told me? When I put the question to her later, she shrugged.

"I didn't really think much about it," she admitted. "I was worried about your game."

But she and Carole, after a good laugh at my agitation, agreed with my decision to enroll in the John Robert Powers modeling school. This "charm school" immediately improved my posture and walk, skills I was grateful for later, when I began a series of speaking engagements across the country.

A mountain of fan mail was waiting for me at Palm Springs, and more came every day until there were thousands of letters— from fans, from people wanting to know how I managed to come back from tuberculosis, and from players seeking advice. I tried to answer them all, to keep up with public appearances, and to practice. Practice never ceased.

Our first day back at the Racquet Club, I finished a workout in tears.

"Dammit, Teach, are you trying to kill me?"

I was red-faced, sobbing for breath, and my arms and back ached. Teach had told my practice partner, Johnny Lamb, to lob to me every chance he got, so for more than an hour I had been backpedaling, leaping, and smashing.

"Sorry, Allie," Johnny said, glancing at my coach before leaving the court.

"I don't want you to get cocky." Teach's voice was level. "You think it was hard to reach the top? Wait till you see how hard it is to stay there. As the challenger, you have nothing to lose; as the champion, you have *everything* to lose, *every* time you step on a court."

Teach was right, but while she was trying to keep *my* head in the right place, she was much less conservative in conversations with friends and the press. She told everyone that the Wimbledon singles title next spring was as good as mine.

"Now that Alice has regained her health," she said to one news-paperman, "nothing can stand in her way. She is the best woman player in the world today."

The year 1936 slipped into 1937, and my celebrity status continued to surprise and delight me. Teach was even more in demand than before, and doors everywhere opened for the two of us.

When the Golden Gate Bridge was completed, Senator Phelan invited me to be the first person to cross the bridge. Again I was treated to a convertible ride, a cheering crowd (San Franciscans love parades), and a ribbon-cutting ceremony at the end of the bridge.

It was thrilling to be a hero in my home town. Sports figures don't get that sort of treatment anymore except in small towns, but in the thirties athletes and movie stars took everyone's mind off a real world that was pretty dismal, and getting worse all the time. The Japanese had become aggressive, seizing Peking, Shanghai, and other Chinese cities; the stock market was declining, and FDR, reelected by a wide margin, was under great pressure to pull the country out of recession.

The tennis world, my world, remained untouched. That winter, I spent two months training at Beese White's. He never told me that he was proud of me, but he did say to Teach, "I should have known she would make it. That girl had a streak of silver in her." That was high praise, coming from the disciplinarian, and I was touched when Teach told me.

When spring came to the desert, Teach and I prepared to leave for England, where I would play in four European tournaments from May to July, culminating with Wimbledon, then return to the States for the East Coast season and the nationals.

Teach would lose the income from four or five months of lessons, but we didn't dare break the spell our partnership had created. Guilty as I felt about my indebtedness to her, I was relieved that she was going with me. With Teach in charge, I had no decisions to make off the tennis court.

14 : EUROPE

1937

"I'm glad you're here," I said to Teach, gripping the ship's rail and watching the distance widen between the dock and the sleek white vessel. We'd had a great send-off, and the sportswriters had turned out en masse to scribble down our parting words. I hadn't much to say, but Teach reasserted her confidence that I would win the Wimbledon singles. She'd never bragged on me like that before, and it made me uneasy. Just being on board ship gave me a frightening sense of déjà vu, in light of my last voyage. *I'm glad you're here, but shut up about Wimbledon*, I wanted to say, but didn't.

The six-day voyage turned out to be nothing like my previous trip abroad. I was in wonderful health and, if Teach had allowed it, would have danced every night away in the ship's palatial ballroom.

Teach, the socialite, was enjoying herself, but I was her first priority, her raison d'être. I wished she were a bit less diligent. I was twenty-three, my hormones were in full tilt, and there were several attractive young men whose attention I found very pleasing. I could have been coaxed into a shipboard romance, were it not for my mentor's nightly tap on the shoulder and firm, "It's ten o'clock. Time for bed."

Eight years had passed since I'd been raped in the shadows of Golden Gate Park. I couldn't forget, but I could put it where it belonged, behind me. It was time.

I had many male friends, and many who wanted to be more than friends, but so far I had avoided intimacy with any of them. The man wasn't right or the time wasn't right, I had told myself, but I knew I was simply afraid. Some of the fear stemmed from the

94

rape, but I was also afraid of Teach, of losing her if I went against her wishes.

"Don't get involved. It'll ruin your game," she warned me every time I showed interest in a man. It was hard to comply when there was love and lust all around me.

There's something about athletes—the obsession with their own bodies, perhaps, or the intensity caused by constant competition—that makes them highly sexual. There were always affairs, heterosexual and homosexual, on the circuit; like the movie community, the players protected their own. A Billie Jean King or Martina Navratilova scandal in the thirties or forties would have been devastating to the sport.

Bill Tilden was tennis's sacrifice to the world's homophobia, though he was hardly alone in his sexual preferences. One of the top women's doubles teams were partners off the court, too. We all knew about it, although when asked, I always said, "I wasn't under the bed."

Eventually they both married and lived seemingly conventional lives, their secret safe.

I envied the lovers' closeness, the looks exchanged, the casual touching of shoulders, the brief clasp of hands before a match. My life was so sterile by comparison. Even Teach had lovers from time to time, though she was so discreet that I never knew for sure who they were. But she guarded me like a maiden aunt, and I let her.

She watched my figure as carefully as my virtue, and I didn't gain a pound during the voyage to England.

"Teach!" I watched her wave off a waiter wheeling a dessert cart. I had set my sights on a frothy chocolate concoction easily worth dying for.

"You'll just get fat." The woman had no mercy.

My weight was under control now. After two years, I had graduated from Dr. Commons's strict diet with some firmly ingrained eating habits (despite an undiminished passion for chocolate). I was fit and slim, and proud of the way I looked. Carole teased me for outweighing her, but it was only because I had more muscle.

"You've become quite a knockout," the actress told me before I left for Europe. "Keep your mind on your tennis and off those handsome Continental men." She winked at me and laughed, but Teach wasn't amused.

I worked out in the ship's gym every morning, then showered and sat in a chair on the upper deck, a lap robe tucked around me, sipping steaming cups of bouillon poured from silver pots by white-coated stewards. I breathed deeply of the cool air, loving the smell of it, and the taste of the briny spray on my tongue. It reminded me of San Francisco, of the long hikes with my brothers to the shore of a different ocean. Porpoises and whales showed off for me, and occasionally I spotted the sinister-looking fin of a shark following the ship.

Afternoons, I took on all challengers at the Ping-Pong table, ran laps, or hit tennis balls against the wall of the gym. When we docked in England, I felt great, though Teach's optimism about Wimbledon still made me nervous. I had been overawed by the European players in France. Was I good enough to beat them now? Was I good enough to beat Helen Jacobs again, if it came to that?

By the time we said good-bye to our cozy shipboard cabin, I had learned another lesson from my coach. I knew exactly where everything was in our twenty-one heavy leather bags. Evening clothes? Suitcase four. The belt to Teach's red dress? Number eight, right front corner. Discipline, Teach said, was crucial to success. I decided that if knowing where my socks were would help me win Wimbledon, I was willing to go along with it.

It was soon obvious that the English-born Teach wasn't comfortable with the people of her homeland, simply because they didn't do things as she did, and refused to be bullied by her.

The British press, a judgmental lot, labeled us both as cocksure about Wimbledon, when in fact I knew all too well what my odds were. Only four women in fifty-three years had won the championship of the All-England Club on their first try. What was it about the place?

The weeks leading up to Wimbledon were good ones. I won a lot of confidence-building tournaments, and Teach was pleased at my quick adjustment to the surfaces. There were some fun matches, too. In Monte Carlo, I teamed up with old King Gustav of Sweden against a pair of French players who apparently didn't know that the king *always* wins. After our defeat, I was changing clothes when Teach joined me, bursting into laughter as soon as the door closed behind her.

"What's the joke?" I wrapped a towel around me, and started toward the bath. Teach's words stopped me.

"Mr. G. [as the king was called] blamed his loss on you. He told everybody you were off your game because you had your period."

"That old fart!" I joined in her laughter.

I had another royal doubles partner that year, one who had been

96

a source of great consternation for his country. Prince Edward VIII had been crowned King of England in 1936, after the death of his father, King George V, only to abdicate the throne before the year was out. I had listened to the coronation of his brother, George VI, on the radio.

Edward, now the Duke of Windsor, was the object of much protocol despite his diminished title. He seemed a rather dissipated, melancholy romantic. He wasn t a bad player, though, and we had a spirited match, ending in victory for our side. The Duchess, the divorced Mrs. Wallis Simpson for whom Edward had given up his throne, was most impressive. She met everyone in our contingent, wrote down all their names, then correctly introduced everyone to her husband. She took wonderful care of him, and I was touched to think that love had the power to alter monarchies.

It began raining a few days before Wimbledon, which was hardly unusual for the British Isles, but I hated the confinement the weather caused. I was in the lobby of our hotel, singing "I've Got My Love to Keep Me Warm" and picking out the tune on the piano, when Commander Frye, a retired World War I navy officer, found me.

"How would you like to have a look at the All-England Club?" he asked. "I have a car outside."

"I'd love it!" I quickly rounded up a group of other players who had never played Wimbledon, and we squeezed into the black Rolls for the ride to the club.

Our voices unconsciously dropped when Frye led us through the players' entrance. We lingered a while at the plaque-covered wall honoring past croquet, badminton, and tennis champions, then followed him toward Centre Court.

I stopped before the famous arch, and read aloud Kipling's words: "If you can meet with Triumph and Disaster/And treat those two impostors just the same . . " It seemed a lifetime since I had heard those words, on my first trip to Forest Hills.

"Make mine 'triumph,' please," somebody muttered, and a ripple of nervous laughter ran through the group. We passed under the arch into one of the most important tennis theaters in the world, and made our way up into the stands. From the royal box, we viewed the hallowed patch of green that was Centre Court, shimmering in the rain.

I suddenly felt the hair rise on the back of my neck.

"Commander," I asked, "do you have indoor courts here?"

"No, my dear, we don't."

"How about sound effects"—I hesitated—"like in a movie?"

The old gentleman stared at me for a moment, then started to smile.

"You hear it, don't you?"

I nodded, mystified. "Where's it coming from?"

From the puzzled looks of my companions, I knew I was the only one who heard the sound of racquets hitting balls.

"Don't laugh," said Frye, "but it happens occasionally. We think what you're hearing, what others have heard over the years, is the ghosts of old players. We've been able to find no other explanation."

I didn't laugh, nor did anyone else. Silently we regarded the court, the arena where generations of hopes had lived and died. What would be the fate of ours?

Everyone attended the draw, the process by which the players were divided into two sets. Fingers crossed and eyes tightly closed, I sat praying. Around me others were probably doing the same, and probably for the same reason. No one wanted to draw into the same half with Hilda Krahwinkel Sperling, the toughest player on the Continent.

When the official called out "Sperling," I opened my eyes and sighed, looking at Teach. Hilda *was* in my half, and we both knew the six-foot German would be a formidable obstacle between me and the championship.

A few days later, I met Hilda in the quarterfinal round with a mixture of trepidation and confidence. Teach and I had watched one of her earlier matches, and had come away dumbfounded. We couldn't believe that she was the fourth-leading player in the world, winner of the past three French championships, and the German champion since 1934.

"She does everything wrong!" I said.

Teach shrugged. "It's not how you hit the ball, but when and where that wins matches."

"Profound," I snorted, "but hardly what you and Beese said when you were making me over."

Teach ignored my remark, and we compared our impressions. German-born, but now representing her husband's country, Denmark, Hilda Sperling was one of the tallest people in tennis, with long arms and legs which made it difficult to lob to her or pass her down the line. She was also the most unconventional player *anybody* had ever seen.

"She is one of the best, yet most hopeless players I've ever seen," Bill Tilden once wrote. "Her game is awkward in the extreme, limited to cramped unorthodox ground strokes without volley or

98

smash to aid her, yet she has been the most consistent winner in women's tennis each year since 1934."*

Her forehand began at knee level, racquet head well below the wrist, and rose up and over the ball. Her backhand was better, but her serve, volley, and overhead were incredibly soft strokes that produced winning points only because they were so well placed.

"There's something peculiar about her grip, too," I said to Teach.

"I checked into that, and you're not going to believe it. Hilda holds the racquet with her thumb and first two fingers. She injured the tendons in her hand, and her last two fingers are useless."

"You're right," I said. "I don't believe I just saw her wipe out a player with two fingers." I remembered my first meeting with Beese, when he had made me hold my racquet as the German did. I had been helpless!

Teach and I decided my best strategy was to come out blasting, in hopes of tiring her, and then force her into errors by changes of pace. We began the first set, and I, not Hilda, was the one committing the errors. I was playing brilliantly one minute, like a novice the next. Hilda seemed confused by my inconsistency (as was I), but she capitalized on my errors, turning them into points. She showed no emotion, but her play was steady, calm, and intelligent—all the things mine was *not*. A sudden shower interrupted the set and gave me a chance to collect myself. When play resumed, I took the set, 7–5.

I began the next set hopefully, but Hilda now took control, covering the backcourt with her long limbs and forcing me to scamper about the backcourt. From a lead of 4–2, she went on to win the next six games.

My mind reeled. Dammit, it was happening. I was going to lose. I couldn't lose. God, not now! But there was no way I could get the ball past Hilda. She was everywhere, and I was helplessly playing her game.

She was leading 3–0 in the last set when I changed tactics. Risking all, I moved to the net and hit drives at my opponent, instead of trying to pass her. That forced some awkward returns, and I was able to put away many of them, relying on volleys and smashes.

It worked, and the crowd loved it. When Hilda and I met at the net, neither of us could be heard over the roar from the stands. We

* Helen Jacobs' *Gallery of Champions*, copyright 1949 A. S. Barnes and Company, Inc.

stood mutely smiling at each other for a moment, gripping hands, and I knew I had been lucky. Hilda was an indefatigable player, and I doubt that I could have outlasted her in a test of stamina, which so many of her matches turned out to be. With Helen Wills Moody out of action, she was the toughest of the lot.

I looked again at the scoreboard, still not believing it: 7–5, 2–6, 6–3. Then I felt Teach's arms around me.

"You're on your way," she whispered ecstatically. "You're going to win it!"

My coach and I would have done well to consider the old saw about counting chickens before they're hatched, or the more modern, piquant "It ain't over till it's over."

I went down in flames against Jadwiga Jedrzejowska, the chunky Polish champion. JaJa had a hit like a mule's kick and it was working for her that day. She blasted her drives deep in the corners, spinning chalk from the line time after time with her deadly placement. She pounced on my returns with unnerving enthusiasm, sturdy legs churning and all the force of her blocky, muscular body addressing the ball. I turned to putty, like papier-mâché in the rain.

Walking to the net, I was aware that I was moving, but I was devoid of physical sensation, like a dreamer. I shook my head, hoping to wake up, and saw the compassion on the Pole's broad face. It was true. I *had* lost. I was out of Wimbledon.

15 : CONSOLATIONS

Pride forced me to hold back my tears until I reached the Wimbledon locker room. When the door closed behind me, I slumped onto a bench, my racquet still in my hand, and began to cry uncontrollably. The pressure that I had felt since the national championships—the pressure to win Wimbledon—was gone, but there was no relief. I had failed, and I had let Teach down. My racquet clattered to the floor, and I pressed the heels of my hands against my eyes until I saw stars, but the tears still came.

Jadwiga patted me on the shoulder as she came in. She knew the misery of losing. She had hammered her way into tennis's top ten the year before, placing sixth in the world rankings (two places behind me), but not without painful losses. This was the first time she had made the Wimbledon finals, and it was to be her last.

The empire's own Dorothy Round, who had won the championship in 1934 only to give it up to Helen Wills Moody and Helen Jacobs the next two years, was not to be denied her country's greatest tennis prize in 1937. Two days after JaJa defeated me, Dorothy beat her in the third set of a final played in blistering (by English standards) eighty-degree temperatures.

Dorothy unaccountably tossed the second set to her opponent with errors and lackluster play, and let the Pole, whose only real weapon was her forehand, take her to 4–2 in the third. Only then did she find the steel that made her such a tough competitor. Tasting victory, JaJa became careless; it was all Dorothy needed. Despite one game lost on a net cord ball, she went on to win the set, 7–5, and the championship.

But in the moments after our match, JaJa was full of her semifinal victory and full of hope, having dispatched the American champion.

101

She searched her English vocabulary for the right words to comfort me. "Do not be hard on yourself. I was . . . lucky today."

She left me then, turned the taps of the lone bathtub in the historic old dressing room, and began to undress. Glancing back at me, she called, "Soon it will be your time. Soon."

I couldn't answer. I was too busy sniffing and mopping my face, a bout of self-pity that was cut short by Teach, who had been outside fending off reporters. The probing English press were particularly irritating when they forced her to eat her own words.

"Wonderful match, Jadwiga," my coach called across the dressing room, then turned to me and said quietly, "Go wash your face, then we'll get out of here. The press is lined up from here to the hotel." She lifted my chin and eyed my blotchy face. "It'll be okay."

Teach didn't show it—she could be so inscrutable when she wanted to—but I knew how disappointed she was. She had told the whole world I was going to win, and now the press was gloating. We had let last year's victory in the nationals go to our heads, and we were paying for that hubris.

I looked in the mirror and considered what I could say. Excuses? No. "JaJa played beautifully today. She was just too good for me." The truth had a way of sounding right.

I dried my face, took a deep breath, followed my coach out the door into the gauntlet of reporters, smiled, and said the words.

I had learned to handle defeat in a mannerly way, without excuses. Why take away from a person's victory by insinuating that she won because I had a blister, or my game wasn't working? When opponents did that to me, it lessened them in my eyes and, I suspect, in everyone's. So I never did it. I shed many anguished tears, but I played the game because I loved it, win or lose. I would no longer love it when losing took away the joy of a good match, and that would be the time to quit.

But I always castigated myself for my mistakes, points I should have won, points that ultimately made a difference. Back in the hotel room after a hot bath, a massage, and a late dinner, I was still moaning."How could I *do* that, Teach? I let her take control. I feel so *stupid!*"

"You *weren't* stupid. JaJa was extraordinary," said Teach. "Will you put it behind you? You still have the doubles." She threaded her fingers in my hair and roughly tilted my head back. "Stop sniveling. You're not going home empty-handed. You're going to be hell on wheels in the doubles."

I don't know that I was hell on wheels, but it was my first match on Centre Court, Don Budge and I won, 6–4, 6–1, and I loved every minute of it. Our opponents in the mixed doubles, Yvon Petra and Simone Mathieu, told the press afterward that "it was like playing against two men."

I took that as a compliment, and my partner laughed when he read it. The red-haired Californian was having his best year ever at Wimbledon, having swept all three events to become number one in the world. My doubles partner for many victories to come, Budge was Bill Tilden's closest challenger as the sport's greatest male player of all time.

"You know, Alice, the men seldom turn out to watch women play," he said, "but none of us, here or back in the States, ever misses one of your matches. You're fun to watch, and if you'll pardon my saying so, you do play like a man."

"Thanks . . . I think!"

My dear mother raised a jock for sure, but I knew she would be proud when she heard the news on the radio. It hurt to think of her. She still wrote to me every day, but I could tell by the spidery line of ink that she was getting weaker.

Kay Stammers and I paired up for women's doubles. She was wearing an outfit like mine for the match, mid-thigh-length white shorts and a short-sleeved sweater. I had worn a dress for a match when I first arrived in England and everybody asked, "Where are they?"

"Where are what?" I asked.

"The shorts!" The British fans had been looking forward to seeing me play in shorts! I never again worried about my unorthodox outfits.

Kay and I were knocked out in the early rounds, but I would still have my mixed doubles trophy to show for the trip.

The day after Wimbledon, I answered a knock on our hotel room door to find one of the bellboys standing there.

"Yes?" I asked.

"There's a car waiting for you, Miss Marble."

"A car? For what?"

"For Lady Crosfield's garden party." He looked surprised.

It was my turn to be surprised. "I hadn't planned on attending." I vaguely recalled the engraved invitation that had arrived earlier in the week. I had opened it and tossed it on the coffee table.

"But you *must*!" he said, rushing on when he saw I wasn't convinced. "Everyone goes to Lady Crosfield's garden party. It's a tradition! Please . . ."

"Okay, okay," I reassured him. "Please find Miss Tennant and tell her."

"Certainly, Miss. Oh, the driver says you should bring your tennis things. The players usually play an exhibition."

The bellboy was right. The picture-perfect lawn at Lord George and Lady Crosfield's mansion was alive with players, patrons of the sport, various London dignitaries, and a sampling of royalty. Queen Ina of Spain, a great tennis buff, was there, as were two of Queen Victoria's granddaughters, princesses Mary Louise and Helena Victoria, sitting in the shade in overstuffed chairs from the drawing room.

"Lady Crosfield's probably a frightful snob," I had whispered to Teach in the car, only to be rewarded with an elbow in the ribs and a "Shhh!" Our hostess turned out to be a delightful woman, bound by protocol, of course, but intelligent and witty in that droll way the Brits have. She became a fan of mine, and when I returned to Wimbledon, came to the locker room to wish me well.

In good spirits, Teach and I boarded our ship for home, and stood a long while at the rail watching the coast of England recede.

"I'll be glad to be back in America and away from these bloody accents," Teach said, exaggerating her pronunciation of "bloody."

"But I have to wait a whole year for another shot at Wimbledon," I said.

"There are a few things for you to think about between now and then." She cocked an eyebrow at me. "Forest Hills, for instance. Helen Jacobs has a score to settle with you."

16: THE SLUMP

After the cool of England, the New York summer dropped on us, wet and nasty as a used locker-room towel, but I immediately began practicing for the national championships, which I was favored to win. Wimbledon was a fluke, the sportswriters said, and for once, Teach and I agreed with them.

But there were other tournaments leading up to the nationals, and it was there that my nightmare began—continued, really—in the form of Jadwiga Jedrzejowska. JaJa, hungry after her near miss at Wimbledon, destroyed me at Seabright, and again at Rye. When she beat me once more at Westchester, I left the court demoralized and desperate.

"I can't beat her!" I said, slumping into a locker-room chair and fighting back tears.

"Not if you keep telling yourself you can't!" Teach's face showed her frustration. She had built me into a national champion, but I was as unstable as a house of cards. One moment I played like a champion, the next like a beginner, and it was all a matter of attitude. Teach had the drive, the confidence, the determination to win, but I was the one on the court. I'm sure she wished our positions were reversed, and sometimes, so did I.

Teach went on, her tone softening, pleading. "She's got one stroke, her forehand. That's all, one stroke!"

"One hell of a stroke!"

"Yes, there's so much topspin on it, it looks like it could tear your racquet right out of your hand, but that's not what beat you."

"Huh?" I stared up at her.

"You beat yourself. You're so worried about whether your *own* strokes are working for you that you don't bother to analyze your opponent's game, to look for holes, for weaknesses you can attack. You have a whole arsenal of strokes, but they're not worth a damn if your opponent controls the game and you don't get a chance to use them."

"Okay," I said without conviction. Still smarting from defeat, I wanted sympathy, not a lecture, and Teach's words had no effect. If they had, perhaps I would not have made the same mistakes the next week at Forest Hills.

The West Side Tennis Club no longer seemed stuffy or imposing, now that I was the reigning champion. When I practiced, crowds gathered to watch, and among them I could see the strained faces of first-timers, no doubt feeling what I had felt during my initiation, and wondering if they would ever be in my shoes.

I showed off for my audience, leaping higher than necessary for smashes. Tennis fans in my day weren't accustomed to seeing women jump; it was so unladylike. The onlookers oohed, and I grinned at Jack McDermott. At the net, I parried his hits with the sharply angled cross-court volleys that were my specialty when I was on. I heard the smattering of applause and lifted my racquet in acknowledgment. It was easy to be on when it didn't count.

"Would you like to take a bow?" Teach asked with mild sarcasm, throwing a towel over my shoulder. She signaled to Jack that practice was over.

He jogged over, kissed me on the cheek, and said, "You look wonderful! Tear 'em up, sweetheart."

I *felt* wonderful, my muscles loose and warm and powerful. I was going to "tear 'em up." I just knew it.

In the fourth round, I played Dorothy Bundy, daughter of May Sutton Bundy, the first American woman to win Wimbledon. I liked DoDo. Everyone did. She was the friendliest player on the circuit, and some said she was too mild-mannered to be a top competitor. Never having given her disposition much thought, I knew only that DoDo had never come close to beating me, and that I was in for a pleasant match.

I took the first set at 6–1, and quickly moved to within two games of winning the second. It was going to be easier than I expected. My confidence in full bloom, I relaxed, which was a mistake. Dorothy wasn't a great player, but she wasn't a pushover, either. Something happened to her; some inner spark got the fuel it needed and rumbled to life.

I had snaked a volley past her, just out of reach of her outstretched racquet. We were so close to the net, our racquets almost touched; I heard her breathing, and saw the flare of anger in her eyes.

Dorothy began to play then, dredging up all her strength and talent, going all out. Now I, who had used change of pace as a weapon so many times, found myself a step too slow. Struggling to catch up, to regain control of the match, I dived for a passing shot and slipped, skidding across the court on the side of my right calf. My concentration shattered, and Dorothy put me away, 7–5.

Helen Jacobs came into the dressing room at the break and silently swabbed my leg with alcohol while Teach talked to me.

"Get back in the game," she said, her eyes burning into mine. "You thought you had the win in your pocket and slacked off, but you can still take her. Go out there and play as if the match were just starting."

I nodded, bending over to examine my leg. It stung from the alcohol and looked like a piece of rare roast beef, but my knee and ankle joints weren't hurt. I replaced my blood-flecked socks with a fresh pair, and returned to the court.

A ripple of sound rolled through the stands. The fans sensed an upset in the making. Or would the champion come back and squash her challenger? It didn't take long for them to get their answer. Showing what a player can do when inspired, or provoked, Dorothy beat me, 6–1, and moved on to the next round. She didn't make it beyond the next round, and never again beat me, but that mattered little at the moment. I would never know if I could defend my title against JaJa. I hadn't given myself the chance.

That night, my calf swelled to twice its size, and I was secretly glad I didn't have to play the next day. But my thoughts kept flashing back to a match early in my career when I scratched my wrist and realized I had an excuse if I lost. I should have won then, but didn't; I played like a loser, and my brother Dan had left before the match was over. Remembering, I felt guilty, wondering if I had done it again. I hadn't used my leg as an excuse to others, but had I to myself? I moved restlessly in my bed.

"What's wrong with you?" Teach spoke softly from her bed across the room.

"My leg's bothering me."

"I don't mean that. I mean, what's bothering you enough to make you lose when you should be winning? I watch you practice, I watch you play, and I think that everything is there, everything is right, but it's not. Something's missing, and I don't know what it is."

"Neither do I." I stared up into the darkness.

Few people remember the 1937 U.S. champion, diminutive Anita Lizana of Chile, though some had compared her to the great Suzanne Lenglen. She loved tennis, and the fans loved her, with her dark eyes and constant smile. The South American was the first competitor to shake hands with all the officials after a match, a courtesy the rest of us quickly adopted. That's not all she taught us. Just five feet tall and weighing about a hundred pounds, Anita was a comparatively soft hitter, but her drop shot, beautifully disguised, was the most frustrating stroke I ever played against.

Anita disposed of Dorothy Bundy in the semifinals and faced the Polish Menace, JaJa, in the final.

"JaJa will blast her off the court," I whispered to Teach. We were watching the match with the Kahns, who had been so morose at my loss that I covered up my own disappointment so we could all enjoy the final.

Teach shook her head. "She'll use her speed and that drop shot."

Teach was right. We watched the little Chilean skip around the court, her smile only occasionally interrupted by a pursing of the lips when she made a mistake, but her mistakes were few. She fell several times, never letting a ball go by without trying to return it. She hit away from her opponent's forehand until that side of the court was wide open for her drop shot.

JaJa looked clumsy next to the sprite in the opposite court, but after being completely nonplussed in the first six games, she fought back from 1–5 to 4–5. Her backhand began to connect and she won several points on well-placed volleys, though the net was foreign territory to her. Anita adapted smoothly to the change, setting up a drop shot to pull her opponent to the net, then passing her down the line to take the set, 6–4.

JaJa began to unravel in the second set, her errors giving Anita a 4–1 lead. The Chilean double-faulted to give the Pole another game, then, at 40–love in the match game, hit a backhand down the line that left JaJa standing flatfooted. The two players embraced amidst thunderous applause from the stands. It was one of the finest matches I had ever seen, and I was humbled by Anita's mastery of her opponent's strength. I should have been able to do the same. Anita had won the championship, 6–4, 6–2, and she deserved it.

The Kahns threw a party for the champion, as they had the previous year when I won, but this time with just twenty or thirty people. When I came downstairs, the subdued atmosphere in the ballroom matched my mood. I caught a warning frown from Teach, and resisted the urge to slip back to my room. I was embarrassed by my loss, and dreaded the obligatory cocktail-hour postmortem.

I found a chair out of the mainstream and sat down. In moments, a pair of creased trousers blocked my view of the dance floor, and a beautifully wrapped package dropped into my lap.

"Freddy! What's this?" I looked up at Fred Warburg, whose Westchester County estate almost equaled Gil Kahn's in size and elegance. I had played many times with Freddy on his wonderful clay courts, often against his famous relative, Lord Lionel Rothschild. The old gentleman was a good player, but he had a weird, swooping serve that Freddy irreverently called "The Lord's Prayer."

"A surprise, of course," Freddy answered, perching on the arm of my chair and waving to the others to gather around.

I tugged at the fancy bow, and the wrapping parted to reveal a silver cigarette box. "Freddy, it's beautiful!" I said, holding it up for all to see. Neither Teach nor I smoked, but many of our friends did; the case would be wonderful in our living room.

"Read the inscription," he said, smiling down at me.

" 'If you can meet with Triumph and Disaster/And treat those two impostors just the same . . .' " I swallowed hard, then threw my arms around Freddy's neck. His was a wonderful gesture, and it brought me to my senses.

"Thank you, my friend, for the reminder," I whispered in his ear.

I grabbed Freddy's glass from the table beside us and lifted it high. "We have a new champion. I'd like to propose the first toast to Anita Lizana. She taught us all a lot today, about playing the game, and about enjoying it."

There was a cheer. Anita blushed and flashed her delightful smile at me. Glasses were raised and clinked and people began laughing and talking.

I went to the microphone and sang a couple of songs with the band. Everybody danced, and it turned out to be a wonderful party. The new champion glowed with pleasure. It had been seven years since the nationals had been won by a foreign player—and what an exciting player she was, quick and fluid in her movements, imaginative in her strategy.

"I admire you very much," I told her when we could talk privately. "I've been trying to beat JaJa all year, and you did it! It was a wonderful match."

"And I admire you," she replied, almost shyly. "I'll never have your courage. I love tennis, but it has never been hard for me. If I had to overcome illness, as you have, I would probably not be here today."

Anita was in her teens when she won the championship, and might well have become one of tennis's greats, but love got in the way. The very next year, distracted by wedding plans, she lost to two English players who didn't belong on the same court with her. A month later, she was married to Ronald Ellis, and dropped from the tennis scene completely. The debate, however, went on. Would she have been a second Lenglen?

Our conversation that night was brief. Everyone wanted to dance with the "senorita," and with the past champion, too.

Finally, I dropped onto a sofa beside Freddy's father, Felix Warburg, a kind Jewish man who had achieved the impossible: amassing a fortune in banking without making an army of enemies. He liked tennis, and always came to watch me when I played in the East.

"Mind if I sit this one out with you?" I asked, giving him a wink.

"You delight me, my dear," he said, his eyes lighting up. We started talking tennis and didn't stop until Teach pulled me away.

"I'm sorry, Mr. Warburg," she said. "Practice tomorrow."

"It's almost midnight," I said, kissing his cheek. "Teach is afraid I'll turn into a pumpkin."

"Goodnight, my dear," he said, rising. "I think I'll turn in, too."

Felix Warburg was found dead of a heart attack the next morning. His family was heartbroken, and begged me to recall everything their patriarch had said during the last hours of his life. I did, and I was grateful that I could use my memory to comfort people who were so dear to me.

17: GABLE

1937

Shortly after we returned to California, my mother died. The whole family was there, except me. She'd insisted that I continue with my schedule of tournaments, but when Dan called to tell me she was gone, I suddenly wished that I'd disobeyed her, and stayed at home during her last days.

My father's courage was always so obvious, but I had overlooked how strong my mother was, and how I drew from her strength. Her principles were simple: Do what's honorable; do what's healthy; don't quit; pray. I seldom made a decision without asking myself, "What would Mother do?"

Her last letter, written the day she died, caught up with me two days later, at a hotel in Northern California. The spidery handwriting was almost illegible: "I love you, Petsy, and I'm very proud of you—not because of your tennis, but because you are a good person. Don't ever forget that. I know you're having a hard time, but if tennis is important to you, don't give up. I'm praying for you. God bless, angels keep. Mother."

The tournament had been a disaster, and my mother's letter deepened my depression. I didn't want to let her go, not without doing and saying all the things I thought of now, when it was too late.

My mother's death didn't cause the downhill course of my tennis, but it did accelerate it. Something was terribly wrong with my game. I double-faulted and my confidence slipped; I missed a volley, and it slipped some more; I dumped five balls in the net and convinced myself that I couldn't do anything right.

Teach was calm, and more sympathetic than she had been at any other time in our relationship.

"You've got to pull out of this slump," she said. "You're number one in the country, you're the best, but you walk onto the court like a loser. You've got to *believe* you can win."

I didn't believe it. Why did Teach keep telling me it was all in my head, when my recent performances were proof that I couldn't win? It wasn't my fault that I was being outplayed. I still played well enough to romp through the early rounds of most tournaments, but when the pressure was on in the finals, I couldn't stand up to it.

In this frame of mind, I entered the Pacific Southwest Tournament at the Los Angeles Tennis Club, the event attended by all the stars and socialites. The setting was beautiful, with banks of flowers lining the courts, their scents rising in the heat of the sun. Stars introduced players and presented trophies, lending a special glamour to the matches.

I advanced through the preliminary rounds without opposition, but in the final I was to face Gracyn Wheeler, a limited but tenacious player who'd recently beaten me.

The morning of the match, Teach and I had breakfast on our small patio. The air was still cool, but a cloudless sky promised another sizzling day on the courts. I absentmindedly stirred my tea, thinking about the turn my career had taken. I pushed away my plate of toast.

"Teach, I don't want to play today." I avoided her eyes. "Tell them I'm sick. All our movie friends will be there, and I can't bear to lose in front of them." I'd had enough of well-meaning friends trying to think of the right thing to say after my losses. I raised my eyes to meet Teach's. "I *should* quit. I keep losing, and what I'm doing isn't fair to you or me. You need a winner. I want to hang it up."

She stared me down before she answered. "I *have* a winner. You just don't want it badly enough . . . yet."

When I started to argue, she cut me off. "You can't quit now, not like this. The tournament sponsors are your friends, too. You're the attraction, and they're counting on you. Give it one more try. If you win, I know you'll change your mind. If not, we'll talk then."

I agreed to play, although I dreaded it. What had happened to the fun of the game?

The men's final was still under way when we arrived at the club.

"You've got some time," Teach said. "Why don't you go see Clark and Carole? I'll meet you back here before your match."

Teach left to make the rounds of her movie-star students. I

wanted to see Carole Lombard and Clark Gable more than I wanted to play. Carole would have a whole new repertoire of jokes, and the easy banter we three always shared would be a relief. I hadn't seen my famous friends since I left for Europe.

It was the anniversary of my first meeting with Clark at the Pacific Southwest Tournament the previous year, when I was winning everything. Carole and I had hugged each other, and then she'd introduced her date. Gable shook my hand and gave me one of those heart-stopping crooked grins. He wasn't nearly as handsome as Errol Flynn, and looked as if he needed to grow into those big ears, but he had an open, guileless face.

Even though it was early in their relationship, Clark was obviously devoted to Carole. After her divorce from Bill Powell, she had dated another young actor, Russ Colombo, only to have him die in a freak shooting accident. She deserved a good turn in her love life.

A year later, the two of them were very much in love, despite being very different, for Clark was as shy as Carole was outgoing.

At our first meeting, I had impulsively asked Clark to introduce my match. He looked uncomfortable, like a boy who had just been asked to dance.

"Allie, I can't!"

"It's easy. I'll give you a slip of paper that says 'Alice Marble and Barbara Banks, best of three sets.' "

"You don't understand," he said. "I don't like crowds. I'd be embarrassed to walk across the court in front of all these people."

I realized he was serious. *Clark Gable!* Uneasy before real people! Before I could react, Carole rescued him. "Honey, don't you think Allie is pretty enough for a screen test?"

"I do," he said, his wonderful green eyes giving me an appraising look. He cocked one eyebrow when I blushed. "Can you act?"

"I don't know."

He laughed at me, teasing, knowing he'd turned the tables on me.

Remembering, I closed my eyes, and leaned back against the coolness of the locker-room wall. I thought the screen test would be forgotten, but a week later, the two of them marched me into MGM Studios.

"She sings," Carole told the director. On his instructions, Wardrobe dressed me in a black spangled gown, put a black wig on my head, and positioned me on a piano seat.

"Do you know 'Bill'?" someone called from the darkness behind the cameras.

"Sure," I said.

"Sing it."

Feeling foolish, I sang the sultry love song. Years of hiding my feelings from opponents across the net were poor preparation for a screen test, and my face felt stiff as a mask.

When we watched the film later, Clark laughed until he had tears in his eyes. Carole punched and scolded him, but soon all three of us were laughing at the caricature in black.

"I think I'll buy it for the times we need a laugh," he said, then added sympathetically, "Don't feel bad. You should see some of my early pictures."

"I have," I shot back, "All of them. I also saw you in that play *The Last Mile.*"

"Oh, God," Clark groaned. His role as "Killer" Mears on the stage in Los Angeles had been his entree into movies, but Spencer Tracy had played the part before him and, in Clark's opinion, had done it better.

Clark and I were friends from that day on. My straightforwardness, he always said, was a welcome change from the flattery of his fans. He was a bit ashamed of being an actor, and preferred talking about drilling for oil with his father or the brief time he'd spent working as a lumberjack, like my father.

Clark's father had tried to "make a man of him" in the oil fields and never, even after his son won an Academy Award, stopped sneering at his chosen profession. "Come on back and do a man's work," he'd say, even after his son made it possible for him to live the rest of his life in luxury.

Carole, who earned ten times as much as Clark when they met, teased him for being a tightwad, but he was desperately afraid of poverty. He was so frugal that his studio had a tough time persuading him to buy dentures.

Teach often coached me on Carole's court, and I came to know Clark well. "Pa," as Carole called him, was an adequate tennis player (here again I compared him to Flynn, who was the best tennis player in the movie colony), but he was more fun off the court, when the four of us would have water battles in Carole's pool, cook steaks on the grill as the sun was dropping, and then sit talking on the darkened patio.

Clark always greeted me with a kiss on the mouth, as family members do. His lips were soft, very sensual, and I often told Carole that she was a lucky woman.

"I am lucky," she agreed one night as we sat talking beside her pool. Teach and Clark were playing cards in the den. She dropped her voice to a whisper, glancing at the patio door, "But I'll tell you a secret. I love him dearly, but wouldn't all those swooning women be devastated to learn that he's not all that great in bed?"

I blushed, and she giggled like a teenager at a slumber party.

Carole's love of Clark was easy to see. An inveterate city girl, she learned to hunt and camp so that she could be with him when he wanted to escape his very public life. They bought a ranch in the desert, and Carole often told me their happiest times were spent there alone together. I worried about her, though, living that rugged life. She was a good athlete, but she was frequently sick and once, to my great distress, told me that she expected to die young.

"Don't say that!" I said. "Did your fortune tellers tell you that?"

"Yes, they did, but it's more than that. It's a feeling I have." She quickly changed the subject and we never talked about it again.

Applause from the court outside snapped me back to the present. I jumped to my feet and hurriedly checked my hair in the mirror. I would have to rush to see Carole and Clark before my match. I worked my way through the crowd toward the celebrity boxes and soon was at the rear of the number one box. Just as I put my hand up to draw back the curtain, I heard Gable's unmistakable voice. "Honey, you know we all love Allie, but I don't want you to be upset if she doesn't win. She just doesn't have what it takes anymore."

I stood motionless, my face burning with anger and embarrassment. How *dare* he! Suddenly I was fed up with my friends treating me like a loser, even if I had been playing like one. I was about to step into the box and confront him, perhaps even give him a punch in his million-dollar smile, when the loudspeaker crackled, "Game, set, and match to . . ."

The match was finished, and I was due on court.

"Damn," I muttered, dropping the curtain unnoticed and hurrying back to the locker room.

Teach was there, checking my racquets. Alarmed at the sight of my red face and clenched jaw, she asked, "What's wrong?"

"Everything." I put a cabbage leaf in my cap, jammed it on my head, and took the racquets from her. Shaking my head at her questions, I jerked open the locker-room door and left. When I reached the court, the petite brunette Gracyn Wheeler was already there, posturing for the celebrities.

I smiled during the introductions, but I was seething inside. Gracyn was smiling too, probably remembering how she'd whipped me a few weeks earlier. I was gonna make *that* ancient history.

Moving to my side of the court, I gestured to the ball boy for balls. Bouncing one on the court, I fingered it, feeling its sun-warmed nap. For the first time in months I felt the surge of my own power. Gracyn was in trouble; I planned to smack that sucker down her pretty throat.

During our warm-up, I watched as her confidence wavered. I was hitting hard, and she was having difficulty rallying with me. When we took our practice serves, mine rocketed over the net, kissing the corner of the service area with accuracy I hadn't shown in months.

At a word from the official, the crowd became quiet and we began to play. I had won the toss, and my first serve was good— low, fast, and deep. Gracyn had trouble reaching it, and her return floated over the net. I pounced on it and put it away.

I took three games before she won a point, and her mouth had closed to a determined, zipper-thin line. She fought back, trying everything in her arsenal, but she didn't stand a chance. I went to the net repeatedly, and left her standing helplessly as the ball angled out of her reach.

The match was over in twelve minutes, 6–0, 6–0. Gracyn's shoulders slumped, and her eyes were filling with tears when she shook my hand. There was confusion and hurt in her expression and, now that it was over, I was sorry I had humiliated her. I had nothing against her; I only had thoughts of humiliating Clark Gable. So I didn't have it anymore, huh?

I smiled for the trophy presentation, told reporters only, "Gracyn was a lovely opponent, but everything just worked for me today," then made my way off the court.

"Alice, you were almost cruel." Teach, trying to suppress a grin and failing, handed me a towel and whispered, "Did I really say you had no killer instinct?"

I ignored her question. "I'll be right back."

A matronly sponsor intercepted me before I'd gone far. "Alice, my dear, you were *delightful*," she gushed, gripping my arm with a jeweled hand, "but why didn't you ask them to stop that miserable band? How annoying!"

I looked at her blankly for a moment. What band? Then I remembered. The military academy next door paraded on Sundays to the accompaniment of its off-key band. It always irked the hell out of me, but that day I was concentrating so hard I didn't notice.

116

"Oh yes, the band . . . terribly distracting," I said. "Gracyn was frightfully upset. Got to run." I planted a kiss on her well-fed jowl and continued my dash.

When I pulled back the curtain on the number one box, I was beginning to realize what had happened, but I *still* wanted a word with Mr. Gable. He stood and turned when he heard me, his arms full of red roses (only Clark Gable could get them so quickly) and his smile would have dropped a dozen strong women in their tracks.

"Congratulations, *Champ*," he said, handing me the flowers and giving me a hug that left me with a pounding heart and the smell of crushed rose petals.

"Oh, dammit, Clark!"

How could I stay angry? I had won! I hadn't concentrated in months as I had that day. I'd let myself be distracted by anything and everything—a scraped leg, the crowd, my own wandering thoughts. I really hadn't *cared* enough about winning.

Teach always told me the most important ingredient in a champion was desire. Hilda with her bad hand, Ja_a with her one-stroke game, gutsy Helen Jacobs, and little Anita Lizana—all of them had the desire to win. Now I understood that it meant going a step beyond playing the game well.

"Clark Gable," I said with what fire I could muster, "I heard you say I don't have what it takes anymore. You're a bastard for doubting me, but you've ended my slump!"

Carole gave a loud whoop, and embraced me. I began to laugh. "Thank you, Clark," I said over her shoulder, "for everything."

Teach appeared at that moment, looking confused. Glancing from one smiling face to another, she bent to smell the roses. When she looked up, her eyes were bright. "I've got a winner again."

18 : WIMBLEDON

1938

Teach put an arm around my shoulder and grinned blindly into the flash of the cameras. Behind the whirring, flashing, probing fringe of the press, a crowd of a hundred or so had gathered at the New York dock to see me off on my second trip to England.

"Good luck, Miss Marble," a teenaged girl called, her face appearing and disappearing as she bobbed on her tiptoes in the throng.

"Excuse me, John," I said, reaching over the shoulder of the *New York Times* reporter to take the notebook the girl was waving. I signed it and handed it back. The reporter smiled at me. I smiled back and said, only half joking, "You guys love me one day and write me off the next. At least the fans are faithful."

"We'll write great stories about you this trip," he said, jotting a few words in his notebook, and then flipping it closed. In answer to the reporters' questions, Teach and I had expressed confidence about my chances at Wimbledon, but none of the bravado of the previous year.

The sound of the *Champlain*'s horn warned us it was time to go aboard. Waiting for us at the rail were socialite Rosalind Bloomingdale Cowen, whose first husband owned the department-store chain, and her four sons.

"What fun!" Roz watched the skyline of New York dipping lower on the horizon. "This'll be my first voyage without a husband since my debutante days!"

With Roz around to keep Teach busy, I hoped I would have a bit more freedom this trip. At twenty-four, I still allowed Teach to run my life, to make all my decisions. Teach wanted to be in control; on the rare occasions when I protested, she pointed out that she was making it possible for me to concentrate on my tennis. I sometimes resented her, especially when she finished my sentences for me, but Teach was very strong-willed. I didn't argue with her.

Before nightfall the first day, a throng of new friends had joined our following—interesting, lively people. Our popularity had much less to do with my standing as the number one tennis player in the United States than with Teach's irrepressible personality.

Wisecracking with a New York restaurateur or swirling around the ship's dance floor on the arm of a famous Paris clothier, Teach was the consummate socialite, and one could hardly imagine the intensity she brought to tennis, and the thirst for excellence she tried to quench through me.

As on our previous voyage, I felt like Cinderella every night at ten. I left the ballroom to rustle along the promenade in my evening dress, bound for the cabin. On the rail, couples stood silhouetted in the moonlight, and I stopped to watch the various stages of romance—the clasped hands, the arms about each other's waists, the first tentative kisses, and the sensual embrace of lovers pausing on their way to bed.

I envied their closeness, their intimacy. Teach had made that impossible for me. "Love and tennis don't mix," she said, or "Love is just a tennis score—a zero." But physically and emotionally, I longed for someone to love me.

Turning away from the trysts on the darkened deck, I followed the passageway to the cabin I shared with Teach, undressed, and crawled into bed. There, I eased my sexual tension in the way every adolescent learns, but nothing could allay the underlying loneliness. I was a champion, but not without sacrifice.

Arriving in England, we were met by many more people than I expected, given Teach's animosity and my poor showing of the year before. Teach was more comfortable with her countrymen this time, and we spent many pleasant evenings in private homes. Over after-dinner sherry, I watched my coach win the heart of many a proper Brit, and I was proud of her. I was *always* proud of her. I was the champion, but I was overshadowed by my coach, who emanated a sense of vibrancy and vitality that drew people to her. Teach loved me for the things I was. I loved her more for the things I was not.

Teach's friend Roz was a good foil for her. She was bright, witty and spoiled, but lacked the vacuousness of many wealthy women, the ones who never worried about anything more serious than a hangnail. Roz was good-natured, and looked at me in mock disdain when I teased her about "roughing it" with only one maid. That maid, of course, was the one trained to pull on Roz's girdle and stockings.

In the days before Wimbledon, Roz discovered that the famous Persian portrait painter Dorothy Bijachai was in London.

"You *must* sit for your portrait," she insisted. "It's a wonderful opportunity. Besides, it's all arranged."

My appeals to Teach were turned down, so I showed up at the studio as expected. Dressed in a long caftan, Dorothy Bijachai was a striking woman who made the lanky Hilda Sperling look like a shrimp. She was nearly seven feet tall, with warm brown skin and pale-blue eyes.

Motioning me to a seat, she said, "Strike a pose." End of conversation.

I sat frozen in position, holding my racquet, for what seemed an eternity. Within my field of vision were portraits of Laurence Olivier and of Sabu, the Indian boy who starred in countless jungle movies. When at last she looked up from the large canvas and motioned for me to relax, I said, "I studied the Baha'i teachings."

She turned to me in surprise, and I knew I had guessed right about the Englishwoman's Persian background. The pacifistic Baha'i teachings were among the many religions Teach and Carole had pursued, and I had learned too, out of curiosity. The artist and I talked freely once we had established that common ground, and the five sittings went less painfully than I had anticipated.

Teach and Roz met me at the studio on the day of the final sitting. After a time, Miss Bijachai motioned me toward the door. "Wait outside. I'll call you when I'm ready."

When the three of us entered the studio, the painting hung on the wall. I hadn't realized what it was like to be captured on canvas, how lifelike it would be. The depth and warmth of the paints made me feel as if I were really looking at myself, at something entirely different from the flat image I saw in the mirror. Miss Bijachai saw my expression and smiled.

"Hmmm," Teach said, breaking the silence and moving closer to the painting, "doesn't look much like my racquet!"

"Teach!" Roz and I protested in unison.

"Well, I can't read my signature," she said defensively. We all laughed at that, even the artist. My coach was the first one at Wilson Sporting Goods to have a signature racquet, and she was proud of it.

I hadn't expected to like the painting. Miss Bijachai knew at the outset that I wouldn't be buying it, and she planned it as part of a

New York exhibition later in the year. Priced at five hundred dollars it would have been beyond my reach; at five thousand . . .

"If I lose in the early rounds, my portrait will probably end up in some smoky bar," I said to Teach and Roz.

"Then see that you don't!" Teach said.

Early defeat wasn't in my stars. I hadn't lost a match since the Pacific Southwest tournament the previous fall, and I allowed myself to hope that 1938 would be my year to win the world championship at Wimbledon. The great Helen Wills Moody was in the draw, but she had proven herself human by losing to Mary Hardwick at St. George's Hill in Weybridge, and to Hilda Sperling at the Queen's Club, the last tournament before Wimbledon.

In the quarterfinal round, I faced Simone Mathieu, the French champion. Her strengths lay in a forehand some said was as good as Suzanne Lenglen's, supported by a steady backhand. She seldom went to the net and her overheads were weak. I saw none of that in the early going, just deep, high-bouncing shots that forced me nearly into the linesmen's laps. The pace plodded, and my irritation grew. I took the first set, 6–2, but Simone jumped ahead of me, 3–1, in the second before I settled down to concentrate on lobs and drop shots, sweeping the next five games for the match.

I watched Hilda's semifinal match with Helen Wills Moody. Now *there* was a slugging match! Helen had learned from her defeat at Queen's, and wasn't about to allow a repeat. The two players blasted the ball from the baseline, sometimes volleying forty times before one of them took the initiative to come to the net and put the ball away. Helen won, 12–10, 6–4, the score giving little indication of how close it really was.

"If I get past one Helen, how will I face the other?" I asked Teach.

"One at a time."

My semifinal match against Helen Jacobs was memorable; discussion as to *why* I lost followed me afterward like an unwanted shadow. Helen made fewer than twelve errors in two sets. She was on; I was not. The score was 3-all in the first set when I forced her into a weak lob. I should have put it away, but I moved too soon and hit long. The failure of my "big gun" distracted me, and before I knew it Helen took the first set.

My trusty smash failed me again at 4–3 in the second set, and I reacted by kicking a ball into the stands, drawing a titter from the crowd and frowns from the officials. That sort of thing just wasn't done at Wimbledon. I moved to the baseline, drawing deep breaths to collect myself, then went to the net again, down 30–40 with the score 4-all. Helen lobbed and I smashed the ball out of bounds again. I succumbed quickly after that, 6–4, 6–4.

Teach took the disappointment better than I expected. "It's no disgrace to lose to Helen Jacobs."

Hazel Wightman, sponsor of our winning Wightman Cup team, had another opinion, which was unleashed when I approached her for sympathy.

"You want to know why you lost?" she said. "You lost it in the eighth game of the first set. You lost it when you started dramatizing yourself all over the court when you netted that drive. You slipped and fell down on the shot, right?"

I nodded. I was behind 3–4 in games and had 40–30 on my service, just one point from tying it up.

"What did you do then? I'll tell you." Mrs. Wighty was warming to her subject, and reporter Herbert Warren Wind was writing furiously. Before twenty-four hours passed, the whole world would be privy to the lecture. "You didn't brush off your shorts and get back into the match. No, you patted your fanny, and you got a nice ripple of laughter from the gallery. So you continued to pat your fanny and, while you were amusing everyone, you netted two more simple shots and tossed Helen the set. Your mind wasn't on your tennis. It took you two full games before you got back to business, and after that you never caught up. Even a girl with your natural equipment can't win if she allows *anything* to break her concentration."*

Well, I *had* asked. Mrs. Wighty never held back when asked her opinion. The winner of forty-four national championships, more than anyone else in the sport, she liked her girls to be aggressive and athletic, but always exemplary in conduct. I'm afraid I gave her pause on many occasions.

"The gallery ate it up when they saw an attractive girl like Alice kick the ball after a bad shot or whack it into the backstop," Mrs. Wighty told the reporter, "but that's where Alice was going wrong. She was thinking of the impressions those displays were making on the galleries, and it was hurting her tennis."

The final between the two Helens was anticlimactic. During Jacobs's quarterfinal match with JaJa, she'd injured her right Achilles tendon, and the long match with me hadn't helped. She leaped for one of Moody's short cross-court shots early in the first

* From "The Fireside Book of Tennis," by Herbert Warren Wind, which appeared in *The New Yorker* in 1952 as "Run Helen."

set, landed hard, and we all knew it was over. Jacobs couldn't run, but she played on, hitting the shots she could hobble to.

I thought back to the 1933 U.S. National Championships, when Helen Wills Moody forfeited to Jacobs, claiming a back injury. Perhaps Jacobs was thinking of it too. It took courage to stay on the court. Moody ran out the first set 6–4, and Mrs. Wightman went out onto the court to ask Jacobs to stop, lest she make the injury worse. Jacobs refused.

The score of 6–0 for the second set went up in a matter of minutes and we all breathed a sigh of relief. It was Moody's eighth Wimbledon victory, and her last; she never played in another major tournament. Perhaps her defeats by Hare and Sperling made her realize her dominance of women's tennis was over. She wasn't the sort to linger, picking up a win here and there as age slowed her game.

Sarah Palfrey and I took the Wimbledon doubles title, defeating Simone Mathieu of France and Billie Yorke of India, 6–2, 6–3. I teamed up with Don Budge again to win our second mixed doubles trophy from Sarah and the German Henner Henkel, 6–1, 6–4.

I felt good. Winning two of three Wimbledon championships was reason to be proud; I held my head up and spoke positively to the British press. Next year would be different. Teach hadn't scolded me for showing off on court—she saw it as a show of spirit—but Mrs. Wighty's words had stung. Next year, my mind would be on the game, not on how I looked to the audience. I wanted that singles trophy more than anything in the world.

The only thing that marred the Champions' Ball for me was a comment by the Wimbledon chairman, Sir Samuel Hoare, who introduced me as "the girl who's so very nice, but never wins." What were my doubles trophies, chopped liver?

The man was "in his cups," my British dinner partner muttered, and everyone in the ballroom tittered when he said "Wimbleship Championship." But his remark was still on my mind a year later, when I managed to repay him in kind.

The American ambassador, Joseph Kennedy, was at the ball, and his words stayed with me, too. "My girl, if you're going to win this thing, you'd better do it soon. There's going to be a war that will make all of us forget about tennis."

19: HANS

When Roz proposed spending a week in Le Touquet, a gambling spot across the English Channel in France, Teach agreed. It would be a good break for me before the nationals, and a rare opportunity for her to gamble.

Roz rented rooms for us all in the best hotel, which also had the largest casino in town. Her younger sons were entrusted to the maid while she and Teach prowled the gaming tables, and her son Alfred and I were left to our own devices.

Alfred Bloomingdale was nearly my age, and terribly embarrassed about being short. Even in his elevator shoes, he couldn't look me in the eye, which bothered him more than it did me. Neither of us was interested in gambling, so we explored the small seaport, which, like Monte Carlo, was a playground for the rich.

One afternoon I left Alfred to buy a few pieces of Limoges china for souvenirs. I was watching a clerk wrap them when through the window I saw Alfred talking with a girl. A woman, actually, one with breasts straining the buttons on her skimpy blouse. Alfred stood so close to her that, given his height, he might have lost an eye had the threads failed. I saw the girl nod, and, with a twitch of her tightly clad bottom, turn to go. Alfred had made a deal.

When I came out of the shop, he was flushed and smiling. "Allie, I have a date tonight, but I know Mother won't approve. Will you tell her we're going out?"

"Sure."

We carried off the lie during dinner with Teach and Roz. Afterward, I sat through a movie in the town theater, following the sappy plot of the melodrama despite my ignorance of French, and walked alone back to the hotel.

124

The lobby teemed with lavishly dressed men and women, their expensive perfumes and colognes scenting the air. The atmosphere was charged with the excitement of the risk-takers, bright-eyed men and women who could wager more money on the spin of a wheel than my father made in his lifetime.

I sat on a silk-brocade love seat just outside the flow of traffic into the casino, studying their faces, imagining I knew what their lives were like. It was more entertaining than the movie.

"Miss Marble?"

I turned my head, started and a bit embarrassed at being caught people-watching, and looked up into the eyes of a stranger.

"It *is* you!" he said, smiling with such pleasure that I automatically smiled back. France had many tennis fans, and a number had recognized me.

"Yes, but . . . ?" My unfinished question hung in the air, but I knew I had never seen him before. I would have remembered. Dashing—that was the best way to describe him—with dark hair, fierce dark eyes, and a disarming smile. He reminded me of Omar Sharif, particularly his eyes, but he was taller than the actor, and with a tan and build that bespoke an active, outdoor life-style. Since the custom cut of his tuxedo ruled out the working class, I decided he was probably a wealthy playboy.

"We haven't met, but I admire your tennis," he said, his voice matching his looks: deep, rich, decidedly European. "I'm so sorry about Wimbledon. Next year it is yours, I'm sure."

He extended his hand, palm up, in a graceful gesture. "I am Hans Steinmetz."*I had watched this scene in so many movies, I almost expected to hear his heels click together. This *wasn't* happening. I put my hand in his and felt his strong fingers close over mine. He bowed and softly kissed the back of my hand.

"And I'm Alice Marble, but you know that."

Hans squeezed my hand and laughed, a throaty, genuine laugh, his teeth flashing white and even.

"Please, would you have a drink with me?" he asked. "Unless you're expecting someone."

I glanced quickly around the lobby. No sign of Alfred. "Well, no. I mean, yes, but I don't drink." So far, I'd managed to behave like an imbecile.

The hotel had several bars: the one Hans led me to was quiet, except for a pianist at the far end of the room coaxing a soft melody from the keys of a baby grand.

* Fictitious name.

We faced each other over a table so small our knees almost touched, and a globed candle flickered over the peach tablecloth. Hans swirled a snifter of brandy, warming it occasionally over the candle, and sipping it with obvious pleasure. "No one can equal the French brandies and wines," he said, offering his glass for a toast. I touched my goblet of iced tea to his.

"To the French, for bringing us together," he said, "and to you, the world's best woman tennis player."

"I can't drink to that," I protested. "I have a long way to go before I'm number one." I changed the subject. "You're not French with a name like Hans. Are you German?"

"My home is in the most beautiful country in the world," he said proudly. "Switzerland. My father is German."

"Why are you here?" I asked, my eyes on his face. Hans was handsome, not movie-star handsome, but striking, with an angular face that softened quickly and often into a smile. Tuxedos so often make men look like mannequins, but Hans wore his as easily as I wore shorts and a sweater to practice.

"A brief holiday before I go home. I had business in London, but I didn't let it interfere with watching you at Wimbledon."

"I'll bet you've never seen me play," I challenged, not wanting to appear flattered.

"Oh, but I have!" He went on to describe the key points of my last match with Helen. We talked at length about tennis and other things, lapsing occasionally into silence to listen to the piano.

Hans worked in his father's bank, he told me, *when* he worked. So far, his father had been indulgent of his only son, allowing him frequent holidays for skiing, or island-hopping in Greece and the Caribbean. So he was a wealthy playboy, but there was a dignity about him that did not fit the image of a dilettante, suggesting, rather, that his responsibilities were more serious than he said.

Rising from his chair, he extended his hand. "The night is beautiful. Let's walk."

"Is it late?" I asked, slipping my hand in his.

"Probably. Do you mind?"

"No." I wondered briefly if Alfred had ever shown up in the lobby. I pushed the thought of Teach from my mind. I wasn't a child. I didn't have to answer to anyone. She was my coach, that was all. It was my life.

When we reached the beach, I slipped off the high heels that matched my gold lamé dress, and wiggled my bare toes in the sand. The dress was my favorite, and I had never felt more attractive in it than I did at that moment.

126

"I never thought I would be walking barefoot on the beach with a stranger tonight," I said.

"A stranger! Now you've hurt me." Hans stopped short in the shadows cast by the beach bar, shuttered and locked for the night. He turned to me, put his index finger under my chin, and tilted my head back until I looked into his eyes, eyes blacker than the sea beyond.

"Perhaps we should get to know each other better." He bent to kiss me, his mouth warm and firm, the sweet hint of brandy on his tongue. It was a long kiss, and I marveled at how good it felt to be held, to be kissed, to be close to a man. Why had I let Teach bully me? Why had I waited so long?

Hans broke our embrace to spread his coat on the sand and pull me gently down beside him. I moved into the circle of his arms as naturally as if we had been lovers for years. And we were to be lovers, I knew. I wanted him. With an urgency that had been building for years, I opened myself to him, welcoming the strange, ultimate bliss that came with our union, our moving together as one. At that moment, we were the only life on the planet, perhaps in the whole universe, and the stars were singing.

"Did I hurt you?" he whispered, cradling me, his lips against my hair.

"You made me happy." I blinked furiously, holding back tears. So very happy.

He held me for a long time, both of us silently watching the ocean, then we dressed and walked hand in hand toward the lighted portico of the hotel. The moon had dropped considerably.

"I'd like to see you tomorrow," he said.

"Today, you mean."

"Yes, today. Noon. We'll have a drive in the country and a picnic."

The casino was still in full swing when we walked into the nearly deserted lobby. Worried that I would be seen looking disheveled, I kissed Hans and went quickly up the stairs, praying that Teach and Roz were still gambling. Had Alfred looked for me? Had he said anything to Teach? If I could just get into bed before anyone missed me, I would be safe. Otherwise, there would be hell to pay.

I pressed my ear against the room door and held my breath. Silence. Quietly turning my key in the lock, I eased the door open. Teach was such a light sleeper there was no way . . . but I had to try.

Every light in the room was on, and Teach sat in a chair, reading, still dressed in her evening gown. I stood in the open doorway feeling stupid, awkward, and very guilty. I'm sure it showed.

Her eyes were twin cannons leveled at me over the top of her book. "It's three A. M. I hope you had a nice evening." Her voice was quiet, but loaded with sarcasm.

"I did." I tried to speak casually, but my voice sounded strained. I'd never challenged Teach's control. This was unfamiliar, shaky ground.

"What did you do?"

Lying to her was impossible, so I didn't even try. "I met a charming man, and we walked down to the beach and sat by the water." I turned toward the bathroom, hoping to end, or postpone, the conversation.

"In your good dress?"

"Yes. He took off his coat and we sat on it," I said over my shoulder. I didn't hear her move, but suddenly Teach was beside me, gripping my arm. I could smell her perfume, and a hint of gin.

"You have sand in your hair." Her eyes were close to mine.

Sand? How did she . . . ? Then I realized. Where I parted my hair down the middle, my scalp was a sunburned pink, and the sand had been easy to see. I dropped my eyes.

"I trust it was pleasurable?" Her words came through clenched teeth, and her grip on my arm tightened.

"Please don't be mad. For God's sake, I'm twenty-five years old. I needed somebody!"

"Needed somebody!" She whirled me around and gripped my shoulders. "Look at me!"

"I can't." I was crying now.

"Look at me!" she demanded, shaking me. I lifted my eyes to hers, tears running down my face.

"Who was there for you when you were sick, when everybody thought your career was over, and even you didn't believe in yourself?"

"You were," I sobbed.

"Who stuck by you last year when you couldn't win a tournament?"

"You."

I wanted to die. People say love is the most powerful emotion, but guilt runs a close second, and I felt enough of it at that moment to last a lifetime. I'd run an emotional gamut that night, from ecstasy to misery.

She dropped her hands from my shoulders and paced, the picture of hurt and rage. "I can't believe you were out there screwing on the beach like a common whore!" She struggled to keep her voice low, but I knew she wanted to scream at me.

"Teach, please . . . I'm sorry."

"Dear God, Alice, you're at the top of your game. There's no place in your life for tennis *and* men! If you don't believe that, I'm wasting my time with you."

Her words were like a slap. What if she left me? The thought made me sick.

"*Never* do this to me again. Never! Do you understand?"

"Yes," I said, sniffing. Tears still coursed down my face.

She relented. "God, you're a mess. Go get cleaned up. And pray you're not pregnant."

I hadn't even thought of that. I went into the bathroom and unzipped the gold lamé dress, letting it fall to the floor. Teach never allowed me to wear that symbol of my indiscretion and rebellion again.

After a long bath, I emerged to find the room dark and Teach asleep. Gratefully, I crawled into my own bed. I was drained from the experience, but sleep wouldn't come. I thought of Hans and knew that I would break my promise to Teach and see him again. I'd do it all again, given the chance, even knowing the consequence.

Alfred intercepted me in the hallway before breakfast, looked at my face, and gave a low whistle. "You look like hell. What happened? When you weren't in the lobby I figured you had already come upstairs."

"You didn't get caught?" I asked. He shook his head. "Lucky. I did. I came in at three, and Teach was fit to be tied."

At breakfast, Roz seemed puzzled at the frostiness between Teach and me, but was much too diplomatic to inquire. I had tea and toast, and was about to excuse myself when the bell captain approached the table.

"Miss Marble, these just arrived for you," he said, handing me a long flower-box.

"How wonderful! Open it," Roz commanded, seizing the chance to lighten the mood of the group, and unwittingly cutting off my escape. I slipped the top off the box to reveal a dozen delicate peach roses, the same color as the tablecloth in the bar the night before. I had said I liked the shade, and Hans had remembered. My spirits soared.

Roz craned her neck. "Beautiful! Who are they from, dear?"

I slipped the card from its envelope. "It says 'From your best fan.' "

I met Teach's gaze for an instant, then looked at Roz. "I think I'll run up and put them in water. See you at dinner."

"Dinner? Where will you be all day?" Teach asked.

"Alfred and I are going on a picnic." I looked at him, murder in my gaze. I had covered for him. . . .

"Yes," Alfred said quickly, "a picnic."

It was the start of a week-long conspiracy in which Alfred and I protected each other's private lives, no questions asked.

Deceiving Teach upset me, but it amused Hans. "You're a grown woman," he said. "Stop acting like a guilty schoolgirl."

"I love you," I said suddenly, looking up from where my head rested on his bare chest. He had taken a room in the hotel, two floors up from the one I shared with Teach, and we had spent much of the week in his bed.

I had known I loved him the first day. I was waiting outside the hotel when the low-slung green convertible pulled up to the door. Before he could get out, I jumped into the passenger seat. "Let's get out of here!"

Laughing, he spun away, squealing the tires like a robber in escape. I sank lower in the seat.

"The car's not stolen," he said, still laughing. "Why the getaway?"

"I just need to be a little more discreet." I explained about Teach while Hans wheeled the car expertly through the narrow streets and onto a country road. In a sport shirt and khakis, he was just as handsome as he had been in his tux, perhaps even more so, with his muscular brown arms bare. He dropped one hand from the wheel to take my hand, and I felt secure and happy at his touch.

We picnicked on the bank of a river that day, across from a seventeenth-century castle that would have made King Arthur proud. In the backseat of the car was a wicker basket with roast duck, liver pâté, caviar, and a loaf of fresh bread. While I spread a blanket under a tree, Hans uncorked a bottle of champagne, poured some into two fine-stemmed glasses, and added cassis from another bottle.

"I know you don't drink," he said, handing me a glass, "but you'll love this. It tastes like currants." He leaned over to kiss me. "And, the French use it to seduce their women."

I blushed, and he kissed me again. "I was the first, wasn't I?"

His words caught me by surprise. Embarrassed, I took a big swallow of the drink, choking and nodding, keeping my eyes on the glass.

"Why?" His voice was gentle.

130

I couldn't tell him. The words just weren't there. "Too busy playing tennis. And I was waiting for you."

"Oh, I'd like to believe that!"

He never asked me again. Our days were filled with gaiety and love, and for the first time in a long time, tennis was not the most important thing in my life.

Every day was different, and wonderful. We drove through the countryside, stopping on a whim for lunch at a castle-cum-restaurant, or a tiny lobster place down the coast from Le Touquet, or a tree-shaded patio café in a small village.

Every day was different, but every afternoon was the same. We went back to the hotel separately, met in his room and made love. I was happier than I'd ever been in my life, and unwilling to think beyond the joy of the moment. First love takes precedence over everything, particularly common sense, and common sense would have told me Teach knew of our affair, even before Hans and I made the newspapers.

Teach and Roz had dinner engagements most evenings, so we were together until almost midnight. Hans always chose restaurants where we weren't likely to be seen, but one evening the gossip columnist of a French newspaper chose the same restaurant.

I was in bed with Hans the next afternoon when there was a light knock. Hans walked across the room, magnificent in his nakedness, and picked up the folded note that had been slipped under the door.

"It's for you," he said.

I read the note, then handed it to him. It was a warning from Alfred. "You made the society pages. Teach may know."

Hans read it, then kissed me lightly. "Go on. Face the dragon. I'll wait for you here and we'll have a late dinner."

I dressed and kissed him. "I love you."

"I love you, too," he said. "Don't worry. It will be all right."

But it wasn't all right. When I got to the room, Teach was dressed for dinner, and putting the finishing touches on her hair. She lay down her comb, and I could see her face in the mirror. She knew.

"Tell Steinmetz it's over."

"Teach . . ."

"Tell him it's over," she repeated, turning to face me. Her voice was calm, and that frightened me more than her anger. "You've had your fun. Now end it. Or find another coach."

She picked up her purse and left. I dropped into a chair and stared after her.

Almost an hour later, I let myself back into Hans's room. He had shaved and showered; I could smell the clean fragrance of his talc when he took me in his arms.

"She knew?"

"Yes."

He kissed the top of my head. "Was it bad?"

"The worst. I have to stop seeing you."

"Honey, you leave day after tomorrow. We can dodge Teach one more day, and by the time I get to see you in the States, she'll have calmed down. She's afraid I'll hurt you. I can talk to her, tell her we love each other. Then she'll understand."

I shook my head without leaving his embrace, loving the warmth of his chest against my cheek. "She won't ever understand. We can't see each other . . . at all."

For a moment there was silence, except for the sound of his heart beneath my ear.

"Teach and tennis mean more to you than I do?"

"No!" I hit his chest with my fist. "Don't ever think that! I love you! I've never loved anyone *ever*. But I've told you all Teach has done for me. She saved my life, Hans, and she made me a champion. I can't do this to her."

He held me then, so tightly it almost hurt, his cheek resting on the top of my head. After a long while, he relaxed, and bent to kiss me.

"Good-bye, my love," he said, and dropped his arms to his sides.

I left him before I could change my mind, before I could say to hell with Teach and tennis and everything my life had been before I met him.

Early the next morning, I went upstairs to his room. I had to see him again. I didn't know what I would say, but I couldn't let it end this way, not with the pain I'd seen in his eyes. The door was ajar and I could hear movement inside. Heart pounding, I pushed the door open, ready to fly into his arms.

Startled, the maid looked up, then smiled politely. "*Bonjour, mademoiselle.*"

At a glance I could see the empty closet, the bare dresser top. "*Bonjour,*" I whispered, turning away, blinded by my tears.

20: ANOTHER DEBUT

1938

During the voyage home, Teach saw how morose I was and relaxed her curfew. We understood, but never talked about why. I could have danced until midnight every night if I wanted, but I didn't have the heart for it. Every man I danced with made me think of Hans, made me wonder where he was, what he was doing . . . and whether he was thinking of me.

In my sleep, I reached for him, seeking the warm circle of his arms, the feel of his skin against mine. Waking, I cursed the loneliness, particularly in those half-lit hours just before dawn, when I knew sleep was impossible. Sometimes I slipped out of bed, put on my clothes and went on deck. The air was wet and cold, the ocean and sky like twin slabs of lead, a perfect setting for my bleak thoughts.

I had no way to contact Hans. All I knew was that his father's bank was in Geneva. He didn't have my address, either, though I would be easy enough to reach through the tennis association if he tried; but I knew he wouldn't. He was a proud man, and I had hurt him badly, at least as badly as I'd hurt myself. Teach had made me say good-bye to my first love, but she couldn't make me forget him, and her control of me would never again be so complete.

I put Hans out of my mind when we reached New York. I intended to take back my national title, and everything I did that summer was in preparation for a showdown at Forest Hills.

Oddly enough, it was my Wimbledon doubles partner, the slight, pretty Sarah Palfrey, who nearly upset my championship plans. When we met in the semifinal round, she showed me straight away that she was prepared to fight.

It had rained, and I adjusted to the slow, heavy balls before she

133

did, taking her to 5–1 in the first set. She rallied then, and began to play with an intensity I'd never seen before. I couldn't touch her. She took the next nine games, winning the first set and leading the second.

The noise after each point was deafening, the crowd loving it when the underdog showed her fangs. I looked for Teach while the umpire quieted the fans. Our eyes met, and she mouthed an expression which always spurred me on, though I never really understood what it meant: "Get off the dime!"

I saluted her with my racquet, and resolved to try harder. I knew Sarah's game as well as I knew my own; there had to be a way to stop her. I broke her serve in the next game, then, using the best serves I could muster, took another. Sarah gave not an inch. Running, diving, and stretching, she returned everything I hit.

Before I knew it, the score was 5–2, 40–15, in Sarah's favor. Two points stood between me and defeat. I couldn't let that happen; I wouldn't! By some miracle, I got my racquet on what should have been match point, sending a difficult backhand volley down the line.

Then Sarah dumped my return of service into the net, and her shoulders slumped in frustration. Committing an unforced error when she was so close to victory was maddening, and distracting. It was my chance to turn the match around.

I'll never understand what makes a player's game suddenly start to click, but that's what happened to me. Shots that I had been hitting wide suddenly started to nick the lines. When the ball left her racquet, I knew instinctively where it was going, and was there to meet it. Sarah continued to press, but could only take five points from me in the last four games of the second set.

She was far from giving up, though. I had to fight for every point in the third set. At 5–4, 40–15, it was my turn to taste the win and have it taken away. Sarah saved match point, and I groaned inwardly. What did it take to beat her? A drop shot and a cross-court volley later, I *had* beaten her, but barely: 5–7, 7–5, 7–5. The match was so close, we had both scored 122 points!

The final was a romp by comparison. It took me only twenty minutes to defeat Nancye Wynne, the Australian champion, 6–0, 6–3, and take back my national championship.

The year 1938 also marked my first "Triple Crown." Sarah and I had taken the national doubles title earlier in Chestnut Hill, Massachusetts, beating Simone Mathieu and Jadwiga Jedrzejowska in three tough sets, 6–8, 6–4, 6–3. The Australians John Bromwich and Thelma Coyne had found Don Budge and me too hot to handle in the mixed doubles, yielding, 1–6, 2–6, in short order. And the singles made three, a clean sweep of the national championships.

Teach and I stayed on in New York for a few weeks after Forest Hills, doing the obligatory round of interviews, radio shows, photo sessions, and public appearances.

I was asked to do many strange things, such as commentating at a football game, but I was caught totally off guard when an agency asked me to audition for a singing job at the Waldorf.

"But I've never sung professionally," I protested. At Carole's urging, I had continued my singing lessons in Hollywood with Ted Streater, who was Kate Smith's long-time coach, but my singing was for my own enjoyment and to entertain friends.

"Emil Coleman says you've got quite a voice," the agent insisted. So that was it! The band leader had heard me sing at the Kahns' after winning my first national championship.

I called Streater to ask what he thought. "If you can't do it now, you'll never do it," he said.

That was all the encouragement I needed; for once, I ignored Teach's protests. I auditioned the next day before Mr. Boomer, the president of the Waldorf, the agent, and Mr. Coleman.

Before I had sung more than four bars of a song, the three men stood and left the room. Was I that bad? I was beginning to bristle at their bad manners when they returned, grinning. "You'll do just fine," said Boomer. "You open in eleven days."

I was given a suite of rooms at the hotel, and a big salary, but I immediately ran up a bill for six hundred dollars at Hattie Carnegie's, one of the most exclusive shops in town, for two evening dresses, which came out of my first salary check. A coach (to help me learn the lyrics and arrangements of the ten songs I started with) was expensive too. Each song was done by an arranger, and the music written for each member of the orchestra at a cost of about twenty-five dollars a song.

The Sert Room at the Waldorf, which held five hundred people, was packed for my opening, and the reviews the next day were good. Dorothy Kilgallen wrote: "The audience could have not been more enthusiastic if Miss Marble had been Flagstad. She has a nice contralto voice and uses it well."

My enthusiastic audience was, of course, largely made up of my friends. The entire Arkell family was there, including their grandson, a cadet at West Point, and gave me a beautiful lei of fresh orchids they had had flown in from Hawaii.

Having sung before audiences many times, I had no stage fright, but I was surprised to discover that singing, like tennis, was physically demanding. I wasn't used to being up at night, and had to train in an upside-down sort of way—sleeping late, hitting the courts in the afternoon, then resting before I had to work. Teach hated it, but I was having a wonderful time with my new career.

I saw familiar faces in the audience every night—Will du Pont was often there, the Kahns, the Bloomingdales, the Loews, the Warburgs—and I made a lot of new friends. Gloria Swanson was staying in the hotel, and we soon discovered that we knew many of the same people in Hollywood. She was a singer as well as an actress, so I asked her for pointers on improving my performance.

She hesitated before answering. "I like the quality of your voice, but you remind me of the English actor who, when he says 'I love you,' sounds as if he's asking for a weak cup of tea."

She went on to explain that my expression never changed, no matter how happy or sad the song, and that I seemed afraid to make any gesture, lest I overdo it.

I realized the truth in what she said, and I knew why. International tennis was serious business. Though Teach sent me on the court with orders to have fun, there was always a great deal at stake, and a great many eyes upon me. A tennis match was a lot like a bullfight. Losing my temper or looking discouraged was like the letting of blood. The crowd would increase its taunts and my opponent would bear down, sensing weakness. No matter how I felt, I couldn't show my emotions on court. Or, apparently, on the stage. I thought about my disastrous screen test at MGM.

I had been so afraid people would laugh because I had gotten a singing job as a result of my tennis, so I worked hard at it, and was better than anyone expected. I knew I was successful when offers of other singing engagements came, but I turned them down. I was a tennis player above all else, as Teach constantly reminded me.

The two months at the Waldorf had been like pages from someone else's life, so different were they from anything I'd ever done. It's odd that people seem surprised when an athlete can talk, much less sing! But letters from fans decried my singing in nightclubs rather than leading the "pure" life of an athlete, and I knew I couldn't keep training on such a crazy schedule. I wanted to have another go at the world championships at Wimbledon, and that meant devoting my time to training with Beese and Teach.

When Teach and I finally made our way back to Los Angeles, after several exhibitions en route, we rented a little house and settled into a routine of practice and lessons at the Los Angeles Tennis Club, and a series of clinics arranged by Wilson Sporting Goods. Wilson now made signature racquets for both Teach and me, and the sales were up since I had regained the title. The company was happy, and so was Teach. The money was coming in.

I was jealous when the results of tournaments in New Zealand, Australia, and South Africa appeared in the newspapers. Other than the English tournaments leading up to Wimbledon, foreign tournaments were out for me, even the French. I had a very good chance of winning abroad, especially in 1938, my best year to date, but there was no expense money available from the tennis associations.

Practice would do me more good than a foreign tour, Teach said, which was a nice way of saying that I couldn't afford to go on unsponsored trips and that she needed me. It was time for me to repay her for the months of lessons lost. Teach put in long hours on the tennis courts, despite the arthritis that had come on her at a very young age. She ignored the pain, as she ignored her other premature sign of age. Teach was only forty-three, but her salt-and-pepper hair had gone completely gray in the time I had known her. (I had something to do with that, she often said.)

Catching up on her paperwork, scheduling lessons, typing her stories for the newspapers, and helping in clinics kept my mind off foreign tournaments, but not off Hans. As soon as Carole Lombard and I were alone, I told her all about the affair with my handsome Swiss.

"If only I could have seen Teach's face when she spotted the sand in your hair!" Carole said.

"Or the look on *my* face," I added drily. "It wasn't funny."

"I know, honey."

"And I just wish Teach hadn't made me end it that way. I loved him. I still do. I waited so long to love somebody . . ."

"I know," she said again, her eyes sad.

Carole changed the subject quickly, asking me about my fan mail, and we were soon giggling again, having found that we received letters from some of the same people, fans who knew that we were friends.

"Look at this one," I said. "He describes a sex position on the first page, a recipe for fudge on the next, and tells me his life story on the last."

Carole looked over my shoulder. "I got one from him, too. But the position he described to me wasn't nearly as interesting. He likes you better."

"Carole!"

One fellow wrote to both of us, asking each to meet him at a department store in Los Angeles a few days hence. We debated showing up together, but opted for a spy instead. Our friend Kay Winthrop agreed to be at the meeting place at the appointed time. When she returned, she reported that our admirer was just over five feet tall, and losing both his hair and his teeth. Carole and I howled with laughter.

"He said he was six feet and handsome!" I said.

"If he had been, I might not have come back." Kay winked.

Carole and I shared everything, from the secrets of our love lives to the spontaneous "private jokes" that sent us into fits of laughter and embarrassed Teach. We were worse than children, she said, but we knew she enjoyed our antics. We both had spirit and humor, but Carole was quicker with words and more mischievous than I.

At one of the many parties we attended together, Carole caught me by the arm and said, "C'mon. I want to introduce you to some people."

I smiled at the strangers, offering my hand, only to hear Carole say, "This is my friend Virginia Bruce."

I kept a straight face. I did resemble Virginia Bruce, a young actress who was doing quite well at the time, but the starlet had a creamy white complexion, while I was walnut brown from hours in the sun. The ruse, which Carole repeated time and again, worked only temporarily. Someone would always say, "You're not Virginia Bruce. You're Alice Marble. I saw you play tennis."

One day Carole met Teach and me for lunch at the Los Angeles Racquet Club. Bertha, a well-known psychic, was with her. Carole introduced the two of us, then waved her hand at the room (all eyes had been on her from the moment she walked in), and said, "Bertha, tell Teach and Alice who all these people are."

"I don't use my skill for that," the psychic said, and I was afraid Carole had offended her.

"Oh, I know," Carole cajoled, her arm around Bertha's shoulders, "but do it anyway, just for fun."

Bertha's round face crinkled into a laugh. She obviously adored Carole, and no doubt was handsomely paid by her. The actress always had psychics around her—"phonies," Clark called them, but he humored her, as we all did.

Bertha proved to be no phony. She went around the dining room, accurately ticking off the names of more than fifty people, and leaving behind her a trail of astonished looks. I felt chilly, though the day was warm; Teach's eyes were wide.

"See?" said Carole triumphantly, and picked up her menu. She was like that, filling her world with excitement, magic, enchantment. Perhaps her premonition of death made her want to wring the very juices out of life. A million times I've wished her premonition had been wrong.

21 : THE PINNACLE

1939

The manager of London's Hyde Park Hotel flung the door open for us, and waved two bellmen toward our baggage, which the taxi driver was stacking on the sidewalk.

"Miss Marble, Miss Tennant, what a pleasure to have you back with us!" Lili Burdette flashed us his most dazzling smile and his wife Gioia left the reception desk and came to meet us. Lili bent with a flourish to kiss both our hands, and Gioia hugged us. I was touched by their welcome. The Burdettes had taken a personal interest in me the previous year, and had thrown a small victory party to celebrate my doubles wins.

"I have a surprise for you," Lili said, snatching a set of keys from the board behind the desk and leading the way. We followed, responding as best we could to Gioia's excited questions about Forest Hills, my singing at the Waldorf (which had made the London papers) and, of course, the movie stars we spent time with during the rest of the year.

"Here we are," said Lili, thrusting the key into the lock and pushing open the door. "I redecorated a suite for you, for when you win the singles this year!"

"Lili, you are wonderful!" I said, stepping into the room. The sitting room was light and airy, the wallpaper a riot of tiny pale flowers. An arrangement of fresh flowers decorated a coffee table. Through the adjoining door I could see the bedroom wallpaper and bedspreads, which had been done in a tasteful, complementary pattern. I glanced back to see that Teach was still in the doorway, a frown on her face.

"Miss Tennant, what's wrong?" Lili's smile faded.

Teach looked uncomfortable. "The room number is eight-oh-three, which totals eleven," she explained. "That's an unlucky number for Alice. We must have a different room."

The Burdettes looked crestfallen. Teach was very superstitious and I knew she would stand firm, no matter what the cost in hurt feelings.

"Do you suppose you could change the number to eight-oh-two A for our stay?" I ventured.

Lili stared at me for a moment, then his smile once more hit full power. "Of course!" He bowed and backed out of the room, giving way to the mountain of luggage arriving on the bell captain's cart. Within the hour, the offending number was replaced.

My defeat of British champion Kay Stammers at Beckenham was a portent of things to come. I was at the peak of my game. I could feel it, and everyone could see it. Excitement charged the atmosphere every time I walked onto a court. The London papers began calling me "Alice Marvel." One said I played like a man but looked like a goddess. That was going a bit far, but I loved it all the same.

If only Hans had been there. I looked for his dark head in the crowd, waited for the delivery of a single peach-colored rose, but neither materialized. There were lots of attentive young men around me now, sleek Britishers with smooth hair and courtly manners, who should have filled the void—but they didn't. I knew better than to expect word from Hans, but still I hoped.

In the quarterfinal at Wimbledon I came up against my old adversary, Jadwiga Jedrzejowska, and put her away in straight sets. The next morning, the sky was a low ceiling of gray clouds. The semifinal match between Sarah Palfrey and Kay Stammers went off, with Stammers triumphing after three sets. Then it began to rain.

I had been in the locker room, still in my street clothes, for what seemed an eternity when the officials said that they were almost certain that my semifinal match with Hilda Sperling would be put off until the following day, but we weren't to leave, just in case.

I looked at the bundle of wool socks I had pulled from my bag. I planned to use them to keep my footing on the wet courts, because I wasn't comfortable in spikes like those the men wore. The socks were Kay Stammers's idea.

"Go buy a half dozen pairs of men's size eleven wool socks," she had told me. "Pull a pair on over your shoes. When a pair gets soggy, replace them." The socks said little for fashion, but they had worked for me in the earlier rounds.

I tossed the socks back in my bag. I was starved, so I wandered over to the hospitality tent, where a table full of little sandwiches and sweet cakes ringed a silver tea set. My mouth watered. Why not? I loaded up a plate of goodies and poured myself a cup of tea. The plate was empty and I was chewing the last bite of delicious cake when the announcement came: "Miss Marble, Mrs. Sperling, Centre Court in five minutes."

I nearly choked. I put down the plate and ran for the dressing room, feeling as if I had a ten-pound weight in my stomach. I changed, cursing myself for my stupidity. Stuffed as I was, I was afraid I wouldn't be able to move, that I would make a fool of myself. Suppose I threw up on Centre Court! The thought was almost enough to make me ill.

I reached the entrance to the court and nodded at Hilda, who looked as shocked as I at the sudden change of plan. Our match was being introduced when I remembered, too late, my wool "traction" socks.

As it turned out, I didn't need them. I had no problems with my full belly, or the footing, or the formidable Dane. It was as near perfect a match as I ever played, despite the circumstances. I beat Hilda 6–love, 6–love in less than twenty minutes. Seven games were on the scoreboard before I realized I'd forgotten to take off my warm-up sweater! Hilda scored a meager nine points in the first set, five in the second. The papers noted later that I made fewer than ten errors in the match.

Teach was ecstatic, and the staid old stands rumbled with the crowd's unusually boisterous approval. In the dressing room, Hilda sat in her dressing cubicle, still holding her racquet, her face wet with tears. I was surprised, and moved. The big woman was always such a stoic; she seldom showed any emotion, least of all tears. I crowded into the small space and dropped to the bench beside her.

She threw me a sidelong glance. "I've never been beaten like that!" There was no animosity in her words, only shock and dismay, feelings I knew all too well. Before I knew it, I was crying too.

The door opened and Lady Crosfield came in on a wave of noise from the slowly dissipating crowd. I had seen her in her courtside box before the match.

She stopped short, looking from one of us to the other. "My dears, who won?"

Hilda and I began to laugh, and to dry our tears.

"Hilda, you have no cause for tears," said Lady Crosfield. "No one could have stopped her today. Alice, you were magnificent."

"Thank you, Lady Crosfield," I said, pleased.

"Both of you are invited to my garden party after the final. Do be there." She looked pointedly at me, a trace of amusement on her aristocratic face. I blushed, remembering the invitation I had ignored two years earlier.

"I promise," I said, and Hilda nodded her assent.

The door flew open again, admitting a beaming Teach. "What are you doing? Change your clothes. The press are ready to beat down the door!" Hilda and I exchanged smiles, and I let Teach sweep me away.

The next day, with my partners Sarah Palfrey and Bobby Riggs, I won the semifinal matches of the women's and mixed doubles. At one point, I stretched to hit a smash and felt a slight pull in my stomach. It didn't seem like much, and I didn't mention it to Teach—until the next morning, when I awoke in agony.

"Teach," I called from my bed, holding my stomach, "I can't move!"

"Don't even try," she commanded, reaching for the phone and mumbling something about the room being unlucky despite the number change. In no time, the hotel doctor was beside my bed, probing my abdomen with gentle fingers and asking questions.

"It's a torn stomach muscle," he said, looking at Teach. "Help me lift her to a sitting position so I can tape her up."

"Can I play?" I asked.

The doctor looked up from his taping, startled.

"I'm in three finals today! I can't default."

Teach turned away so I wouldn't see her despair, but it was apparent in the slump of her shoulders.

"It will be painful," the doctor said hesitantly, "and you certainly can't expect to perform at your best."

"Teach," I called across the room to where she stood staring out the window. "I'm playing. Help me get dressed."

She looked at the doctor, who answered her with a shrug.

Teach finished tying my shoes and straightened, her hands on my knees. "Are you sure you can do this?"

"Yes. I'll meet you in the lobby. I'll just be a minute."

When the door closed behind her, I shut my eyes tightly and prayed, not for a victory—that was out of the question now—but that I wouldn't make a fool of myself.

The singles final was first. I walked onto Centre Court with Kay Stammers, sweat trickling down my back despite the coolness of the sullen gray day. Teach and I had said nothing about the torn muscle, for two reasons. My opponent could lob me out of the court

143

if she knew my weakness, and if I lost I wanted no excuses to spoil Kay's victory. She was a wonderful competitor, and my friend. It just wouldn't be fair.

Kay looked at me strangely when I only hit a few balls on the warm-up and didn't practice my serve. She won the toss, and chose to receive first. I groaned inwardly. That meant I had to serve.

Moving cautiously to see what I could manage without hurting, I dropped the first game. I took the next, then lost the third when a quick stretch for the ball made me wince and back off. Kay was too perceptive; I wouldn't be able to hide my injury much longer that way. I knew I had to ignore the pain, to think only of my next shot.

I gritted my teeth and stepped into the ball, using my whole body to avoid the pain of twisting. I chanted Beese's words, "Step and swing. Step and swing. Find your rhythm."

I did find my rhythm. The left-hander, always a daring shot maker, was playing near-perfect tennis, but somehow I managed to stay one step ahead of her, anticipating her moves, hitting the lines, returning shots which should have put points on the board for Kay. *Everything* about my game was working.

I hardly knew when it was match point. I hit a backhand down the line, catching Kay out of position, and she began walking toward me. There was noise from the crowd, but it was subdued, not anything like the response when I beat Hilda. Many of the spectators had waited outside the stadium all night in the rain in order to get a seat for the final. To end it so quickly with the defeat of their very popular contender shocked them.

It was a shock to me, too. If I had not taken the chance, if I had listened to the doctor, if I had not decided to try . . . I looked up at the umpire, then at Kay walking toward me, then at the scoreboard, where the numbers were going up: 6–2, 6–0. I had done it! I was champion of the world!

I was crying before I got to the net, where Kay hugged me, smiling. "Time for you to meet my queen," she said.

I whirled around to look at Teach. She was caught in a vortex, a swirling mass of reporters and well-wishers, but her eyes were on me, and her smile was glorious. My victory was her victory, the culmination of a lifetime of striving. I was the best in the world, and so was she. I hugged my racquet to my chest, prouder than I'd ever been in my life.

In moments, I was approaching the royal box on the arm of the American ambassador, Joseph Kennedy. The Dowager Queen Mary looked as queenly as a person could, dressed all in white, even to the hat on her snowy hair.

"Your Majesty, Miss Alice Marble," said Kennedy, stepping back. I looked into large violet eyes, eyes that held mine in a direct, steady gaze. Fine lines crinkled the delicate rosy skin at the corners of her mouth and eyes. She turned in her wicker chair and extended her hand. I curtsied and grasped it, surprised at the strength of her grip.

"Thank you for a fascinating match." Her voice was as I somehow knew it would be: low, assured, sincere. Her eyes sparkled. "And I like your cap," she added. I grinned at her and said something that I cannot, for the life of me, remember.

In a daze I walked away, out into the sunshine that had finally broken through the clouds. Then I stopped short. I'd forgotten to back away from the queen! Teach had drilled me a dozen times on protocol, yet I had just strolled away like an ignorant bumpkin. I turned to look back. She was watching me, and smiled. Kay had been presented and was just leaving the box.

A phalanx of officials and reporters swamped us, shouting above the sound of the fans who were on their feet, cheering. I was happy, and grateful, and proud. I thought of how my mother would have loved this moment. My brother Dan would hear the news on the radio. Dan, who had forced that first racquet into my hands. He would be so proud.

"How does it feel to be the world champion?" a reporter yelled in my ear.

"Better than anything I've ever known," I said, trying to sort out the emotions rioting inside me. I held the big trophy and smiled while the flashbulbs popped. Beside me stood Kay with her runner-up trophy. The newspapers that afternoon reported that she had hit more winners than errors, a feat which would have earned her a victory in any other Wimbledon.

"She was too good, I'm afraid," Kay told the press. "She played beautifully. She made no mistakes. Even if I hit the ball well, it didn't make any difference."

Teach finally made her way through the crush and rescued me. "She still has two matches to play," she explained, steering me toward the dressing room. "There will be time for interviews later."

"I don't know how you did it," she said when we reached the relative quiet of the dressing room. She shook her head and knelt to untie my shoes. "How do you feel?"

"Great," I said simply. The dull ache of the torn muscle was no match for my euphoria. I couldn't stop grinning. Teach glanced up at my face and laughed. "God, you were wonderful, Alice. You were simply wonderful. If you never play another match in your life, I'll still be a happy woman, having seen you play like this. I always knew you could."

"Not without you, Teach. You made me."

"Now, don't cry!" Teach scolded. "Think about your doubles matches. God only knows how you'll survive them."

The Marble family in 1920:
Harry and Jessie (top); Dan,
George, Hazel, Alice, and Tim
(bottom).

Alice as mascot of the San
Francisco Seals minor-league
baseball team—"The Little
Queen of Swat."

All photos collection of Alice Marble

Early highs and lows: the 1933
Pacific Coast Championship, and
collapse in Paris during the 1934
Wightman Cup preliminaries,
later diagnosed as pleurisy and
tuberculosis.

Eleanor "Teach" Tennant and Alice.

Carole Lombard and Alice: close friends and confidantes.

Alice with Clark Gable and Caesar Romero.

Alice lunges for a volley in Beckenham, England, during a tournament in 1937.

Alice during her 1937 singing debut at the Waldorf Astoria in New York City.

Wimbledon 1938: *(left to right)* Sarah Cook, Dorothy Bundy, Helen Wills Moody, Alice, Hazel Wightman, and the Duchess of Kent.

Alice with mixed doubles partner Don Budge at Wimbledon.

Enjoying a moment with
Princess Helen Victoria
(Queen Victoria's
granddaughter).

Scenes from Wimbledon
1939: hitting a forehand.

Dancing with Bobby Riggs at the Wimbledon Ball, after both won the singles, doubles, and mixed doubles titles.

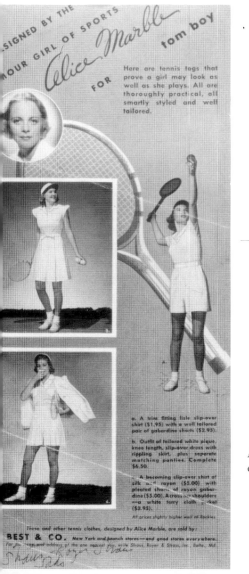

Alice's glamourous image led to a part-time career in designing sportswear.

At the U.S. Open at Forest Hills, New York, in 1940.

With Polish champion Jadwiga Jedrzejowska, who would be tragically killed at the outset of World War II.

Walking onto court with Britain's Kay Stammers.

With Tica Madrigal, author of the Madrigal language books, and her brother Miguel in 1940.

With WACS on the exhibition tour.

Alice and Mary Hardwick (left of Alice) meet the Duke and Duchess of Windsor at a Red Cross benefit in the Bahamas, 1943. (Alice and Mary played over five hundred exhibitions for troops during World War II.)

Alice and Bill Tilden.

Will du Pont, Jr.

Mary K. "Brownie" Browne.

Alice and two promising pupils in 1961: Billie Jean King and Carole Caldwell.

Alice holding the *Life* magazine August 28, 1939, issue that featured her on the cover as the top-ranked woman tennis player in the world.

22 : THE TRIPLE

The doubles matches. Could I last? My stomach ached, and I longed to sink into a tub of hot water, but couldn't because of the tape around my abdomen. Instead, I tried to relax while Bobby Riggs battled Elwood Cooke (later Sarah Palfrey's husband) for the singles title. It took two and a half hours for Bobby to win in five sets, during which time my muscles stiffened in the chilly dampness. Teach's face was pensive as she tied my shoes. I stood and twisted carefully, testing my range of painless movement.

Sarah Palfrey came in the locker room and stopped suddenly. "Alice, what's wrong?"

"She's torn a stomach muscle, but for God's sake keep it to yourself," Teach answered before I could speak.

"I'll be okay," I said. "Both of you stop worrying. This is my day!"

And it was. Sarah and I won easily, dispatching Helen Jacobs and Billie Yorke, 6–1, 6–0. The match took surprisingly little out of me, and loosened me up for the mixed-doubles final with Bobby Riggs.

When Bobby first asked me to play doubles with him, I refused, then at Teach's urging, consented.

"You never try hard enough in doubles," I told him. "I've won twice here with Don Budge. I'd like to do it again."

"I promise you I'll play as hard as I can," Bobby said in his most contrite little-boy voice. "It's really important to me. We'll win, I promise." I didn't know until later how much he had at stake.

Bobby and I were usually on opposite sides of the net, and I often wished us on opposite sides of the world. Since Teach had started coaching him, he had been the bane of my existence. He was an arrogant rascal, and Teach constantly pitted us against each other, using all of her mind-bending tactics to bring out the competitiveness in both of us.

Five years my junior, Bobby was born in Los Angeles and became the tennis protégé of coaches Easter and Jerry Bartos when he was twelve. He was a rowdy little kid, but Teach saw his potential. She taught us both on Carole's court, and made us practice together. He was a perfect practice partner for me (though I wouldn't admit it at the time), because he hit the ball softer than most men.

He was also a scoundrel and a hustler. One Thanksgiving, after an early-morning lesson at Carole's, the actress asked Bobby, "What are you doing for Thanksgiving?"

He shrugged, looking sad. "Ma never does anything for holidays."

"That's terrible!" Carole said. She went inside, raised her grocer on the phone, and insisted that the poor man open up his store, whereupon she bought a turkey and all the trimmings for Bobby, his parents, and his three brothers. Bobby never made it home with the feast. He stopped off at the Los Angeles Tennis Club, and lost it all on a bet.

But there was no losing for Bobby or me on the final day of Wimbledon. He played his heart out, as did I, both of us flying on the sheer adrenaline of our previous victories. We won in straight sets, and when it was over, we had both won the "Triple Crown" of singles, doubles, and mixed-doubles championships. I was the first woman in the century to win the triple, but Bobby's feat was even greater. He became the only player in Wimbledon history to win all three championships on his first attempt.

The day had become a magnificent dream, and I wanted it never to end. Everywhere I turned, there were flashing cameras, mobs of autograph seekers, and reporters asking me about everything from my shoes to my sex life to my diet. Bobby and Teach were going through the same treatment. How does it feel to be the coach of both "Wimbly" champions, the press wanted to know, barraging her with questions about technique and training methods.

"How *does* it feel?" I teased, when we made it back to our hotel and were relaxing over a glass of champagne with the Burdettes before changing for the Champions' Ball.

"It's the most rewarding day of my life," Teach said, her face serious. "I knew there was a fighting spirit in both of you, if I could only bring it out. You've both made me very proud."

"Hear, hear," said Lili, raising his glass. At that moment, Gioia came running, her dark Italian eyes wide. "Clark Gable's on the phone!"

"Honey, what wonderful news!" Clark said when I got to the receiver. "We're so proud of you!"

"I still can't believe it," I said, listening to the echo of my voice on the transatlantic line. "So much has happened. I'll never forget this day!" Then Carole's voice was in my ear. "Hullo, world champion! Our love to you and Teach and Bobby."

"I wish you were here. It's been incredible!"

My excitement scarcely dimmed even when Teach stripped the tape—and what felt like a layer of skin—off my middle so that I could bathe and put on my evening dress. The muscle was very sore to the touch, and I couldn't lift my arms above my head without hurting. I gratefully took the pain pills I'd shunned before the competition.

More than fifteen hundred people attended the Champions' Ball that night at the elegant Grosvenor House. I looked out from the dais into a sea of faces as Kay Stammers introduced me. Applause rumbled through the ballroom, and I started to choke up. Then my eyes fell on Wimbledon chairman Sir Samuel Hoare, and I remembered his remark of the previous year.

When the room was quiet I said carefully, "I'm so glad to have been a part of the *Wimbleship* championships—and to have won at last!" There was a roar of laughter. Hoare blushed and joined in the laughter. I went on to thank Teach, my family, and my supporters.

"Sing for us," someone called, and others joined in. Everyone knew about my brief career as a singer. I sang "Stardust" and, when they demanded an encore, "This Can't Be Love," then stepped down from the stage into the arms of a smiling Bobby Riggs.

"We have the first dance," he said. The music started and we swept around the empty dance floor, all eyes on us. I was wearing a grand dress, the red chiffon in which I had made my debut at the Waldorf. I didn't care that my heels made me two inches taller than Bobby, or that his broken tooth gave him a "Dennis the Menace" look. I forgot everything, except the joy of being champion.

"Aren't you glad you decided to be my partner?" he asked.

I nodded. "I'm sorry I doubted you. I've never known you to care about doubles."

"*Everything* depended on our winning."

"What do you mean?"

"The odds against my winning all three championships were so great I couldn't resist. I bet every dime I had, and every dime I could borrow, on myself."

"You bet on the match? Bobby, you're impossible!"

"I know. I'm also a lot richer!" He threw back his head and laughed, spinning me around.

"Don't make me laugh! It hurts!"

I wanted the night to go on forever. We all felt the specialness of the moment, and there was a closeness, an intimacy, among the international players that I had never known before. Would we ever see each other again? Europe was preparing for war, a war that would alter the course of the world—and the lives of us all. We danced as if we could delay the dawn.

23 : CELEBRITY

My torn stomach muscle improved enough for me to play—and win—in Ireland before we sailed home on the *S.S. Champlain.*

The Statue of Liberty was a tiny figure on the horizon when Teach and I went to our cabin to dress and to prepare the last of our things for arrival in New York. I put on a very stylish black-and-white dress and wide-brimmed hat I had bought in one of England's fanciest shops. "I feel like a million bucks," I said to Teach, "and I want to look it."

Waiting to descend the gangplank, I whispered to Teach, "I've waited a long time for this."

"*We've* waited a long time," Teach agreed.

Together, we stepped onto the gangplank and into the sight of those waiting on the dock below. There was a cheer, and I could hear my name being shouted over and over. The Brits had been wonderful to me, despite the defeat of their beloved Kay Stammers, but the New York fans were *my* fans and they showed it. I was thrilled, and still a little dazed when we were engulfed by the crowd, all of whom seemed to be shouting questions and flashing cameras. It was just the beginning.

We had expected a grand reception but were unprepared for the maelstrom of activity. It went on for weeks, threatening to destroy any semblance of a training schedule for my upcoming matches. Perhaps the knowledge that the world was soon to be at war made people more passionate about everything.

The phone in our hotel room rang constantly, and Teach and I were both exhausted from trying to deal with offers, make the right decisions, and not offend anyone. Within the first week, I had four film offers, countless requests to sing, speak, write, be a guest commentator at sporting events and, of course, play tennis. Only when I signed with Frank Orsatti, the Hollywood agent who represented skater Sonja Henie, did some sign of order return to our lives.

"Thank God," said Teach, shaking the agent's hand. "Now I can go back to being a coach."

Orsatti lined up four screen tests, to take place when we returned to California.

Teach and I moved into the Sherry Netherland Hotel on Fifty-ninth Street and Fifth Avenue. Roz Bloomingdale Cowen's parents spent the summer at the shore, and had graciously offered us the use of their suite.

I agreed to several speaking engagements, and asked the help of Amy Scherer, who worked on the First Lady's speeches and was one of the most sought-after socialites in New York.

"I've prepared a speech on the will to win," I told her, "but I'd like to have a trial run before I give it in public."

Mrs. Scherer immediately arranged a tea at Roz Cowen's house, inviting several theater directors and producers—and Mrs. Eleanor Roosevelt. No tennis opponent ever made me tremble the way I did standing before that semicircle of stage legends and the First Lady. This wasn't like playing tennis or singing songs before a group. These were my thoughts, my opinions, and though I knew the words were firmly locked in my memory, I was unsure as to how they would be received. For the first time, I worried about boring an audience.

As I spoke, I scanned the listeners' faces. They seemed attentive and interested. I finished, and looked at Mrs. Scherer.

"Mrs. Roosevelt, comments?" she asked.

The First Lady smiled at me. "I was so impressed, I'm going home to straighten all the dresser drawers in the White House."

I was puzzled for a moment, then realized that my speech had hit the mark. It had inspired the First Lady to *do* something. I joined in the group's laughter. The others were complimentary, as well, and it was with some confidence that, a week later, I addressed a women's club in New Jersey.

Halfway into my speech, I saw a familiar figure in the audience—Katharine Cornell, the first lady of the theater (before Helen Hayes). Afterwards, she came backstage and congratulated me.

"I can't believe that you're coming to see *me*," I said, thinking

152

of all the times I'd slipped backstage after her plays, and we laughed together.

Teach masterfully coordinated my public appearances with practice and tournaments, and my winning streak remained intact going into the national championships.

Helen Jacobs was always one of my toughest opponents, and the 1939 national final was as fierce a match as the two of us ever played. It was more than skill that had earned Helen one Wimbledon and four national singles titles; it was pure guts, and she proved it that day.

The weather was terrible. Strong winds gusted across the court, carrying dust and papers from the stands, playing havoc with the ball. It was impossible to know where our returns would go once they left our racquets. The press said I had a slight edge because I hit the ball harder, but I felt no such advantage as I struggled to keep the ball in bounds.

I took the first set at 6–0, going to 5–3, mostly on the strength of my serve, in the second. Then Helen rose to the challenge, the way I'd seen her do so many times, and scrapped her way to an 8–10 victory.

I went into the third set rattled, feeling the nervous anticipation of the crowd. I pulled my hat tighter on my head. The wind had threatened to whip it off several times, an annoying distraction, but I needed it to keep my hair out of my eyes.

Breaking Helen's service, I won the first game, then lapsed into one of the fits of inconsistency that had plagued my whole career. Teach never tried to coach me from the sideline, but suddenly I heard her bellow, "Get off the dime!" when Helen led, 3–1, and I was committing errors on both my forehand and backhand. I had to concentrate! I took a deep breath and blocked out the crowd, the wind, the flopping brim of my cap.

We both sought the net at every opportunity, trying to escape the vagaries of the wind. Twice Helen fought back from match point. The match could have gone either way, under the circumstances, and I felt more relief than triumph when I finally hit the winning point to end the set, 6–4, and clinch my third national championship in four years. We had been on the court an hour and a half.

Bobby Riggs followed me, handily withstanding the threat of a nineteen-year-old unseeded upstart, Welby Van Horn, to win the men's singles championships.

I teamed up with the Australian Harry Hopman to win the

mixed-doubles title, and with Sarah Palfrey to take the women's doubles over Kay Stammers and Freda James Hammersley, winners of two Wimbledon doubles championships, 6–4, 8–6, at Chestnut Hill, Massachusetts.

"Next time," said Kay, smiling as she and Freda came to the net and offered their congratulations.

"Next time," I replied, my voice catching in my throat. The four of us knew that there wouldn't be a next time, not for a long while. Though the United States championships would continue, it would be without most of the international competitors. Europeans had concerns more important than sports, with the ugly specter of war drawing closer.

A month later, it happened. On September 1, Germany invaded Poland, and two days later England and France declared war on Germany. The British began flying huge balloons over London to interfere with enemy planes. When the planes strafed the balloons, anti-aircraft guns fired on them from the ground. I thought of Wimbledon, of the ghostly match I had heard on my first visit, and my curtsey to the queen on my last. I thought, too, of the beautiful houses and estates we had visited just a few months before. What would happen to them, and to our friends?

FDR proclaimed the United States a neutral nation, but we all wondered how long that could last. Could we stand by and watch the destruction of our allies?

Then the news reached the States that JaJa Jedrzejowska was dead, the victim of a German bomb, and the war took on a new reality for me. The tennis world mourned JaJa, and knew the grief had just began.

In the early days of World War II, another war caught the imagination of the American people—the War Between the States. *Gone With the Wind*, more than three years in the making, premiered in Atlanta on December 14, 1939.

When Carole and Clark asked me to go with them to the premiere, I said yes to what was every movie fan's dream. I met Margaret Mitchell and the cast, many of whom I knew. Atlanta teemed with celebrities, and Loew's Grand Theatre at Five Points, the heart of the city, was a magical place. Marquee lights reflected off gleaming cars as the stars arrived, stepped into the blinding flash of cameras, and paraded past a gauntlet of excited fans to the marble lobby.

Despite the fanfare over the search for Scarlett, and all the hype leading up to the premiere, I was unprepared for the sheer grandeur of *Gone With the Wind*. It was the best movie I had ever seen—

154

the best movie ever made. Clark seemed pleased when I told him so, but he felt smothered by the outpouring of public adoration for Rhett Butler, as if his own identity had been eclipsed by that of the suave Southerner.

Clark refused to stay in the big hotel where the other cast members were, opting for the quieter Georgian Terrace. Every day he liked to have some quiet time for himself, for though he loved Carole, she was a chatterbox. One day, she rapped on the door between our adjoining rooms and came in.

"Quick," she whispered. "You have to see this."

Mystified, I followed her back into their suite. "He's taking a bath," she whispered, nodding toward the closed bathroom door, and leading me to the window.

"Look." She pointed to the hotel across the street. In every window we could see binoculars trained on a common point: Clark Gable in the bathtub. Carole and I shook with silent laughter.

I finally gasped, "Don't you want to go in there and draw the blinds?"

"What? And spoil their fun? Let them look. Besides, if they see his 'manly weapon,' they'll find that it's a dinky little thing."

"Carole! You are a devilish woman!"

"Yep," she said, and we again smothered our laughter.

The year 1939 was like no other in my life, and nothing that had gone before prepared me for it. Every athlete dreams of reaching the top—an Olympic gold medal, a world championship, whatever title is the dearest in that sport and proclaims that he or she is the best in the world—but only a few make it. Months after Wimbledon, I still had trouble believing that I was the world champion, even when the honors kept coming. The sportswriters voted me Woman Athlete of the Year; the fashion writers added their Best Dressed Woman in Athletics, and I was one of ten women named to *Who's Who*.

Before the year was over, I knew I had changed, and Teach knew it too. People expected me to be my own woman—mature and capable of handling myself in all circumstances. I couldn't let Teach continue to make my decisions and finish my sentences. I began to pull at the restraint she exercised on me.

I found myself in social situations where the talk was not limited to sports, and realized that I knew nothing but tennis. That wasn't too surprising; I had had no education beyond high school, and my world for the past eight years had been the tennis court. Traveling had been wonderful, but I knew nothing of classical literature or world affairs or politics.

When Roz Cowen jokingly introduced me as "my friend Alice, whose knowledge is a mile wide and a half-inch deep," I realized that I wanted to change that image. Attending a Spanish class with Roz was my first real gesture of independence, and immediately put a strain on my relationship with Teach. When I returned to the hotel late one night, Teach was furious, even after I explained that several of us had gone out to dinner after class.

"I didn't realize I was too old for you," she said.

"What are you talking about? Roz is your age, and the Kaltenborns are in their sixties!" Teach had met the people in the class at Roz's parties: radio commentator H. V. Kaltenborn and his wife, Olga; Ben Grauer, announcer for Walter Winchell for fifty years; Charles Hoagland, head of research at the Rockefeller Institute; and the rest.

I knew what Teach meant, but I ignored her insinuation. I had been seeing a lot of our Spanish teacher, Margarita "Tica" Madrigal, and Teach was jealous.

Tica, the daughter of a Costa Rican English teacher and a Kansas housewife, spoke English with a terrible accent, but she made Spanish and Portuguese sound like poetry, and she was a talented teacher. Her classes at Duke and New York University were always filled, and her books were considered the best language manuals available. I went from beginning to advanced Spanish in six months, and into a relationship with Tica that was as intense as it was unexpected.

She was my age, shorter than I by several inches, and chubby, with short black hair and animated black eyes. She was always bursting with energy, and quick to laugh, especially at herself. When Tica offered to teach me to play the guitar, I was delighted.

One Thursday we were to have a lesson at my place. Tica came early, and found me sitting on the floor, intently fretting the strings of the guitar. She knelt behind me and reached around me to adjust my position. Something in me stirred at the touch of her hands on mine. I could feel her breath on my cheek, and the closeness of her body made my heart race.

Surprised and confused at my feelings, I started to pull away. Tica held me, gently pulling me closer to her, closing her arms around me. I could feel the fullness of her breasts against my back. She murmured an unfamiliar phrase in Spanish.

"What does that mean?" I asked.

She gave a low laugh and kissed my ear. "It means that you are ripe and ready to fall from the tree."

"But I've never . . ."

"Been with a woman? That's obvious, too, but something in your eyes these past few weeks has been telling me you want to."

I turned in her arms to look at her. Before I could speak, she kissed me, and I returned the kiss. Her lips were soft, and I thought fleetingly of Hans, the rough brush of his mustache, the firmness of his mouth. Then I was mesmerized by Tica, by her gentle love-making, at once strange and wonderful. *Who knew how to please a woman better than another woman?* I thought.

I hadn't had any sexual contact since my affair with Hans; Tica satisfied that need, and was a bright, witty, enjoyable companion, too. I adored her, and when her live-in lover left in tears, I assumed Tica and I would be together.

But Tica found someone else. Doris Dana, a cute little English teacher at Columbia, caught her eye and it was my turn for tears. Tica ended our affair as gently as she could, but I was heartbroken. I had loved her, and now I felt foolish and miserable beyond words. I was alone again.

Teach had been like a gathering storm, knowing full well what was going on, but powerless to do anything about it. I steeled myself for a tongue-lashing, but when I said to her, "Let's go home. Let's go to California," she looked at me with pity, and said nothing. We packed our bags and headed west.

24: WILL DU PONT

The country was shifting gears. Plants across the country, even the car companies in Detroit, were turning out war matériel: planes for the army and navy, weapons, ammunition, uniforms, parachutes, and boots. Europe writhed as Hitler's troops continued to lance into ill-prepared countries almost at will.

Teach and I were back in Los Angeles when I received a note from Howard York, a very good tennis player from Philadelphia. Howard and his wife had met a man who gave them access to his five indoor tennis courts all winter. "He's coming out to California soon," the note read. "Will you show him around? We told him to look you up at the L.A. Tennis Club. His name is Will du Pont."

The name meant nothing to me, and I didn't give it another thought until one morning when I stayed home to work on the books in the pretty little Beverly Hills apartment Teach and I rented. The phone rang; I put down my pencil to answer it.

"There's a strange guy here looking for you," said the club hostess. "You'll die laughing when you see him. Says his name is du Pont."

"Good Lord, I didn't expect him so soon!" I said. "Ask him to wait and we'll have lunch. I'll be right over."

Even with the warning, I wasn't prepared. Will du Pont had found someone to play with, and was just coming off the court when I arrived. Several club members were all too willing to point the stranger out to me, as if it were necessary. He stood out.

I watched him walk toward me in a rambling, farmer's gait, his long arms swinging loosely. He wasn't a big man, and his aquiline face and long nose gave him a sorrowful look. He was dressed in high-top black basketball shoes (he had weak ankles), rumpled

158

khaki pants, a sweater fastened with a big safety pin, and a badly stained tennis cap. I glanced down at the nice dress I had worn for the occasion, and stepped into his path.

"Mr. du Pont, I'm Alice Marble."

"How do you do? I'm a great fan of yours!" He shook my hand with an almost comic formality. We walked into the lounge and found a table. I saw the club regulars glance at my companion, but he didn't notice.

"The Yorks think very highly of you," I said. "Is there anything I can do for you while you're in California?"

"I'm planning to build some hard courts at my place in Wilmington that can be used year-round. I'd like to see how it's done here."

"I can show you dozens of courts, and introduce you to the people who built them," I said.

He smiled. "Wonderful!"

I saw Teach in the doorway and waved her over. "Mr. du Pont, my coach Eleanor Tennant."

I saw Teach's eyes flick curiously over the man's outfit. She shook his hand and accepted the seat he offered.

"Where are you from, Mr. du Pont?" she asked politely.

"Wilmington, Delaware."

"Are you related to the munitions family?"

"I'm the head of it."

Teach's eyes widened slightly. Money always had that effect on her, so I guessed that du Pont was a wealthy man.

"Why don't we have lunch at the house?" Teach suggested.

"Don't you have lessons?" I asked.

"I'll cancel them," she said. At that, *my* eyes widened. "I'll call S. T.," she said, rising from her chair. "What do you like to eat, Mr. du Pont?"

"Red meat would be fine," he said, and excused himself to shower and change.

"We're all set," Teach said when she returned from the phone. "S. T. will have a nice rare filet ready in an hour, bless her." S. T. Bratton was a delightful black woman who had been Tallulah Bankhead's maid until a heart condition forced her to stop traveling. She ran her own catering business and worked for us part-time, another victim of Teach's persuasive talents. She was a great cook, and absolutely charming to company.

I eyed Teach with suspicion. "Why are you doing this?"

"The man's a millionaire."

"It won't rub off."

"It can't hurt."

Teach was fascinated by wealth, but I had learned that a millionaire's money could not buy peace of mind. Such was the case with Will. The heir to a fortune, he had quadrupled the holdings his father left him, owned nineteen farms in Maryland and Virginia in addition to his forty-room Wilmington estate, and raised some of the finest race, show, and steeplechase horses in the country. Yet he was an unhappy man, trapped in an unhappy marriage. Will and his wife, Jean, showed horses in Madison Square Garden and all the other big shows, but had little else in common. Tennis was very important to him, but not to her.

Born at Montpelier, Virginia, the home of James Madison, Will spent all his time in the stables and preferred the company of grooms and horses to his social peers, who called him Dirty Willie. His language could be as rough as his wardrobe, but he was a gentle, caring man.

When we walked together, I would change sides so that he was next to the curb.

"Why do you do that?" he asked, and I could see that he was serious.

"Because a gentleman is supposed to walk on the curb side, to protect the lady from runaway horses and splattering mud—that sort of thing."

"Oh," he said. "I always put you on my right hand because that's the way you lead horses and cows."

"Thanks for the comparison," I said, tucking my arm in his and laughing. He was one of the richest men in the world, yet beguilingly innocent.

Will stayed three weeks in California, and had lunch or dinner with us every day. He never took us out to dinner or invited us to the hotel where he stayed. When people found out who he was, they plied him with invitations, but he said no. Though he seldom drank back east, he drank bourbon—quite a lot of it—with us, had a late-afternoon swim, and retired at seven-thirty every day. He was up at three A.M., tending to masses of paperwork and talking on the phone with his East Coast interests.

Will was a year younger than Teach, and like her, a great storyteller. The three of us had fun together, visiting the stars and other people we knew who had courts that would interest Will.

After he had learned what he needed, Will went back east to his mansion, wife, and five kids, and built some of the finest all-weather courts in the country. They were heavily used in good weather, for Will loved to entertain tennis players. There were even a few diehards, like James Michener, who spurned Will's lovely indoor courts, shoveled the snow off the outside courts, and played in mittens in the dead of a Delaware winter.

Every year, Will left behind his businesses, farms, and horses to spend three weeks in California. And, until the day he died, my life was to be linked to his. He was one of the best friends I ever had.

Teach's lack of interest in the movie business (beyond teaching its stars) changed when I began doing the screen tests that agent Frank Orsatti had set up. All the major studios were interested. I was the number one woman tennis player in the world, undefeated for more than a year, and a salable property in the eyes of the movie moguls. Teach thought we would get rich.

But as her interest grew, mine diminished. The fantasy on the screen was a far cry from the gritty reality behind the scenes, the convoluted business in which people were chattel and careers were often made or broken on whim. I was further disillusioned by the Academy Awards, which went to the very deserving Vivien Leigh and Hattie McDaniel for their roles in *Gone With the Wind*, but not to Clark Gable. Clark shrugged it off, but I considered the result a travesty.

"Teach wants me to try for a career in movies," I told Carole, "but I just can't. It's not me. I love the actors, but I hate the business. Some slimy little bastard is always trying to use me, or get me in bed."

"There are plenty of them," she agreed. "Enough to make you swear, isn't it?"

"How can I get out of this? You know how Teach is."

"I think we can redirect her," Carole said. "Leave it to me."

When the actress suggested a tour of small towns across the country on our way to New York for the nationals, I picked up her cue.

"There are so many towns that never get to see good tennis," I said.

"Wilson can book the tournaments, you can do clinics," Carole said, "and you'll make a bundle of money by the time you get to New York."

"And I promise not to lose a match," I added. "Let's get away from this movie stuff for a while, before it affects my game."

Tennis was the most important thing in Teach's life. She took Carole's idea, and perfected it. Wilson Sporting Goods set up a series of thirty tournaments across the country, and when other players heard that I was playing, the rosters filled. Everyone wanted a shot at the champion. Wilson would pay Teach to conduct clinics at each stop, and we carried a supply of signature racquets, Teach's and mine, to sell.

Carole saw us off. Our bags were in the trunk of a brand-new Studebaker Teach had talked Wilson into providing for the trip. Shaking her head, Carole admired the car. "How does she do it?"

"Teach could charm the spots off a leopard." I hugged her. "Don't shoot your foot off on one of those hunting trips, and tell Clark he's the best, no matter what the Academy says."

"I will. Don't let Teach drive too fast. This honey looks like it can move."

Teach had invited Lillian Lyford Yeates to go with us. Lily, whose husband had lost a considerable fortune in the 1929 stock-market crash, was from Minnesota, one of the stops on our itinerary.

We had left our first stop, Phoenix, and were headed for Shreve-port, Louisiana, when Teach got sleepy and agreed to let me behind the wheel. The roads were wide open, it was a sunny day, and I felt gloriously alive, purring through the countryside in that new car. The speedometer was marked to 104 miles per hour. I glanced at Teach, asleep on the seat beside me. In the rearview mirror, I could see that Lily had dozed off in the back.

I gradually increased the pressure on the gas pedal, and watched the needle climb: 90, 95, 100.

"You're going too fast," Teach said quietly, without opening her eyes. I sighed and eased off the gas. If I hadn't, we'd probably all be dead. The car was going about sixty when I entered a curve and saw a huge truck straddling the center of the road. High in his cab, the startled man whipped his wheel to the right, but it was too late to get the big trailer out of the way.

"Watch out," I yelled, though there was no time for anyone to react, and steered for the shoulder of the road. The outside front tire hit the ditch and skewed the car around so rapidly that it turned over three times and came to rest on the opposite side of the road, facing back toward Phoenix.

I stared stupidly at the windshield, which had two starbursts where Teach and I had shattered the glass with our heads. My head and neck hurt terribly, and my ears were filled with a shrill, piercing noise. Another sound penetrated my fogged senses, and I turned to look into the pale face of the truck driver. He was tapping on the window and motioning for me to unlock the car door. When I did, he jerked the door open, and crouched to peer in the car.

"It's all right!" he yelled, and the shrill noise trailed off. It had been Lily, screaming. The silence was a relief, but the throbbing in my head and neck continued. A knot was beginning to swell on

Teach's head. Lily, despite the screaming, was unharmed. We were all shaken enough to offer no protest when an ambulance came for us.

In the hospital emergency room, the three of us were examined in separate areas cordoned off by curtains. I lay on a stretcher, my head immobilized by sandbags, and listened to scraps of conversation: ". . . broken neck," I heard the doctor say, and my name, then an unintelligible reply from Teach.

I bit my lower lip, fighting panic, and felt the salty taste of my own blood. Oh God, no. Please don't let me have a broken neck! I visualized months in bed, maybe even paralysis. I might never be able to play tennis again! I was sweating and almost in tears when the doctor, followed by Teach, pulled back the curtain.

"Okay, Miss Marble, the X rays show nothing's broken, but you're going to be very stiff."

I was still shaking when a taxi took us to a hotel. After a sleepless night, I started trembling all over again the next morning when I had to get back in a car. Teach wanted to move on, in hopes of staying on schedule. Our car was totaled, but Wilson had arranged for a replacement from the local dealership.

The schedule suffered anyway when, in Shreveport, I came down with strep throat and spent a week in the local hospital. My neck was painfully stiff; I had difficulty putting my head back to hit a smash. At each stop, we found a chiropractor to manipulate my neck and relieve the muscle spasms. We managed to keep the injury out of the papers. In Washington, D.C., an up-and-coming Pauline Betz, who would be Wimbledon champion in 1946, could have beaten me if she'd only known to lob.

As it was, I didn't lose a match, and we met some delightful people. The wealthy scions of Minneapolis—the Pillsburys, the Johnsons, and the Bells of General Foods—were every bit as hospitable as Lily promised, but I got just as much pleasure from playing in the small towns, where the people had never seen first-class tennis. We were house guests wherever we went, and Teach was delighted because that meant we could bank our ten-dollar daily expense allowance.

Everywhere we went, people talked about the war. I read the newspapers that spring as I never had before: world news first, *then* the sports. In April, Norway and Denmark fell to the Germans, followed by Holland and Belgium in May, causing the bloody retreat at Dunkirk. Teach and I heard Churchill's impassioned "blood, toil, tears and sweat" speech on the radio, and rubbed the goosebumps it raised on our arms. I had been too young to know what was going on in the first world war, but I knew it would be different this time.

We were staying at Will du Pont's in Wilmington when the news came that Paris had surrendered to the Germans. The Roland Garros Stadium, where I had collapsed, would soon be used by the Nazis as a detention center for prisoners on their way to the death camps. The Battle of Britain was on, and London was being bombed every night. I worried about my friends, and sent CARE packages, though I didn't always know if they arrived. Wimbledon would be hit sixteen times before the war was over; a five-hundred-pound bomb fell on the Centre Court stands in October.

The grass courts of the du Pont estate were excellent, and Will was thrilled to have us there, but it was obvious that Jean didn't share his enthusiasm for tennis—or for me. They were divorced before the year was out, and Will's daughter (also named Jean) always blamed me for breaking up her parents' marriage, though the divorce had nothing to do with me. The marriage was doomed long before Will and I met. In California, Will had confided that he'd been miserable for years, and sometimes hoped that his private plane would crash.

"Shame on you, Will," was all I could think of to say. "What about your cousin, the pilot? Would you wish his death, too?"

"No, but I wouldn't mind dying. I wouldn't mind it at all."

I shrugged off the animosity of the du Pont women. Years later, I was to discover just how much young Jean hated me.

25 : WAR

I prepared for the 1940 nationals at Arthur Loew's estate in Glen Cove, Long Island. Teach and I always enjoyed staying with Arthur, whose father, Marcus, was one of the founders of MGM. At Pembroke, we were treated like members of the family. The chauffeur drove us to Forest Hills in the limousine or, if the water was calm, Arthur took us up Long Island Sound on the family yacht.

I never felt deserving of such grand treatment, but that didn't keep me from enjoying it. It was part of the magic of tennis in my time. There was no real money to be earned as an amateur player, but the sport provided a glorious life-style. Teach and I always lived well beyond our means.

"I feel as if I should be doing something more important than playing tennis," I told Teach one evening.

"Such as?" She looked at me over the book she was reading.

"The Selective Service Act just passed," I said, tapping the newspaper I had just put down. "Men have to register for the draft."

"So?" Teach lowered her book another inch.

"So I want to serve my country, too. I want to enlist. We're going to war. Everybody says so."

"You do serve your country. You take people's minds off war," Teach said, her book on her lap now. "That's where you belong, on the court entertaining, doing what you do best."

I defeated Helen Jacobs, 6–2, 6–3, in the last national final we were to play, completing another triple sweep of the championships with Sarah Palfrey and Bobby Riggs in the doubles. Helen was still a tough opponent—I never had an easy match against her—but I was a month short of twenty-seven, while she had just celebrated her thirty-second birthday. And I was at the peak of my game, with an unbroken string of twenty-eight tournament victories. I hadn't lost since Helen had beaten me at Wimbledon in 1938.

"What's left for us now, with international tennis on hold?" I asked Helen in the locker room.

She finished untying her shoes and slipped them off her feet before answering, and then her answer began with a sigh. "I'm going to hang it up for a while," she said. "I'm going to join the service, if they'll have me, and do whatever I can to help end this war."

The military wanted her, all right. Helen became an officer in the WAVEs, the new women's branch of the navy, and was busy throughout the war. She continued her career in the navy afterward, and eventually retired with the rank of commander.

I tried to enlist, too, but the armed forces gave me a slightly different reception.

The door of the U.S. Army recruiting office in Manhattan slammed harder than I'd intended, and I glanced back to make sure the glass was intact. Inside, at the desk, the sergeant touched a finger to his temple in salute and grinned at me.

"Dammit," I muttered to myself. "What does he mean, 'unfit'? I just won the national tennis championship and I'm not fit?"

When I reached the navy recruiting center, I stopped scowling. By the time it was my turn to see the recruiter, I was smiling again, having spent a pleasant half hour talking with several young men who were signing up. *They* were pulling for me to make the grade.

I sat down in the straight-backed chair before the recruiter's desk and waited. The interview didn't take long. The officer tapped a folder on his desk and spoke. "I looked over your records, Miss Marble. I'd love to see you in a navy uniform, but with your health history, I have to turn you down."

"Turn me down! Why?"

"Tuberculosis."

"But I was cured years ago! Do I look sick?"

He smiled and shook his head. "Certainly not, but . . . that's just the way it is."

Three hours and two recruitment offices later, I had completed a full sweep of the military. The marines and coast guard didn't want me either. All of them were eager to enlist the world champion—until they looked at my health history. I walked slowly back to the Sherry Netherland.

"No luck?" Teach asked, as if my expression weren't evidence enough. I shook my head and slumped into a chair.

"L. B. Icely [the president of Wilson Sporting Goods] called again, about your joining the pro tour he's setting up," she said. "Why not earn some money while you're at the top of your game? It's rotten luck that you reached the top just in time for this damned war, but you're the best, and people want to see you play tennis. You're better off doing that than typing requisitions on some god-forsaken military post."

"I hear you," I said wearily, but my thoughts were elsewhere. I could always join the Red Cross. At least I would be in uniform. Brownie had been a Red Cross officer in World War I, and, at forty-three, was planning to join up again as soon as her school in Cleveland could find a replacement teacher.

A few days later, my career decision was made, but not in a way I expected. I answered the phone and heard the words, "Miss Marble? It's the White House calling. Please hold on." Then the unmistakable voice of President Roosevelt came over the line.

"Yes, sir?" I said. "Thank you, sir. . . . I will, sir. . . . Thank you, Mr. President."

I dropped the receiver back in its cradle. Teach's eyes were on me. "Did you just say 'Mr. President'?"

I nodded, trying to grasp what had just happened. "It was FDR himself," I said slowly. "He wants me to cochair a physical-fitness program for the Office of Civilian Defense with Jack Kelly [Grace's father]." I looked at her. "Can you believe it?"

"I'm afraid I can," she said dryly, and I could read her thoughts. There went the pro tour.

"I need to do this," I said. "Will you be my assistant?"

"Certainly not. I've had my war."

Brownie said yes, she would work with me, and promised to be in New York within the week, replacement teacher or no. Meanwhile, the president's secretary had set up a meeting for me with the FBI. "It's a routine check," she assured me, "to see if you have a shady past."

I laughed. "No dark secrets."

The "routine check" was a barrage of questions directed at me by two agents in almost identical dark suits who scribbled occasionally on identical clipboards. Even their close haircuts matched. After a couple hours, I wearied of the cookie-cutter twins and said, "Boys, you're repeating yourselves. First, you ask me a question," I said pointing at one, "then after a while, you ask me the same thing." I pointed at the other. They exchanged glances.

"You're right, Miss Marble," said Tweedledum hesitantly. "The trouble is, your answers are the same, word for word, and you recall every trip you've taken out of the country, right down to the exact dates and all the details."

"Those are things we're trained to pick up on," said Tweedledee. "Foreign agents memorize their cover stories." He raised a hand as I started to object. "We *know* you're not a foreign agent, but we don't know what to make of you."

I grabbed a magazine from the table next to me, opened it, scanned a page, then handed it to one of them. "Listen carefully," I said, and recited the page from beginning to end. The agent looked at his cohort, then at me, and cleared his throat.

"Did I miss anything?" I asked.

"Not a word. You have a photographic memory?"

"It's always been easy for me to remember what I read, if that's what you mean."

The two looked at each other again, then back at me. "You should be working for us."

I laughed. "Thanks, but tennis is my game. I'm not cut out for intrigue."

I gave them my diary, to check against what I had told them, and they came up with one small discrepancy about my Canadian trip when I was sixteen. The FBI cleared me to accept the president's offer, and to enter military bases, then filed my records away with thousands of other routine checks. Or so I thought.

The president launched his new fitness program, presenting Jack Kelly and me to the nation with a grand flurry of publicity. Proudly I posed for photos in my new uniform, the drab green of the Civilian Defense Corps. Brownie and I alternately spent three days a week in Washington or on the road, extolling the value of exercise to factory workers, college students, and women's groups.

I was surprised to hear from the FBI again so soon, and almost amused at what the agent who met with me had to say.

"We want you to report anything you hear at the parties and political functions you attend."

"What do you mean, 'anything'?" I asked.

"Anything out of the ordinary, particularly anything that seems unpatriotic."

I agreed, though it all seemed a bit cloak-and-dagger to me. I was given a Spanish typewriter on which to write my weekly reports, and the number of a post-office box to mail them to. The language was enough to conceal what I was doing from anyone accidentally seeing my work. It became a part of my routine to tap out newsy notes of functions I attended—who was there, who said what—like an ersatz gossip columnist. I told Teach I was practicing my Spanish, and she was none the wiser.

Unfortunately, the president's physical-fitness program ran out of gas. Everyone was working. Women spent long hours on assembly lines beside men who would soon leave the work force for the military. The few hours between work and sleep were devoted to caring for their families, leaving no time for exercise.

I needed to work, too. As lofty as my title was, the political appointment paid a dollar a year. Brownie and I called it quits. The Red Cross happily put her back in uniform and sent her abroad, sometimes to places as far away as Australia, where tennis balls had become a luxury item. Her home base when she was in the States was the New York apartment I shared with Teach.

I picked up where I had left off, helping Teach with clinics and speaking to various groups on "The Will to Win." At Carole's urging, I agreed to design a line of clothes for Best & Company department stores—dresses, coats, and blouses with a sporty look, and tennis outfits for the "Tomboy" line. Based on my short time in the Civil Defense uniform, I designed a much-needed oxford for women in the service, which was manufactured by Sadler of Boston. I was pleased with my work, as were the buyers, but I was beginning to think of my future, and the debt I owed Teach. I only saw one way to repay her.

Christmas in New York had been wonderful, though I missed my family, and spent more than I could afford on phone calls to follow up the presents I had sent. Teach and I had shuttled by limousine from one Long Island estate to another for a marathon of parties, and were finally back at our apartment for a rest before the New Year's celebrations.

Christmas carols played softly on the radio. Teach was reading, and I had been curled up in a cushioned window well for more than an hour, enjoying the quiet, watching snowflakes dance in the light of street lamps below. I looked at Teach, considering the enigma of our long relationship. She gave, and I took; she taught, and I learned, parlaying the lessons into fame, if not fortune. What was really in it for her? I knew my teacher better than anyone on earth, but I *didn't* know her. She had an answer for everything—except her personal feelings. I only knew I was in her debt for making my dreams come true, for making me a champion. I watched snow gather on the dark hat of a man hurrying by.

"Still snowing?" Teach asked.

"Uh-huh. Tell Icely I'll play."

"What?" Teach leaned forward in her chair.

"I'm ready to turn pro."

"You're sure?"

"Yes."

"Why? What made you change your mind?"

I shrugged. "What's left for me? There may not even be a national tournament next year. I'm champion. Let's make the most of it."

I loved to see Teach smile. It was a beautiful expression, reflecting everything that was bright and charming in her. I saw it now, and was glad.

The morning editions of the papers carried the news, and Will du Pont's phone calls caught up with me by lunch.

"Have dinner with me tonight?"

"I'd love to." Will came over from Wilmington a couple of times a week to take me to dinner or the theater. The scenario was always the same. We'd go to dinner, walk back to my apartment, and he'd ask me to marry him. My answer was always the same. "No, Will. You're very dear to me, but I can't marry you. I'm not in love with you."

But he never stopped asking. His divorce from Jean had been finalized and he was anxious to have a woman to share his life. When we went to the Broadway opening of *Oklahoma!*, Will's eyes had been on me throughout the play. I sometimes wished my feelings for him were different—the situation would be so simple then—but they weren't, and I wanted to be fair to him.

"I'd like for Teach to come to dinner too," he said.

The three of us had just settled into our seats at '21' when Will, never one to mince words, said, "I understand you want to turn professional."

I nodded.

"I'll give you a hundred thousand dollars not to."

Teach's martini—our regular waiter always had one waiting for her—sloshed over the rim of the glass onto the tablecloth. She blotted the spill with her napkin and stared at the millionaire.

"No strings attached," he added, his eyes on me, reading my thoughts about his desire to make me Mrs. Will du Pont.

"Why would you do such a thing?" I asked, ignoring the nudge of Teach's toe against my shin.

"You're turning pro to make money. Take my offer and you won't have to."

170

"But I haven't earned it."

"Why don't you take some time to think about it?" Teach interjected, giving me a harder kick.

"I don't have to think about it. I could never pay Will back. Whatever I make on the tour, at least I will have earned it." I took Will's big, rough hand in both of mine. "But thank you, Will. It's very nice of you to offer."

He shrugged. "If you've made up your mind, then tell me all about it—who's playing, and where? And let's eat." He lifted a hand to catch the waiter's attention.

Teach reached for her martini, bewildered. She would have accepted Will's offer, I knew. She loved money. She worked hard to make it, but she liked to throw it around the way our wealthy friends did, and it never lasted long.

Teach had a great deal of respect for L. B. Icely, which clouded her thinking when she negotiated my contract for the pro tour. The company's first president was a brilliant man, having turned a meat-packing company into the country's largest sporting-goods supplier and a household word in tennis racquets. And he was a canny businessman. I readily signed the contract he and Teach worked out, thinking that twenty-five thousand dollars was a lot of money, and the most I could expect. We were to open in Madison Square Garden on January 6, 1941.

26 : PROFESSIONAL

1941

The night of my pro debut, I was exhausted. For two weeks I had been singing in four shows a day at Loew's State Theatre in New York. I had a small part in the vaudeville that accompanied the musical *The Thief of Bagdad*. Twice a day, I took a taxi to the tennis club, changed, practiced for an hour, then hopped another cab back to the theater.

I managed to get enough practice, but Teach objected to the schedule I was keeping. She was right. I was tired and stressed when I faced Mary Hardwick Hare, my old Wightman Cup opponent, before a sellout crowd in Madison Square Garden. I won, but I played a rotten match, and felt bad about it. Teach said nothing but I felt her disapproval when I joined her and Will du Pont to watch the match between Don Budge and Bill Tilden.

At the post-match party, Icely pulled me aside and said, "You were very smart to give her so many games."

I felt as if I had been struck. He thought I had lost games on purpose, to make the match more interesting. "Mr. Icely, I don't give anybody games," I said, and walked away before I lost my temper.

I meant what I had said to him. I had learned that it's dangerous to take pity on an opponent. If you give her a couple of games so she doesn't look bad, she's likely to catch fire and beat the hell out of you. It had happened to me often enough.

The pro tour was exciting, at the start. Then, at our third stop, Chicago, I discovered that Don Budge was making seventy-five thousand dollars for the tour, plus a percentage of the gate. Teach was not the businesswoman she thought. I went to see Icely alone.

"I'm not playing," I told the head of the world's largest sporting-goods company, pointing out the discrepancy in pay. Tilden was on salary to Wilson, as was Mary Hare, whose husband was the vice president of the company. I was the lowest-paid player on the tour.

"You will play," he replied, "or we'll sue you."

"Go ahead," I said, and walked away. I was still furious when I found Teach.

"I don't know what you're going to do," I told her, "but I'm not playing tonight, and I'm not going one stop further on this tour."

"What's wrong with you?"

"You! How could you sell me out for less than a third of what Budge is making? Icely made a fool of both of us, but mostly you. You made the deal."

An hour before we were scheduled to play, Icely capitulated. We were booked for seventy-five matches all over the country, and he knew I had him cornered.

"Here's your new contract," he said. "It's just like Budge's." I signed the papers, and shook the hand he proffered.

"I thought Teach was the business manager," he said.

"I think I'm old enough to manage my own affairs." I returned his smile. There was no animosity between us. The company would make a bundle, despite the hard bargain I drove, and the publicity the tour would generate for Wilson was inestimable. Icely was ahead of his time in recognizing the value of sponsorship.

It was the first time I interfered in Teach's handling of my tennis, and though my action benefited us both, it was another sign of the change in our relationship that began after I won at Wimbledon. I wanted control of my life. I wanted to choose my friends, lovers and career, but I was bound to Teach, because of all she had done for me. Would I ever be free of that debt?

Of the seventy-five matches we played, Mary Hare won only three, but she was always optimistic and good-natured. She practiced her serve constantly in the hopes of picking up extra points, and she never gave up.

The forty-eight-year-old Bill Tilden was no match, either, for Don Budge in his prime. Before every match Bill good-naturedly vowed, "I'm going to give that youngster a lesson tonight," but he only beat him seven times.

I watched each time the two of them played, no matter how tired I was after my match. The greatest male player of the first half of this century, Bill still had the strokes and the genius, but his legs were gone, and constant smoking affected his wind. Every day he said, "I'm quitting tomorrow. Got a cigarette?"

Mary and I adored him. If one of us broke a fingernail, he sent an orchid. He was witty and charming, and very cultured, as befitted his Main Line Philadelphia upbringing. His father had been a politician, and Bill had been raised by his mother, whom he idolized. He liked good food (though he never drank), music, and bridge, and was a wonderful dinner partner when I was able to lure him out with the promise of a bridge game. He loved the theater, and actually produced and starred in several shows—bad ones. The tennis court was meant to be his stage.

Budge was condescending to Tilden, which disturbed me, but I understood. Bill had a high voice and an effeminate way of walking and standing with his hand on his hip. He should have lived in today's world, when being gay is more acceptable. As it was, he agonized over his homosexuality, and was treated like a criminal. Of course, what he was accused of doing *was* a crime. He was sent to a work camp, a sort of white-collar prison, after one incident with a minor. The second time, he went to prison.

Bill always drove himself to tournaments, and roomed alone. Perhaps he picked up boys in the towns where we played; I don't really know. He talked to me only once about his homosexuality, trying to find the words to express his torture. He didn't need to; it was written all over his face. Later, he lost pride in himself, and stopped bathing and taking care of his clothes. Other players on the men's tour called him "Tilly" and treated him cruelly, a pitiful situation for such a brilliant athlete.

Bill was about sixty when he died. On his last day, he played five sets of singles, went home to his funny little apartment, and just quit living. I died a little, too, when I heard that no one from the tennis community planned to go to his funeral. I called all the players I knew and shamed them into going with the reminder that Bill Tilden was one of the greatest players and gentlemen in our sport. Like du Pont, he just didn't fit in.

Despite the fact that Bill and Mary were mismatched with Don and me, fans turned out to see us wherever we played, and we put on a good, honest show for them. Our tour, covering seventy cities, was so tightly scheduled there was hardly time to do laundry or get my hair cut. Teach's clinics were always packed, so I often helped her during the day, then played at night.

Every city was an adventure, every court a new challenge. In Trenton, New Jersey, we were booked into a basketball court so short that when Mary tossed up her serve, a boy in the balcony caught it. She turned to stare up at him and said, in her British accent, "I say, young man, we both can't play, you know."

In Los Angeles, our canvas traveling court was stretched over an indoor ice-skating rink. At either end of our court, behind the netting, kids were skating while we played. Clark and Carole were in the audience, along with Barbara Stanwyck and many other stars. Bob Hope and Bing Crosby introduced us that evening, Hope with the words "And now we bring you the chairman of the board of adrenaline of California, William Tatum Tilden II."

We went up into Canada, then back down to Santa Barbara, where Beese and Alex White came to see us play. In San Francisco, my whole family was in the stands.

We played a cow palace in El Paso that smelled strongly of its usual occupants. Every time I put my foot down, it made a depression in the canvas stretched over the dirt floor.

"God knows what-all is under there," I whispered to Mary when we changed sides, and we both laughed.

Toledo, Ohio, was no laughing matter. I had the beginnings of a cold, and when they decided to sweep the dusty canvas right before we played, I threw a temper tantrum reminiscent of my earlier days. During the first set, I sullenly swatted the ball. Down by about four points, I was toweling my face during the change of sides when I heard someone behind me say, "Why don't you start playing tennis, Miss Marble?"

"Why don't you shut up?" I shot back, then I looked into the eyes of a white-haired man in the black collar of a minister. I turned away, embarrassed and ashamed. It was no way for a champion to act, even if I didn't feel well.

I vowed to give the crowd the kind of tennis they came to see, but on the next point, I tripped over a seam in the canvas and fell, badly spraining my thumb. It hurt like hell, but I played the rest of the match as if the world championship were at stake. After the match, the others didn't speak to me, and went out to dinner without me. I learned my lesson. It was my last show of temper on the pro tour.

In Minneapolis, the governor and mayor introduced us; then Mary and I went out to warm up. Mary hit a ball to me, and it didn't bounce. I hit another back to her, and *it* didn't bounce. Our canvas court was meant to slow the ball, but not that much! Workmen hurried out to stretch the canvas tighter, but it didn't help.

I met Mary at the net. "I played here as an amateur," I said, "but this never happened!"

Then one of the ball boys (who happened to be the grandson of the Bells, owners of General Foods) yelled, "I know what's wrong," and ran off the court. In a few moments, he reappeared, breathless, and said, "I closed all the windows in the basement. Try it now."

I never understood why, but the balls bounced, and the kid was a hero. Mary and I started hitting balls with him, and the crowd loved it. Pro tennis was battling an unsavory reputation, and I was always happy when incidents like that gave us a chance to establish a personal rapport with the audience, something that would make them see us as real people.

When the tour was over, a doctor put me on glucose for several days, saying I was suffering from malnutrition and exhaustion. But I had cleared a hundred thousand dollars, a fortune in those days. Back in New York, Teach and I put the money in a joint account in one of Will's banks.

I started seeing Will again, but my friends stopped pushing me to marry him. One evening after he had fallen asleep at the dinner table, someone said, "You can't marry him. Will's such an automaton, he would probably say, 'Alice, we'll have intercourse at eight thirty-one P.M.'"

I laughed, but I felt bad that Will was so alone.

The du Pont companies were coming up with all sorts of new products, and Will tried them out on me: nylon stockings that never ran (they were taken off the market), nylon racquet strings, and Corfam tennis shoes.

Every Thursday, Will and I played tennis with Bishop Fulton J. Sheen. Then we'd sit in the bar and have a drink. The bishop always ordered a horse's neck, ginger ale with a spiral of lemon peel.

The bishop was the worst tennis player I'd ever seen, but he was enthusiastic. One afternoon during doubles, someone gave me a real setup and I put it down the line, right into the bishop's private parts. He walked off the court white-faced. When he returned, I was laughing.

"I don't think that's funny!" he said.

"I'm so sorry. I was thinking of my mother. When we got hit, she always told us to rub it."

The bishop told that story from coast to coast, and for many years men in black mentioned it to me.

Jack McDermott, my favorite practice partner in New York, was a broker, and like so many people, wanted me to influence Will to invest in the stock market. I always refused him, and he finally said, "Well, how about you?"

"I'm not much of a gambler, Jack!"

"Can you spare five hundred dollars?"

"I suppose so."

"What do you want to invest in?"

I opened my purse, rooted about in it, and pulled out a Tangee lipstick. "This," I said. Within a week, the stock doubled in value and I sold it.

The only other gambling I did was with Will, who taught me to bet the horses. I attended the Kentucky Derby, the Preakness, and the Belmont Stakes with him when his horses were running, and shared his excitement when his horse ran third in the Derby.

It was Will who introduced me at a party to a Mr. Gaines, who produced comic books. We were chatting about Wonder Woman and Superman, the current rages with the kids, when I asked, "Why don't you do real-life wonder women, the women who have made history?"

"Such as?"

"Clara Barton, Dolley Madison, Eleanor Roosevelt . . ."

Before the evening was out, I had agreed to do some research and rough out the dialogue for a few comics. In less than a month, I had my own desk in the Lexington Avenue offices of All-American Comics, as associate editor for the Wonder Woman series.

My cocktail-party inspiration netted me nearly fifty thousand dollars, but I was restless and discontented with my life. Amateur tennis had gone on without me. Bobby Riggs and Sarah Palfrey won the national singles titles. Everybody else seemed to be involved in the war, and I was writing comic books! I wanted to do something important, something to serve my country, like Helen Jacobs.

Teach watched me rattle around our New York apartment, alternately staring out the window and opening the refrigerator door on the off chance a chocolate cake had appeared there.

"How would you like to play exhibition matches at some military bases?" she asked.

"Ha! Those guys aren't interested in tennis. They want to see Marlene Dietrich."

"A general I know thinks differently. Will you give it a try? Bill, Don, and Mary are game."

"It's all set, then?"

"More or less," she hedged.

"And you knew I'd say yes?"

"You wanted to help the war effort. Just consider your tennis whites a uniform of sorts."

27 : JOE

In the fall, we started playing exhibition matches at military bases on the East Coast. At first I thought the soldiers turned out just to see girls in shorts, but I changed my mind when they stomped and cheered every point of the match between Tilden and Budge.

"It sounds more like a boxing match than tennis," I whispered to Mary. We were playing at a base in Yonkers, and had joined the soldiers in the stands after our match.

Mary nodded agreement. Tilden sliced a backhand down the line that caught Budge napping, and the soldier next to Mary whistled shrilly through his teeth. The Brit winced and laughed, "Well, they sound like they're enjoying it."

On December 7, Teach and I were at Arthur Loew's Long Island estate. After divorcing his first wife, Arthur had married Melitta, an ardent tennis player and fan who insisted that we come to Pembroke whenever there was a break in our schedule. The mansion was a treat after bunking in army barracks.

Since brunch, we'd been playing on the indoor court with several of the guests, among them skier Andrea Mead Lawrence and Paul Lehman, a member of the famous stock brokerage and under secretary of the navy under James Forrestal.

When Loew's butler interrupted us, Lehman and I had wrested one set from Arthur and Melitta and led, 40–30, in the first game of the second.

"Mr. Lehman, there's a phone call for you."

"Who the devil . . . ?"

"It's your office, sir. They said it was urgent."

178

Lehman snorted. I tossed him a towel. "Don't be long," I said. "We can put these two away in no time."

The Loews and I were standing at the net chatting when the butler returned, looking distraught. "Mr. Loew, the Japanese have bombed Pearl Harbor!"

We looked at each other, then heard the sound of a small plane taking off from the estate's landing strip. The naval under secretary was on his way to Washington, still dressed in sweaty tennis whites.

I had a sick feeling in my stomach. The war was no longer something happening across the ocean in Europe; it suddenly seemed close, and very real, and American boys were dying.

Soldiers weren't the only casualties of the escalating war. On January 17, 1942, Teach and I were back at Pembroke. Arthur's wife Melitta was having her early-morning lesson with Teach when I came down to the dining room for breakfast.

"The usual, Miss Marble?" one of the maids asked.

"Yes, please. Where's Mr. Loew?"

"He ordered breakfast sent to his room this morning."

"Is he ill?"

"I don't think so, miss. He didn't say." She dropped her eyes and hurried into the kitchen.

Arthur probably had work to do. Having joined the Coast Guard right after Pearl Harbor, he now had military duties as well as his responsibilities to MGM Studios. I ate alone, then changed and went to the indoor tennis court. I was hitting lobs to Melitta while Teach coached her on her smash when Arthur walked onto the court. I had never seen him so distressed. He looked at me, then Teach, and there were tears in his eyes. Alarmed, Melitta put her arm around him. "What's happened?"

"There was a plane crash near Las Vegas yesterday." He swallowed. "All twenty-two people on board were killed, including Carole Lombard and her mother."

"Oh God, no!" Teach's voice seemed faraway. I went to my room like a sleepwalker, and slumped in a chair, dry-eyed, staring into space. This couldn't happen. Losing Carole was like losing a sister. We had such a wonderful kinship, an intuitive understanding of each other. I loved being with her because she was caring and fun, and had become my closest confidante. Just the week before, we'd had a long phone conversation when she was in California between tours of bases overseas.

"Clark wants to enlist," she'd said, "but the studio is raising holy hell. They're trying to convince him to take a desk job, but you know Papa. He wants to be in the thick of it. I'm frightened for him, and for me, if they let him fight." Her voice was full of anxiety and fatigue.

"I worry about *you*. Don't push yourself so hard."

"You sound like Clark. I'm fine. Visiting the bases isn't much, but it's something I can do to help. I just wish this damn war would end. I want to try again to have a baby!"

"God bless," I said.

"Angels keep," she responded.

When I was little, my mother had taught me a prayer: "God bless us, and angels keep us safe from harm." Over the years it had shortened to the exchange "God bless, angels keep" within the family—and with Carole.

We had promised to see each other soon. Now she was gone.

Teach came in to comfort me, but the moment our eyes met, we both started crying.

"I keep thinking about Carole's brothers, and poor Clark," Teach said.

I nodded, unable to speak.

"I called," Teach said, "but nobody knows where he is. He's probably gone to the ranch where he can be alone."

"Nothing will stop him from enlisting now."

"And he won't care that much about living, with Carole gone."

"I can't believe it. Damn this war!"

Teach suddenly sobbed; it was the painful sound of her self-control giving way. Awkwardly, I put my arms around her, and she clung to me, her face buried in my neck. It was the first time I had seen Teach grieve, and I held her tightly, not speaking. There were no words to comfort either of us.

Soon after Carole's death I found out Clark was in New York, and left a message at his hotel: "Alice and Teach send their love and sympathy." Photos of him after the tragedy showed him looking haggard and twenty years older. I was glad he found happiness later with Kay Spreckles, who was so like Carole.

I stepped up my own war effort. I wanted to *do* something, so I started visiting the military hospitals near New York. I sang, played cards with the men, or just talked to them. They were starved for attention, and I felt as if I made a difference. At the Stage Door Canteen in New York, a famous hangout for servicemen, soldiers from all branches challenged me daily at the club's Ping-Pong table. I was too quick for most of them, having played the game since I was a child, but we had fun.

When Brownie was in town, she loved to go to the Canteen. On one of those evenings, I bowed out of the Ping-Pong wars to watch her dance with a tall marine captain. At five foot two, she looked like a child in his arms. Some child! If that marine wasn't careful, he would fall in love with her, because Brownie was so easy to love.

Hearing the opening chords of "Taking a Chance on Love," I wandered over to the piano and started to sing. The pianist smiled up at me, and Brownie peeked around her marine's arm and winked. When the sound of a rich baritone blended with my voice, I turned to look at the man who had joined in.

He was an army captain, tall, with dark, wavy hair and genial brown eyes. Something about those eyes made me blush and forget the words to the song. What was it? He was handsome, but I was accustomed to handsome men, and all lonely soldiers looked at me the way he did. With my heart hammering, I leaned over to read the sheet music and regain my composure.

When the song ended, I looked up and asked, as casually as I could, "How about another song? Your choice."

"Miss Marble, if I beat you at Ping-Pong, will you have dinner with me?"

"It's Alice, and you're on."

"Joe Crowley, Alice."

Joe was an excellent player, and I managed to lose without being obvious. I was sorry when the game was over. I liked watching the easy grace with which he moved, and the way his hair curled against his forehead in the heat of the game.

"You won," I said, "but it's late. Suppose we have that dinner another time."

"Only if you let me walk you home."

"Sure." I glanced at Brownie. She was still in the circle of the marine's arms, and seemed likely to stay there. I gave her a wave and accepted Joe's help with my coat.

We walked quickly, heads ducked against the winter wind. Teach was asleep when we entered the apartment, so I poured Joe a glass of wine and we sat in the living room, talking quietly. Joseph Norman Crowley was a Kansas farm boy who had put himself through Ohio State University, graduating with a degree in engineering. The intelligence branch of the army had snapped him up when they discovered he had studied five languages.

"The army taught me to fly," he said, "and I never know where I'll be going or what I'll be doing next."

That's all he could say about his reconnaissance work. He was a decent tennis player, he told me, a skier, and a scratch golfer. And he knew all about me, having followed my career in the newspapers.

With a glance at his watch, Joe thanked me for the wine and rose from his chair. "I leave on assignment tomorrow," he said. "It may be a while before I get back. May I call you?"

"You'd better! You owe me dinner."

He grinned, put his cap at a jaunty angle, and said good night. I sat alone for awhile after he left. I hoped that Captain Joseph Crowley returned safely, and that he remembered me.

Nearly three months later, he finally called. "I'm loaded with money—I haven't been anyplace I could spend it—so pick out the nicest restaurant in New York and we'll go there for dinner."

Not much had changed in my life since he had left. Tilden, Budge, Hare, and I were playing at bases in the States and Canada, Teach had her hands full with clinics, and I was still entertaining soldiers at hospitals and the Stage Door Canteen.

But Joe looked different when he came to pick me up—leaner and more serious than I had remembered him. His face broke into a warm Kansas-farm-boy smile when he saw me. We didn't talk about his work; I knew the war was getting worse, and suspected that he was in the thick of it.

The Japanese had captured Singapore, Java, and Rangoon, and reports of the Bataan Death March had trickled back to the States. There were rumors that the Nazis were murdering millions of Jews in gas chambers, but they seemed too heinous to be true, and most people discounted them. The war kept creeping closer and closer to home. Sugar, gasoline, and coffee were added to the growing list of rationed items in the States.

The owner of Le Pavillon Restaurant had reserved a quiet corner table for us. It didn't stay quiet long. Within moments, Gloria Swanson and Mary Pickford arrived, and stood chatting at our table. Joe politely asked them to join us and, when they accepted, whispered to me, "I'm not that loaded!"

"Don't worry," I whispered back. I knew Gloria and Mary wouldn't let any soldier pick up a check. Joe had seen most of their movies, and was wonderfully gallant. The actresses enjoyed the company of young men, so I hardly got a word in all evening. I was content just watching and listening. Not since Hans had I felt so attracted.

A man stopped at our table to tell me he enjoyed my tennis, and Joe, starry-eyed from the wine and the attention of the two actresses, looked up at the stranger and said, "I hope to make Miss Marble my wife. If she marries me, I'll be the proudest man in the world."

Joe seemed as surprised at his words as I was, and both of our faces reddened. Gloria and Mary clapped their hands with delight. "Alice, what do you say to that?" Mary asked.

"Captain Crowley is moving a bit fast!"

We all laughed, and moved on to another subject. Marriage! I didn't want to get married. Too many of my friends had husbands overseas, and I knew the fears they lived with. On tour, I had met hundreds of women who rushed into marriage with their soldiers, sometimes after knowing them a few weeks or a few days. And I had seen grief on the faces of those whose soldiers didn't return—more often than I wanted to think about.

"No more talk of marriage," I said during the walk back to my apartment.

He didn't answer, just put his arm around me, and it felt good being close to him.

At my door, we said good night several times, but each time one of us thought of something else to say, prolonging the moment. "I'll walk you to the elevator," I said finally.

Joe pressed the button, and we stared up at the lighted numbers as the elevator made its way to my floor, eleven stories from the ground. The door opened. "You remind me of my best friend," Joe said softly.

"Who's that?"

"Rusty, my dog."

I should have laughed, but there was something so touchingly innocent about his remark that I wanted to cry. God only knew what he had been through since I saw him last, but he missed his dog. He was a long way from Kansas—might never see it again. I blinked furiously at the sudden tears, took his hand, and pulled him from the elevator.

"I think I need to hear more about Rusty."

We had the apartment to ourselves. Teach was out of town for a week, and Brownie was overseas. We talked well into the night, sharing our secrets, laughing over moments in our past. It was rare for me to be alone like this, getting to know someone new. When the words stopped tumbling from us, we snuggled together in my big bed, he in his shorts, me in my pajamas. I drifted off to sleep with the steady beat of his heart in my ear. Somehow, we knew that the moment wasn't right for our relationship to go further.

The smell of coffee roused me from a deep sleep. I stared at the rumpled pillow beside me. I wasn't dreaming; there *had* been a man in my bed. Running my fingers through my hair, I walked into the kitchen, where Joe was expertly flipping pancakes.

"Morning, Sunshine," he said, leaning over to kiss me lightly on the lips.

"Are you always like this in the morning?"

"Yes, since I met you."

I sipped at the coffee he handed me and eyed the pancakes. "I think I'll keep you. I can't cook worth a damn."

In the days that followed, we were seldom out of each other's sight. Joe was on leave, and I managed to postpone most of my obligations. Every day he watched me practice, then we wandered the streets of New York like teenagers in love, browsing the museums and shops, going to movies or the theater.

At night we slept in each other's arms, as we had that first night, but he made no move to make love to me. We talked, laughed, and drifted off to sleep, happy to be together. Nearly a week had passed when I suddenly knew I wanted him. "Joe . . ." I said, reaching for him.

"Shhhh," he whispered, pulling me to him and covering my mouth with his. Just as he had waited patiently for me to come to him, Joe was slow and gentle in his lovemaking, fanning the passion in me with his hands and lips.

At last, I lay spent in his arms. He kissed my cheeks, whispering "I love you" until my breathing steadied. We fell asleep, our bodies entwined, then woke at first light to make love again.

"Are you happy?" he asked, propped on one elbow, stroking my breasts with his other hand.

"Yes." I caught his hand and brought it to my lips. "I'm especially happy that we were friends first, then lovers."

"Not that it matters, but I think it's been a long time since you made love."

I nodded, kissing the palm of his hand, and enjoying the shiver it caused in him.

"Was I worth the wait?"

"Yes, you egomaniac!" I slapped his chest. "Are you cooking breakfast, or are we going to live on love?"

Groaning, he rolled out of bed, and I soon heard him singing in the shower.

We were both dressed and lingering over coffee at the kitchen table when I heard the rattle of a key in the lock. "It's the wrong day for the maid," I said, sloshing coffee into my saucer. "Teach is back early."

"So I get to meet the dragon at last." Joe smiled, covering my hand with his.

I took a deep breath and called, "In here, Teach." I didn't want

184

her popping into my bedroom and seeing the mess we had made of my bed.

"I caught the sleeper car on the train rather than stay another night in that damn hotel," Teach said, pushing open the kitchen door. "What a—" She stopped short at the sight of Joe.

"Teach, this is Captain Joe Crowley," I said quickly. "Joe, Teach Tennant, my coach."

"Hello, Miss Tennant. It's a pleasure." Joe stood, offering his hand.

Teach shook his hand briefly, her eyes flickering over the breakfast dishes and settling on me. "Bit early, isn't it?"

Joe and I both started to speak at once, then stopped. Teach was gone, the kitchen door swinging in her wake. The sounds of slamming drawers came from her bedroom.

"I'll meet you for lunch at the Stage Door Canteen," Joe said, bending to kiss me.

"Coward." I hugged him. "Bring bandages."

28 : MARRIAGE

The ensuing battle with Teach lacked none of the fireworks of her tirade over Hans, but there were two important differences: I didn't cry, and I didn't give in.

"It's my life, Teach! I have a right to something beyond the tennis court, to happiness, and I won't let you stop me this time. I love you, and will always be grateful for what you've done for me, but I won't stop seeing Joe. We love each other."

"Love or lust? He's in the army, for God's sake," Teach shouted, her face crimson. "It's a one-night stand!"

"Teach!" There was a warning in my tone.

"Even if you do mean something to him, he could get killed. How many times have you seen it happen? How many times have you told me how sorry you felt for the women left behind? Do you really want to be one of them?"

"Whether I do or not, it's my choice."

Teach stared at me, then turned back to her unpacking.

Joe shipped out the next day, and I felt lost. In such a short time, he had filled the empty spaces in my life and made me happier than I thought possible. Mary, Bill, and Don teased me about being lovesick, but I could tell they were pleased.

Brownie called during a stopover in Florida, and was ecstatic at the news.

"Are you going to marry him?" she asked.

"I am. I know I haven't known him long, and I've cautioned so many girls against marrying their soldiers, but now that I'm in their shoes . . . Brownie, I love him so much. I want to be his wife more than anything in the world."

"Then do it, honey. You won't be sorry. That's what Carole

186

would have told you, too. We're all living on the edge. Teach breathing fire?"

"She's livid that I'm sleeping with him. I'm not about to tell her we're getting married."

"Chicken."

I made squawking noises into the phone, and we both laughed.

"I wish you could be at the wedding," I said. "Joe has a friend, a navy chaplain, who is going to marry us on board ship."

"I wish I could, too. I'd given up on you getting married." After offering some risqué advice on keeping Joe happy, Brownie rang off with the promise to get to New York as soon as the Red Cross allowed.

Joe phoned whenever he could, and the sound of his voice, even over a crackling long-distance wire, was a joy and a relief. He managed some leave in New York every few months, depending on his assignments. To avoid confronting Teach, we checked into a hotel when she was in town.

My "affair," as she preferred to think of it, was a personal affront to my lifelong mentor, but she was quiet. I suppose she thought I would come to my senses, or something would happen to break us up, and decided to wait it out. She was friendly to Joe when we were together; she didn't dislike him, just his intrusion in her grand plan for my life. She tried to hamper us by not telling me when Joe called, or by telling him I was out of town when I wasn't, but nothing altered the course of our relationship.

Joe and I envisioned a small wedding, but we were in for a surprise when we boarded the ship docked in the Hudson. More than a hundred sailors in dress whites gathered around us on the deck while Joe's friend performed the ceremony. When Joe slipped the silver band on my finger, and gave me my first kiss as Mrs. Joseph Crowley, everyone cheered and threw their hats in the air.

In the taxi on the way to our hotel, we were still laughing at the scene. "How long do you suppose it took to get their hats sorted out?" I asked.

Joe shook his head. "How long do you think it will take you to get used to being my wife?"

"Not long. Friend, lover, husband—a natural progression."

"Friend, lover, wife—would you like to add 'mother' to the list?"

"Arthur Brisbane wrote in his column that I should have a dozen children. We can work on it."

We spent most of the weekend in our hotel room, living on room service and love, not wanting to share each other with the outside world even long enough to go to a restaurant. A real honeymoon would have to come later; Joe's leave ended on Monday.

I'm sure Teach heard the rumor that Joe and I had been secretly married, but she didn't confront me, and I gladly postponed telling her what she probably already knew. Others did ask me, but I laughed it off as a rumor. I had to. Because of Joe's work in army intelligence, there was to be no formal announcement, no fanfare in the press until after the war. German spies had been caught in New York and Florida, and Joe's superiors worried that I might become a target for kidnappers. I continued to use my own name, and my wedding ring stayed in my jewelry case.

Teach had more to occupy her time than my sex life. We were constantly on the go, touring more than five hundred bases through the duration of the war. We played all over the United States and in Panama, Guam, Mexico, and Canada—wherever it was safe for us to go. The routine was exhausting but because the men enjoyed it, it had its own reward.

Mary and I played with the enlisted men, and often teamed up with out-of-shape officers for doubles. My worst fear was that one of them would have a heart attack while showing off, but instead we often hurt ourselves trying to cover for them.

During play, we kept up a running line of chatter about things back home, which the soldiers liked. Mary, with her clipped British accent, had a better knowledge of the geography of the United States than I did, and a remarkable way of relaxing the soldiers who played with us.

"Where are you from?" she would ask, and then exclaim, "Oh, I remember that town! There's a charming little drugstore on the corner, and the movie theater down the street . . ."

"Mary," I said to her, "every town in America has a corner drugstore and a movie theater down the street."

"I know. It works, doesn't it?"

She could be a devilish snob at times, but I loved the effect she had on homesick GIs from towns like Macon, Georgia, and Plainview, Texas.

Wherever we went, I visited the base hospitals to sing and talk with the wounded. Sometimes a dark-haired soldier with dancing eyes reminded me of Joe, and I consoled myself with the thought that I was showing somebody's "Joe" that I cared.

My husband and I were to spend two and a half years living on notes, phone calls, and days stolen from the war. We weren't to-gether enough for anything to become commonplace. Everything we did together was special to me, as if I had just been born and was seeing the world for the first time. And what a glorious world it was with him.

Joe was a good athlete, and I liked watching him play golf as much as he enjoyed my tennis. He rallied with me when I needed a practice partner, but he never challenged me. Most men in that situation are curious; they want to find out just how good they are, and whether they can beat a woman champion. Joe had nothing to prove. Golf was his sport, and I was content to walk the course with him while he played.

"With your coordination, you'll make a good golfer," he told me. "When the war's over and I'm home for good, I'll teach you."

"I'll try to beat you."

"I bet you will." He laughed.

"You can thank Teach for the killer instinct."

"I have a lot to thank Teach for."

"I want you two to be friends, and I want her to under-stand . . ."

"Honey, I like Teach, but you have to be the one to tell her. When are you going to do it?"

"She knows. It's just a question of my putting it into words. I'll do it when the time's right."

One wonderful winter interlude we spent skiing in Stowe, Ver-mont. After a few beginner's lessons with former Olympian Andrea Mead Lawrence, I fell in love with the sport and was ready to throw myself into it. Joe, who had spent the morning on the expert slopes, caught up with me in the ski shop where I was trying on equipment.

"Planning to get serious, are you?"

"Yep. I want to ski where you ski."

"And how do I tell Teach that I let her star break a leg?"

"I'm in good shape. I won't break anything."

"Honey, should you risk it, in the middle of the war and your tour?"

"You're beginning to sound like Teach." I was frustrated, but knew he was right. Skiing went on the back burner.

Every time we settled into a semblance of normal life—the simple pleasures of being together, of waking up in each other's arms, sharing the newspaper, planning for our future—the war shredded our moment of peace. Joe would be off on some dark mission, and I would be packing for a ride to another base.

The tennis courts we encountered were even more diverse than those on the pro tour. We played on the rolling decks of ships, on baked-earth courts, and in a variety of gyms, armories, and Quonset huts.

After playing all day with the men (or women—there were often WACs, WAFs, or WAVEs on the bases), we spent the evenings dancing with the men.

Every night, I massaged my aching feet. "I don't know which is worse," I told Mary, "the rough courts, or being trampled on the dance floor."

"We should get hazardous-duty pay," she agreed.

There were emotional hazards on the tour that I hadn't anticipated, and that I didn't discuss with Mary, though I'm sure she encountered them too.

Most of the time we slept in base WAC, WAF, or WAVE barracks. Officers gave up their private rooms for us, or we bunked in with the enlisted. I frequently had late-night visits from women whose interest in me went beyond tennis. It was courageous—and foolhardy—for them to admit they were lesbians, but they did. I knew their loneliness only too well, remembering the joy I'd had with Tica, and the hurt when she left me for another woman.

Of course, I didn't talk about my lesbian relationship, but it made me more compassionate in a time when few tried to understand.

"I know you didn't choose to feel the way you do," I told a young woman who confided in me. "It just happens, and only a person who has experienced it knows that love *is* blind; it can't tell the difference between the sexes. If you happen to fall in love with a man, the world gushes its approval; if you fall in love with a woman, you're treated like a monster. You're *not* a monster; don't ever think that you are, or be ashamed. There are many people like you, and you can find happiness."

Invariably, those late nights were followed by five thirty A.M. reveille, and I remembered my earlier eagerness to join the military. Seeing it firsthand, I realized it was a hard life, and I developed a great respect for the women, as well as the men, who were serving our country. I only lived it days or weeks at a time, always with the knowledge that I would be going back to civilian life. Those in uniform had no control over their lives, and never knew what the next week might bring.

Panama promised to be an ordeal the day we arrived. It was sweltering, and I was still a little woozy from the battery of injections we had had before leaving the States. "God, we have six weeks of

190

this humidity," I said to Mary, who looked as wilted and nauseated as I did.

"A tropical paradise," she agreed, mopping her face. "What I wouldn't give for a cold, damp English summer."

Before the week was out, the weather was the least of my miseries.

29 : TRAGEDY

1944

"Aren't you going a little fast for these roads?" I asked the young GI who had been assigned to drive me the fifty miles from the army's Gulick Fort Military Reservation in Cristobal to Coco Solo Naval Base in Cologne. Mary Hare had gone on ahead, but I had plenty of time to make it to the match. I rubbed the back of my chronically stiff neck, thinking how close I had come to breaking it outside Phoenix. I had good reason to be nervous in cars.

"Don't worry, I'll get you there safely," the driver said. I glanced at his boyish face, so full of confidence, and leaned back in the seat. I'd have to ride this one out, and pray.

Seconds later, all hell broke loose. The car skidded in loose gravel and slipped over a precipice, coming to rest against a tree stump. The crash had thrown me onto the floor in front of the backseat. I fumbled for the door handle and, ramming my shoulder against the door, forced it open. Crawling quickly out, I looked around and froze. Rocks and dirt skittered down a fifty-degree incline, bouncing into space twenty feet away, where the mountainside dropped perpendicularly to a valley a thousand feet below.

Groaning and holding his bloody nose, the driver fell out of the front seat, landing almost on top of me, and looked around.

"Mother of God," he whispered, following my gaze.

The hair prickled on the back of my neck. I didn't want to move, not even to turn my head, but my eyes were drawn to the sound of groaning metal. Our vehicle slewed gently off the stump, and began to slide, rapidly gaining speed until it launched itself off the ledge into space. In a few seconds there was an explosion, and a rising column of black smoke.

I panicked. Turning, I clawed my way up the bank, the driver close behind me. I could hear him gasping for air, just as I was, and groaning with pain and fear. Loose earth and stone sloughed like quicksand from under our hands and feet and knees. My terror increased. At any moment, I knew I would lose my grip and be caught in a landslide, following the car down the mountain. Falling. That's all I could think of. Even when I reached the roadside, I lay clutching the earth, my face in the dust.

The driver, his face streaked with blood, dirt, and sweat, knelt beside me.

"Oh my God, I'm sorry!" His voice cracked. "Are you all right?"

I looked up at him and nodded. I was shaking too much to answer. He helped me to my feet, and supported me. Then he glanced down.

"You're hurt! Jesus, look at your hands!"

I looked at the bloody mess, and wished I hadn't. In my panic, I had torn the skin of both hands on sharp rocks, and had ripped out several fingernails. I stared at him, and it was a toss-up which of us was going to faint first. The tooting horn of an army Jeep at that moment was the sweetest sound imaginable. Before the shock wore off and the pain set in, I was in the army hospital at Cristobal.

"What some people won't do to get out of a match," Mary said. She stood beside my bed, her face still showing her fright. I tried to laugh, but found myself crying instead.

"It's over now," Mary soothed, dabbing my face with a tissue.

I looked down at my bandaged hands, then at her. "I've ruined a perfectly good manicure."

She laughed, relieved. I'm sure she wished, as I did, that Teach, Budge, and Tilden had come with us to Panama.

"The doctor says your hands will heal," she said, "and from what the driver says, you're both lucky to be alive."

It was two weeks before I could use my hands, a wretched, helpless two weeks. When Joe's plane landed, it was a dream coming on the heels of a nightmare.

"The general has to be here several days," Joe said when we finally stopped kissing each other. "Can you work a honeymoon into your schedule?"

"Well, I *am* here to entertain the troops," I said, waving to the GIs who had whistled and cheered when I threw myself into Joe's arms.

"Let's find someplace more private." Joe shouldered his bag and put his arm proprietarily around my waist.

We had several days together, sandwiching intimate moments between his duties and my schedule of play. We even had the luxury of sleeping together, in accommodations arranged by Joe's commanding officer. We were discreet, but Mary, the proper Brit, seemed a bit scandalized. I didn't care.

"I thought you were safe and I was the one in danger," Joe said. He lay on his side, his head resting on my belly, the bedclothes a tangled mess from our reunion. I couldn't see his eyes, but his voice betrayed him. My close call had frightened him, though I tried to make light of it. Warm and contented in the afterglow of our lovemaking, I played with his hair.

"Please be more careful," he said. "I can't bear the thought of losing you."

"I feel that way every moment you're away from me." I traced the outline of his ear with the tip of my finger. He reached up to take my hand and, pulling it to his lips, kissed my fingertips one by one. They were still a mess, but the skin had healed and the nails were growing back.

"I love you so much," he said, rolling over on his back to look at me. I kissed him, and we made love again, slowly, without the urgency of the first time.

Joe was in the audience every time Mary and I played, and knowing he was there made the sultry heat and the pain in my hands easy to bear. When he left, time once more slowed to a crawl, and even the trip back to the States seemed to take forever. I walked the deck of the ship, missing Joe, aching for him.

I was in New York a short time before I started having morning sickness. When a doctor confirmed my suspicions, I knew it was time to come clean. I told Teach about our secret marriage, the Panama honeymoon, everything.

"Pregnant! I thought you'd picked up a bug in Panama!" I could see a vein throbbing in her temple. She'd not yet recovered from my story of the car crash.

"Pregnant. I picked up something else in Panama."

"How could you?"

"It was a pleasure." I struggled to keep from laughing. I was euphoric. Joe and I were going to have a baby!

"Don't be a smart-ass. You have obligations, a career."

"Being a wife and mother is part of that career from now on. I can play for another six or seven months, the doctor says."

After a few days of acting like the world had ended, Teach

194

grudgingly accepted the situation, and became even more of a tyrant about my health.

Joe and Brownie both arrived in New York and heard the news together. Brownie was overjoyed, and when Teach saw the tears in Joe's eyes, even she began to soften.

"I never thought I'd see this," Brownie said. We were watching Teach and Joe laughing over a shared joke.

"And I never thought I could be so happy." I patted my stomach, which was still quite flat. "This little one is going to be surrounded by wonderful people, starting with you and Teach."

"With you two as parents, he—or she—will need all the friends he can get," Brownie quipped.

When I was five months pregnant, I was driving home from a party on Long Island when a drunk driver swerved onto my side of the road, forcing me into a ditch. Again I opened my eyes in a hospital room, but this time a terrible sense of loss accompanied the pain. On opposite sides of my bed stood Teach and Brownie, and the answer to my question was on their faces.

"The baby?"

Brownie shook her head, her eyes brimming. "But you're okay. You and Joe will have another chance to start a family."

"I'm just thankful you're all right," Teach said. "The hemorrhaging . . ." She swallowed, and hurried from the room.

"Poor Teach," I said, my words slurred and hoarse from the anesthesia. "She doesn't like to lose control of her emotions."

"Poor Teach, my eye," Brownie snorted. "She didn't—"

"Please," I interrupted. "Don't fight. I need you both so much."

When I woke again, several hours later, both my friends were there, and a truce was obviously in effect. I tried to lift myself up on my elbows. "You haven't told Joe, have you?"

"No," Brownie answered, gently pushing me back. "We wanted to ask you first."

"Don't. He'll be home on leave after New Year's. I'll tell him then."

Christmas has never been a joyous occasion for me, not with the memory of my father's death on Christmas Eve, but this year was different. I had recovered from the miscarriage, physically if not mentally, and I knew everything would be all right when Joe came home. Everyone said the war was almost over. Maybe he wouldn't have to go away again. His letters, though heavily censored, gave me hope. Please God, just let it be over.

And there was cause to celebrate—Brownie was home for good. In her honor, Teach and I had a small Christmas Eve party in our apartment. Will du Pont was there, and Tica with her little English teacher, Doris. It still tugged at my heart to see Tica with another woman, but I was glad we had remained friends. A part of me would always love her.

We were singing Christmas carols to Tica's accompaniment on the guitar when the doorbell rang. Balancing her drink, a slightly tipsy Teach flung the door open, expecting a late guest. Instead, a man in uniform stood in the doorway. Teach put her drink down. In answer to a question from the stranger, she gestured toward me, and took the telegram from his hand. She closed the door behind him and started across the living room toward me.

I stopped singing and met her halfway, eagerly opening the telegram. It had to be from Joe. That morning a package had arrived from him with a bottle of my favorite perfume and a wonderful letter. Wherever he was now, he had managed to send a telegram. I quickly scanned the blocky words on the yellow sheet, and felt my heart die. It wasn't from Joe. It was from the War Department.

"We regret to inform you that Captain Joseph Crowley was killed in action when his plane was shot down over Germany. . . ."

I felt a scream rising in my throat, but when I opened my mouth nothing came out. Teach was staring at me, her smile gone. Behind us, our guests had launched into "God Rest Ye Merry, Gentlemen," oblivious to the fact that my world had just disintegrated. I looked down at the telegram, now a crumpled ball of paper. I opened my hand, letting it drop to the floor, and walked slowly to my bedroom. Inside, I closed the door and leaned against it, my eyes tightly shut.

"No!" I whispered in a voice I didn't recognize as my own. Again and again I said the word, over and over until it was a wail, like the cry of an animal. Yet the tears didn't come. What good would crying do? Joe was gone, and all my dreams with him. There would be no more reunions, no more nights of passion, no more plans of a family and our future together. There was no future. If only the baby . . . at least Joe had died thinking the baby still lived inside me. Dear God, if only I had something of him. . . .

There was nothing left for me but pain, and I couldn't face that. I had been forced to be strong all my life, and I was tired of it. I didn't want to be strong anymore. I didn't want to *be* anymore.

There was a bottle of pills on my dressing table, a sedative prescribed for me when I had trouble sleeping on tour. I rarely took them, so the bottle was nearly full—and offered a way out. Choking down a handful of pills, I sank to the floor, hoping it would be over soon.

196

* * *

Brownie sensed something was wrong, and was at Teach's side when she smoothed the crumpled telegram.

"Dear God," Brownie said. She and Teach looked at each other, then at the group. Tica saw the look on Brownie's face and her fingers paused on the strings of her guitar.

"Joe?"

Teach and Brownie nodded. Silently the guests gathered their coats and left, Tica last of all.

"Take care of her," she said to Brownie and Teach.

"We will, somehow," Brownie said.

Staring at my closed door, Teach asked, "Should we go to her? Is there anything we can do?"

"It may not be the right thing to do, but I don't want her to be alone," Brownie replied.

She knocked softly on my door, calling my name, then entered the room to find me unconscious on the floor.

"Teach! Come in here!"

Teach dropped to her knees beside Brownie, who was shaking me. "Has she fainted?"

"Yeah, with a little help from these." Brownie held up the empty pill bottle.

Teach grabbed it from her hand. "I'll call an ambulance."

"Then help me get her on her feet. We've got to get her walking!" She shook me again. "C'mon, Alice, don't do this! Stick with us, honey!"

I was released from the hospital on Christmas morning.

"I understand your grief, Miss Marble," said the doctor, "but I hope you won't try this again. If your friends hadn't found you . . ."

I looked at Teach and Brownie, at their drawn faces and the dark circles beneath their eyes. They had been with me all night, and from the looks of them, had not slept. My throat ached unbearably from the tube used to pump my stomach.

"Merry Christmas." The words came out in a hoarse whisper, but left no doubt as to my bitterness.

"Let's go home," Brownie said.

In the taxi, she put her hand in mine. It was warm, reassuring; I gripped it tightly all the way home.

"I know how you must feel—" Teach began, but I interrupted her.

197

"No, you don't know how I feel," I croaked, "and I don't want to talk about it. Please."

I turned my head to stare out the window. Bright garlands of red, green, and gold spiraled up the lampposts, and storefronts vied with each other for the most elaborate decorations. When we stopped for a red light, a pair of young boys dashed across the intersection, carrying new ice skates. A church service had just ended and the parishioners lingered outside, smiling, shaking hands, exchanging the season's greetings.

I closed my eyes and gripped Brownie's hand. I was sorry I was alive. My mother had raised me to trust in God, but how could I? He had allowed everything to be taken from me—my baby, Joe, even the right to die. Was that the way a merciful God worked?

When we reached the apartment, there was a stack of messages from friends who knew about Joe and me. I couldn't look at them.

"You two look awful," I said. "Why don't you get some rest? I'm going to."

At the door to my bedroom, I turned back to face them. "I'm sorry I put you through this, but I won't thank you for saving my life." Alarm swept over their faces, and I quickly added, "Don't worry, no more suicide attempts. I just want to be alone."

"We're here for you," Brownie said.

Teach nodded. "Anything we can do . . ."

I closed the door. Never before, not even in the sanatorium, had I felt such total despair. What was to become of me?

30: TURNING POINT

I looked at Teach and Brownie. They had taken turns being with me since my return from the hospital, making me eat, sitting with me until I fell asleep, and trying to talk me out of my depression. I hardly heard them, and nothing could change the way I felt. Hours dragged into days, days into weeks, but I was aware of nothing but my unbearable losses.

How could God be so unfair? I'd had it with Him. I wouldn't play his game anymore. How many times could Alice Marble be knocked down before she stayed there? There was no reason to pull myself to my feet, to be brave, to set an example, to be a champion—because there was nothing left I cared about. Nothing. I tried to explain that to Brownie and Teach.

"I love you both, but why didn't you let me die? I *want* to. My life doesn't matter anymore."

"Don't say that," Teach said. "You have a lifetime of tennis ahead of you. Tilden wants to set up another pro tour with—"

I cut her off with a wave of my hand. "I don't give a damn about tennis. I have no heart left. Understand? Don't try to bully me. It won't work this time. Just leave me alone."

The hurt in Teach's face made me sorry I had been so abrupt, but we'd been through all this before.

"We just want to see you get out," Brownie's soothing voice cut in, "even if it's just for lunch. You've hardly left the apartment. You've got to face people and get on with your life."

Before they could say more, I jumped up, went to my room, and flopped facedown on my bed. I didn't cry. I had stopped crying weeks ago. Now I just felt hollow, like everything had died inside me, and I didn't want mourners.

I had tried to go out, at first, but I always ran into people who had heard about Joe. They all said how sorry they were, and asked about my plans. They meant well, but their sympathy felt like the ends of a broken bone grating together. There was no comfort, no way to heal this kind of hurt. I could never feel whole again.

To add to my misery, every time I left the apartment I had the feeling I was being followed. Someone—I didn't know who or why—was watching me. Teach said I was just slightly paranoid, that it had to do with the shock. I had lashed out at her then, just as I had now, and she had left the apartment rather than argue with me.

Several days later, three dozen red roses arrived, filling the living room with vibrant color and their glorious scent. Brownie put them in vases and fussed over their arrangement while I watched with mild interest. She thrust the accompanying note into my hand.

"Brownie, you shouldn't have . . ."

"I *didn't*, silly. Look at the card."

I slipped the card from its envelope and read, "If I can do it, so can you. Clark."

"Brownie! They're from Clark! He's still overseas. How'd he find out about Joe?"

She shrugged, but I could see the shine in her eyes.

"You and Teach got word to him?"

She nodded.

Deeply moved, I hugged her, rereading the note over her shoulder. Then I held her at arm's length.

" 'If I can do it, so can you.' That's what Carole said to me when I was in the sanatorium."

I looked into Brownie's eyes, something I hadn't been able to do since the night I had my stomach pumped.

"Clark was devastated by Carole's death, but he's learning to live without her, isn't he?"

She nodded, then looked away, tears in her eyes.

I blinked back my own tears. "I've started over so many times. Maybe I can do it again. You two won't leave me alone until I do, so . . . I'll try."

"I know you will. We'll help."

"Speaking of Teach . . ." I grabbed the phone and dialed the Court House, the indoor club where Teach was giving lessons. Her voice came on the line.

"High noon," I said. "Lunch at '21.' And I'm buying."

I hung up, looked at Brownie, and laughed. It felt good to laugh again.

200

Brownie rushed off on an errand, promising to meet us at the restaurant. I put on a creamy wool dress that was much looser than the last time I'd worn it, and shrugged into the polo coat I'd designed for Best & Company. Carole'd had one just like it.

"*Good* to see you, Miss Marble!" the doorman said, stepping out to hail a taxi.

"No, thanks, John. I'll walk." I answered his smile with one of my own.

I pulled the coat collar higher as a bitter wind tugged at my hair, and had a pang of homesickness for California, but as I walked down Fifth Avenue, the chilly air made my skin tingle, made me feel alive.

Around me was the usual cacophony of taxi horns and squealing tires, the patter and rustle of pedestrians. New Yorkers always hurried, whether they needed to or not. I purposely slowed my pace so the crowd had to flow around me, like a logjam in a river. I dawdled before shop windows, studied the new spring styles, then I turned to watch traffic sprinting down the avenue.

"Miss Marble? Alice Marble?" asked a voice behind me.

I turned to face a chubby teenager, her cheeks ruby from the cold and her obvious shyness. "We . . . we love you," she blurted, squeezed my arm briefly, and darted away through the crowd. I looked after her, touched, but was quickly distracted by the feeling that other eyes were on me. I set off at a brisk walk, and arrived at the restaurant before Teach and Brownie.

"It's been too long, Miss Marble," the maître d' said. "Welcome back! Your usual table in the corner?"

"Yes, please."

Several people came over to speak to me, and with each one, it became easier for me to talk. There was a lull, and a man in army uniform approached the table.

"Miss Marble, it's good to see you out in public again."

"Thank you," I said, steeling myself for another round of condolences. The man was a stranger, but he might have known Joe. *Why* had I arranged this outing, and *where* the hell were Teach and Brownie?

"I'm with army intelligence," he said, more softly than I expected of an army man, and showed me an identification card. "We'd like to talk to you."

"But I'm expecting friends," I said uncertainly.

"No, not now. May I call to set up a meeting?"

I hesitated, then said yes, expecting him to tell me more, but he just nodded and left. Was he the one who had been following me?

Teach arrived like a whirlwind, Brownie on her heels, and my first lunch out in weeks turned into a celebration. Our favorite waiter doted on us, bringing a bottle of champagne, compliments of the management. Teach drank too much and became very mellow, Brownie's grin turned more than a little lopsided, and I had a few glasses of champagne with orange juice, a lot for me.

I knew Teach was high when she insisted I have dessert, and it was with a mouthful of heavenly chocolate cake that I asked, "How can I thank you two for sticking by me through all this?"

"By living," Teach said. Brownie nodded in agreement.

By living. In that moment of wonderful camaraderie, I hadn't a clue that "living" was soon to take on a new and exciting dimension.

The next morning, I was plowing through long-overdue correspondence when the phone rang. I waited for Brownie to get it, remembered she was out, and grabbed the receiver.

"Miss Marble?"

"Yes?"

"It's Captain Jones.* We met yesterday at the restaurant."

"Yes. What can I do for you?"

"There are people in the government who think you can help your country. We know how hard you tried to enlist."

"How's that?" I asked.

"I'll pick you up in an hour at Fifty-seventh and Fifth. This isn't something we can discuss on the phone."

"All right," I said. "I'll be there."

My heart beat faster as I dressed quickly in a dark-gray tailored suit—nothing too flashy for what, in my mind, had suddenly become a "secret" government meeting. I laughed at myself for letting my imagination run wild. They probably wanted me for doubles with some fat general.

I was standing in front of Tiffany's when Jones pulled up to the curb in a plain dark-green car. Hesitantly, I got in, noticing that he wasn't in uniform.

"I like the way you play, Miss Marble," he said, driving toward the East Side of Manhattan. "I saw you in the Wightman Cup in thirty-eight."

"You went to England for the matches?" I asked.

"No, I was there for graduate school." He turned briefly to smile at me. His face was pleasant enough, but the smile didn't show in his eyes, which were hard and assessing. The captain (I wondered

* Fictitious name.

202

why he wasn't in uniform) was in his thirties, learly built, with dark hair in a traditional military cut.

We crossed the Brooklyn Bridge and turned onto a side street. "I'm not exactly a tennis fan," he said. "I went to the matches because I like to watch girls."

Alarms went off in my head. Dammit. What had I gotten into? I edged closer to the door and wrapped my fingers around the handle.

"Relax, Miss Marble," Jones said calmly. "I'm not a masher. This is strictly business. Besides, we're here."

Jones pulled up to a high chain-link gate and handed the guard some papers. My photo was apparently on one, because the guard leaned into the car to scrutinize my face for a moment before opening the gate.

Even if he wasn't a masher, there was something about Jones I didn't like. When he parked next to one of several dingy-looking warehouses, I got out without waiting for him to open the car door. He showed the papers to a guard at an unmarked entrance, then ushered me down a corridor and into an office.

"Miss Marble, Colonel Linden."* Jones waved toward a tall man in uniform. The colonel appeared to be in his fifties, with hair graying at the temples and small lines around his eyes, but the uniform didn't conceal the fact that he was very fit for his age. This was no paunchy pencil-pusher. I shook his hand, noting the rows of ribbons on his lapel. Linden gestured toward a grouping of chairs, and the three of us sat down.

Without preamble he said, "We've been watching you, Miss Marble."

"Well, *thank* goodness," I began. "My friends thought I was going crazy. Wait till I tell them—"

"This meeting cannot be discussed with anyone," he interrupted. "In fact, I must have your word on that before we go any further. Even if you decide not to help us, nothing you see or hear may leave this building.

"You were thoroughly checked by the FBI when President Roosevelt appointed you to the Office of Civilian Defense, and the reports you made for the bureau were acceptable."

"The Spanish reports?"

Linden nodded.

"But that was so silly. I never heard anything important."

* Fictitious name.

"You don't know that, and I'm not at liberty to discuss how the information was used," he said. "Miss Marble, we have reason to trust you, but you must understand that this is very serious business."

"I do," I said. "No, actually, I *don't*. I don't understand a bit of this so far. I promise not to say anything to anyone, but why do you think I can help you? Every branch of the service turned me down because of my tuberculosis."

"We *know* you can help," Linden replied. "In fact, you're the only one who can do what we have in mind."

"Go on."

"It has to do with Hans Steinmetz."

"Hans? What do you know about Hans and me?" I regretted my words, and knew I was blushing. Jones's face was impassive, but his eyes seemed to mock me.

"We know of your . . . relationship," said Linden. "The European gossip columnists had a field day with it at the time. But tell me, why did you break it off? Was there an argument?"

"No. Teach—my coach, Eleanor Tennant—talked me into ending it. She didn't want anything to distract me from tennis. But what's my private life got to do with helping the army?" I was confused, and a bit angry.

"Don't be offended, Miss Marble. Please." Linden's face was kind. "There's a point to all this. Were you and Steinmetz on good terms when you broke up?"

I nodded. "We didn't argue. He didn't like it, of course. Neither did I. We were both hurt. I . . . loved him very much."

"Have you communicated with him since 1938?"

"No." I shook my head. "And then later I married Joe. I loved Joe more than Hans, more than anybody."

Linden cleared his throat. "I know. We're sorry about that," he said quietly. "I think we can assume Steinmetz would see you again if he could, which is exactly what we want you to do."

I sat stunned, incredulous. "What? What are you talking about?"

"Hans is a very important link to a lot of high-ranking Nazis," Jones said.

"Hans? A Nazi?"

"No," Linden said, "but he's close to them. They know they're losing the war and the smart ones are smuggling the riches they've acquired—gold, jewels, paintings, currency, anything of value—out of Germany, mostly into Switzerland. Later, when they run—and they will—they'll be able to set up dynasties in places like South America where no questions will be asked as long as they can pay."

"The Nazis are keeping their treasures in Hans's bank?" I asked.

"We're not sure," Jones said, leaning forward intently. "He's becoming very rich, quite possibly off the Nazis. We suspect that he keeps the records of these transactions in a private place, like his vault at home, rather than at his bank."

I sighed. Hans, dealing with those murderous pigs? My spirits, which were shaky at best, sank, and I suddenly felt weary. "I don't want to see him. What good could it possibly do?"

"A great deal," Jones said. The man's gaze made me uncomfortable.

"We want you to get together with Hans, gain his trust, and find out where he keeps those records," Linden explained. "We know it's a long shot, but we hope you can get to the records and photograph them for us."

I couldn't believe what I was hearing. I almost expected someone to yell "Cut!" and the actors to relax, light up cigarettes, and start talking about their social lives. This wasn't real!

"Do you know what you're asking? That's impossible. Even if Hans didn't find it strange that I suddenly popped back into his life, he'd hardly open his safe for me and say, 'Here's what I do for a living, honey.' And his Nazi buddies . . . I could get killed!"

"We'll teach you everything you need to know," Linden said patiently. "We'll send you to Switzerland for some well-publicized clinics and exhibitions, and let Hans find you." He paused, then added, "It may be impossible, as you say. He may not even contact you. Maybe he has another woman. Who knows? All I can tell you is that this is a chance to get evidence we can use to stop the Nazis from getting away, from starting up again in other countries. Nobody wants to fight this war all over again."

Linden looked at me levelly, probably wondering if I had any guts. "As you say, it'll be dangerous, very dangerous. If you say no, we'll certainly understand."

"I need some time to think about this."

"Tomorrow. I'll call you."

I expected Jones to try to persuade me on the drive back into the city, but he was silent until he let me out a few blocks from my apartment. "We need your help," he said simply.

"You're all crazy," I replied, slamming the door and walking away without a backward glance.

I moved in a fog the rest of the day. Teach and Brownie came home late and tired from teaching, and we all turned in early. I went to bed, but there was to be little sleep for me. I'd had many sleepless nights since Joe's death, but now Hans intruded on my thoughts. I'd loved him and hurt him before. Could I bring myself to spy on him, to betray his trust? And could I make love with him? Linden and Jones hadn't spelled it out, but I knew "regaining Hans's trust" would mean sleeping with him.

I hoped that Hans wasn't helping the Nazis, but if he was, then what he was doing was wrong—maybe not illegal in his country, but wrong nonetheless. If I could do what Linden and Jones wanted, it could hurt the bastards who shot Joe's plane out of the sky. I tossed in my bed as if the Germans had already caught me and were torturing me. I could get killed. Was I prepared to die for my country? I got out of bed and paced quietly, careful not to wake Brownie in the adjacent room.

I was hunched over a cup of coffee at the kitchen table when Brownie came in, yawning. "Boy, you look like forty miles of bad road. Rough night?"

"Yeah."

"You know you can wake me."

"Thanks. I had to work this out alone." I mustered a smile for her. "I'm okay. Don't look so worried."

When the phone rang an hour later, I nearly ran over Brownie to grab it. She looked at me strangely.

"Hello? Okay. Sure, Teach, I'll meet you there." I hung up. "Teach has a practice partner set up for me," I told Brownie. "She's putting me back in training."

"Good," Brownie said, pulling her coat from the closet. "I'll be home early. Don't try to cook dinner. I'm too young to die."

She dodged the little rubber ball—my ever-present "squeezie" —and closed the apartment door laughing.

I retrieved the ball and was still squeezing it when the phone rang. I froze. It rang again. And again. I took a deep breath and answered it.

"Miss Marble, Colonel Linden here."

31 : TO BE A SPY

"I've thought about your offer."

"And . . . ?"

"Well, I've nothing left to lose."

"You do," he said quietly. "Your life."

"I'll take that chance. What do you want me to do?"

"A car will pick you up at two o'clock tomorrow, same place. I'll set up a training schedule for you; you have a lot to learn, and not much time. And, of course," he added, "say nothing to anyone."

I hung up, and stared at the phone for a moment, not believing what I had done. Late for Teach, I stuffed my tennis clothes in a bag and rushed out the door.

I was dripping with sweat when Teach called a halt after one set. "That's enough," she said, looking pleased. "Talk Brownie into giving you a rubdown when you get home."

I had spent more than a month holed up in the apartment, doing no more than squeezing my rubber ball. My muscles protested the sudden return to activity, but every day workouts became easier. I got into a routine: I played tennis every morning, then slipped away to the Brooklyn warehouse and my other life, under the guise of taking classes at New York University as I had before.

I've always been good at keeping secrets, but it was difficult not to tell Teach and Brownie that I was involved in something that really mattered, not to tell them all the new things I was learning. They attributed my improved spirits to tennis and I let them think that, for I *was* happy to be playing again. But I was more excited about the intensity with which I was being groomed as a spy.

The warehouse was a training center for agents; that much was clear to me from what I saw, and there was a lot I wasn't allowed to see. My schedule was staggered so that I never met any other trainees, a precaution that made sense. Agents in training never knew who their companions were, but my persona made that impossible. And it could blow my mission, and my life, if someone somewhere in this hideous business knew I was a spy and was coerced into saying so. For the same reason, there was no need for me to know the faces of other agents.

I knew I might be killed; what I hadn't considered was that I might have *to kill*, a possibility made patently clear from the first day of my training.

The gun issued to me was a small one, a .25-caliber automatic with a six-shot clip in the handle, one shell already in the chamber.

"This is a peashooter compared to the weapons most of our operatives carry"—in my instructor's burly fist it looked harmless enough—"but it's the best gun for you. It's easy for a woman to conceal on her body, and quite effective if your target is close. I don't know the details of your assignment, but I understand you'd most likely use it in close quarters."

I shuddered. "I certainly hope not."

"I hope not, too, but it's my job to make sure you can use it if you have to." He paused. "It's a small caliber, but it can kill."

Maybe it could, but could I? I took the gun from him; it was an ugly, sinister thing, and heavier than it looked. I'd never held one before and I shifted it awkwardly in my hand until it felt right.

"Well, my coach tried to make me a killer on the court." I tried to joke, feeling entirely out of my element.

"That's a start." Dave grinned. At least, he'd said his name was Dave. Everyone knew who I was, but I only knew first names, and I suspected those were phony. I would never know enough to endanger the operation.

Dave was a good teacher. In two weeks, I was completely comfortable with the weapon and the small shoulder holster that concealed it under my arm. I could pull the clip and reload it in seconds, even in total darkness. On the indoor shooting range, I "killed" countless paper targets, first little bull's-eyes, then man-sized cardboard silhouettes.

"Fire!" Dave clicked his stopwatch. Holding the gun with both hands at arm's length, I fired. Two tiny holes appeared in the heart of my target, then two in the head and two in the groin.

"Ouch!" Dave laughed, stopping the time on his watch. "Very funny. But remember, don't get fancy. Shoot for the body. Keep pulling that trigger until he drops, and then reload on the run. Got it?"

"Yessir." I gave him a mock salute.

He returned it. "Get on over to the gym. See you tomorrow."

I changed into sweats in the locker room and walked into the mat room—the padded cell, I called it, because the walls as well as the floors were padded. I appreciated the cushions after I was bounced off the walls a few times.

"Hi, sadist," I said to the young blond giant waiting for me.

"You say the sweetest things," replied Grunt. He had told me his nickname the first day, and it fit, though I grunted as much as he did in the process of learning how to defend myself and give an attacker something to remember me by.

Grunt insisted on calling me Miss Marble "out of respect," which seemed incongruous, when you consider the body contact that went into the training. I tried to remember that he "respected me" when he was sprawled on top of me with a massive forearm across my throat.

I had a healthy respect for Grunt. When I hit him hard in the groin one day, accidentally failing to pull my kick, he said as calmly as he could, "Good move," and disappeared into the locker room to compose himself. He wasn't the slightest bit angry then, or ever.

Grunt weighed twice as much as I did, but under his tutelage I learned to use his bulk against him and send him flying with a variety of throws. At night, in the scant minutes before I fell into an exhausted sleep, I tried to imagine circumstances that would cause me to stick my thumbs into a man's eyes, or ram the bones of his nose up into his brain with the heel of my hand, or crush his windpipe with a chop of the hand, or a kick. . . .

"That old standby, the kick to the groin, is useful," Grunt told me, "but your target will expect it from a woman. I can teach you ways to hurt or kill that most people have never even dreamed of."

He was right. Sometimes our practice sessions involved practices so heinous, I'd leave feeling sick.

"For a sweet-faced guy, you're a real bastard," I said with genuine irritation. I was lying on my back, gasping for breath. Grunt had caught me off guard, slammed me to the mat, and now his hands were on my throat. I smacked both of his ears gently with my hands, then placed both thumbs lightly against his eyes, just to show that I had access to them. "Break," I said, and he rolled away. I sat rubbing my shoulder.

"Did I hurt you?" He hovered, a look of concern spreading over his broad face.

"You *always* hurt me, Grunt. I've started playing tennis in long-sleeved blouses to conceal the bruises."

"I'm sorry, but if something I teach you saves your life, it'll be well worth it. Besides, since when are you such a sissy?"

"A sissy!" I bounced my first off his hard abdomen, and we both laughed.

Compared to sessions with Grunt, map reading was a cinch. My instructor, a slight young man with glasses, had a faint air of irritation when Linden left us alone for our first meeting. I suppose he thought I was going to be a pain.

"Where do we start?" I tried to sound cheerful. We would both have to make the best of it.

"Here." He turned on the lamp, illuminating a huge map, and picked up a pointer. "This is Geneva. Here's the Steinmetz estate twelve miles away, on the road to Chamonix. You have a choice of several roads. . . ." His voice droned on as I listened and watched.

After half an hour, he put his pointer down. "Okay, I'd like for you to study this map. When you're ready, I'll ask you to identify as much as you can on an unmarked map. Eventually you should be able to reconstruct the map from memory."

"Uh huh." I eyed the map speculatively. "Give me a sheet of blank paper."

I spread the paper on a drawing table, and began to sketch the map we had been discussing. "Here's Geneva," I said, drawing a small circle. "Here's the road over the mountain to Hans's place twelve miles away. . . ." I continued until I had drawn a serviceable map of the area.

"You've seen this map before." His voice was accusing.

"No, I've seen it only just now." I watched a question begin to form on his lips. "I think it's what you call a photographic memory."

He smiled, his dourness gone. "I want to give you as many escape routes as I can, so let's get on with it."

I was passed from one instructor to another in the secret nerve center that lay behind the plain facade of the "warehouse" in Brooklyn. One afternoon when I reported to Linden's office, he and Jones were waiting with a sheaf of plans and photos of Hans's home.

"The place is a castle, really," Linden began. "At least, it was when it was built back in the 1600s by Steinmetz's ancestors. It's been added onto and remodeled many times since then." He handed me a photo of a breathtaking stone château nestled against a backdrop of the Alps.

"It's everything he said!" I glanced up at the two men. "It's beautiful! He used to threaten to steal me away from Teach and lock me up in his castle. It might not have been so bad." My mind was suddenly flooded with memories of Hans.

210

Jones stirred in his chair, unmoved by my memories. "Here's the floor plan of the place." He unrolled a large blueprint and anchored the corners with ashtrays.

"How'd you get this?" I asked.

"Mostly it's guesswork," Jones admitted, "*educated* guesswork. We got our hands on blueprints from some of the remodeling projects and surmised the rest from research. The original structure was much like that of other houses built in that era. It was stylish to have a wide central hall with a drawing room on one side"—he pointed to the floor plan—"the formal dining room on the other, and a grand staircase leading to the rooms above. Here, under the staircase, is probably where you'll find the doorway to the basement. You can be sure there's a wine cellar down there, and that's probably where the vault is."

"Why would Hans keep records at home?" I asked.

"Discretion," Linden answered. "Everyone on his household staff has been with the family for many years. They're loyal. Employees at the bank come and go—they might be nosy, or Russian agents. The Russians want this information, too, and undoubtedly have men watching Steinmetz's house and bank. They're as concerned as we are about Germans escaping the country with their stolen fortunes and someday coming back to power. The Russians also are in desperate need of money for their military; they might simply want to loot Hans's safe for their own use. In either case, I suspect they have operatives working in the bank and on neighboring estates."

"What about us? Don't we have spies in the area?"

"Yes," Linden answered vaguely. "We hope to keep an eye on you while you're there, but don't count on anyone coming to the rescue."

He placed in front of me a photo of a small shop front and another of a slight, bearded man with a gnomelike face. "This is your contact, Franz Regenbogen.* He works as a goldsmith in the oldest part of Geneva, on La Grande Rue near the Hôtel Les Armures, where you'll be staying. When you have the film, take it directly to Franz, then get to the airport. Our people will put you on an army transport any time you show up."

He hesitated, then said, "If you get in trouble, get to Franz. He'll know what to do. It'll blow his cover, but we'll pull you both out if things go wrong. Otherwise, don't contact him for any other reason until you have the film."

* Fictitious name

I stared at the photo of a stranger who was my link to safety. His face, together with images of Hans and Joe, would swirl through my dreams that night.

The compact spy camera I would use to photograph the documents had just been perfected by Kodak for undercover work. It was a snap to use, but the safecracking was anything but.

"I can't do it!" I threw down the screwdriver and pulled off my headband, which held a small, intense light. Cursing under my breath, I rose from my knees and defiantly kicked the heavy safe door.

"Relax," my instructor said, sitting back on his heels. We'd both been kneeling for more than an hour while I futilely picked away at the lock. "It's a lot to learn. We can't be sure of the type of safe you'll encounter, so we need to cover the possibilities. The vault was probably installed when the last wing was built, and is most likely Swiss made, so that narrows it down a bit."

He rose to his feet and handed me the screwdriver. "Besides, you've gotten pretty good at locating and disarming the alarms we've set up, so you won't trigger the explosives and blow your head off before you get to work on the safe. That's progress."

He sounded so cheery I laughed in spite of myself. "Wonderful."

The first time I heard the tumblers click into place and felt the handle of the big door turn, I let out a war whoop that brought a guard running. The next day, there was an entirely different locking mechanism in its place, but I mastered it, too, and all the rest that followed.

"You've done a remarkable job," Linden said, dropping a thick file on the table around which he, Jones, and I were seated. "I wish we'd had you earlier in the war."

"I tried."

"Speaking of which, the doctor's report from your exam two days ago says you're in excellent health." Linden gestured to the file.

"I know." I had a right to be smug. "And I beat the socks off Sarah Palfrey the other day, too."

"Your . . . mental state has improved, too, hasn't it?" The colonel's eyes were serious.

It took me a moment to answer. "I have a purpose again, more important than tennis, something that may make a difference."

"Then I say you're ready to give some clinics in Switzerland."

"Am I?"

212

"We've taught you all we can. The war's winding down, and we have to move before Hitler's own officers kill him and all the rats run for cover. You'll leave Monday."

I could barely breathe. Two days!

"Tell your friends—the ones you have to tell something—that you're doing some clinics in Switzerland for the army. It's the truth, you know."

Telling Teach and Brownie wasn't as simple as that.

"What? Without me?" Teach was obviously miffed.

"You have students here. It's only a few clinics." I tried to be firm. I wanted Teach to relinquish her grip on me, but old habits die hard.

"I just wish you wouldn't go to Europe now." Brownie frowned. "There's still a war on."

"Remember, Switzerland's neutral." I wanted to end the conversation. "Look, you two, I love you for being concerned, but I need to go. I need to feel useful. Understand? Please?"

"Why do I get the feeling there's something she's not telling us?" Brownie asked Teach.

"Indeed. She can give clinics anyplace in the States." Teach eyed me suspiciously.

32 : SWITZERLAND

The army transport banked on its final approach to landing, and I could see the Geneva international airport, its runways like neat cross-stitching against the smooth white of the snow. Geneva lay at the tip of Lake Leman, an azure crescent of water swollen by the spring runoff from the mountains above.

The mountains. I couldn't take my eyes off the peaks jutting four thousand feet or more above the lake. The rocky summits of the Alps were white against the sky, and I could see the thin ribbons of roads leading around the fringe of the lake to Martigny and through the mountains to Chamonix. Someplace on the road to Chamonix was Hans's château. I shivered, and turned from the window to gather my things.

The flight had been long; I was anxious to be on the ground again. Sitting still gave me too much time to think. What would it be like seeing Hans again? If he didn't contact me, I wasn't sure if I'd feel disappointed or relieved.

I stepped out into sunshine, but shivered descending the ramp. I felt as if the word "spy" were painted across my back. Switzerland was a neutral country, but I had been sent to interfere with the Nazis' stash. People had been known to disappear in neutral countries.

Looking out across the field, I *really* wanted to get on the next plane back to the States. I smiled my way through countless introductions, reporters' questions, and photos with the local tennis and political figures. Then I was driven to the beautiful Hôtel Les Armures, where the tennis association had booked a lavish suite for me.

Dinner that night was a wonderful, light-hearted affair. I was

214

so immersed in tennis talk that the real reason for my visit to Geneva didn't cross my mind until I said good night to my hosts, and closed the door of my room.

Exhausted, I undressed, turned off the lights, and pushed back the heavy drapes. The Alps glowed whitely in the moonlight. Hans was out there somewhere. Did he know I was in Geneva? Did he care? My heart beat faster at the thought of what I had to do.

"God bless, and angels keep me safe from harm," I whispered, and snuggled deep under the eiderdown comforter.

I woke to sunlight pouring through the open drapes, and tried to shake off the grogginess of jet lag while I dressed. The tennis pro of the local club met me for breakfast in the hotel dining room; then we were off to the club's indoor courts for my first clinic.

Three days of clinics and luncheons, and three evenings of parties flew by without incident; I began to wonder if everyone had been wrong to assume Hans would want to see me.

I had played Ingrid, a strong young Swiss girl with a powerful serve, and was making my way to the locker room, dog-tired and not paying full attention to the people around us, when a girl handed me a single long-stemmed pink rose and a card. I thanked her and once inside the locker room, put down my racquets and opened the card.

Beneath an ornate family crest were words written in a bold hand: "You're more beautiful than I remembered. Have dinner with me tonight. I'll call at your hotel in an hour." My heart jumped when I saw the signature. It was from Hans.

Back at the hotel, I changed dresses three times before finally deciding on a red one that I knew showed off my figure and went well with my blond hair. I was perfecting my lipstick when the phone rang.

"Hello?" I silently cursed the tremble in my voice.

"I'm downstairs," said a voice I thought I would never hear again.

"I'll be right down!" My heart was racing.

I descended the wide staircase, my eyes searching the lobby. Then I saw him watching me with a look of approval that I recognized in his dark eyes. Seven years had passed since Le Touquet, but he'd not really changed. The touches of gray in his hair and the fine lines in his lean face only added to his good looks. He wore a beautifully tailored blue suit and carried a dozen roses to match the one he'd sent me at the tennis match.

"Alice," he said simply when I stood before him, "you still take my breath away." As I cradled the roses in one arm, he bowed low

215

over my hand and kissed it softly, the touch of his lips warm and tantalizing.

"Hans, I thought we'd never meet again."

I kissed him quickly on the cheek. His eyes held mine and I slowly rose on my toes again to kiss him lightly on the mouth. Who cared if people were watching? I handed the roses to a smiling desk clerk with instructions to take them to my room.

The restaurant Hans chose was a short drive from the hotel, and we were soon facing each other across a small table in a candlelit room. Seven years of separation fell away layer by layer while we talked. He had followed my career in the papers, and even watched me play a few times in England before the war.

"I wanted so much to call you, just to spend an evening with you," he said, "but I knew how Teach would react!" We both laughed at that, old wounds nearly forgotten.

"She made me a champion," I said, looking in his eyes, "but she cost me a lot, too. I couldn't make the same mistake twice, Hans. She couldn't talk me out of marrying Joe."

My eyes filled with tears. I had talked too much, opened too many closed doors. Hans raised my hand to his lips again. "Be happy," he said softly, kissing the inside of my wrist and running his lips gently the length of my thumb before lifting his eyes to mine again. "Let me make you happy again."

If Hans had asked to come to my hotel room that night, I doubt that I would have resisted. The physical attraction was still there, as powerful as it had been that night in France when we met and made love on the beach. Back then, we'd been the cosmopolitan man and a nervous girl taking her first lover. Now, nothing stood in our way. Hans's kiss in the car before he walked me to the door of the hotel left no doubt as to his feelings, yet he bade me good night in the lobby.

It was the next night before we ended up in bed. The evening started with dinner at his château, which really did stand like a medieval castle on the flank of the mountains above Geneva.

Silent servants came and went, appearing at just the right moment to serve the next course, only to vanish until the next. Our only company was Hans's ancestors peering down from their portraits on the walls of the formal dining room.

Hans laughed when I told him the paintings made me nervous, took my hand, and pulled me up from my chair. "Never mind them. Let me show you the house they built me."

He led me across the wide central hall to the drawing room, a vast room hung with fine old tapestries and decorated with antiques and works of art. Tall windows and French doors looked out on formal gardens that would be magnificent when spring broke.

"I'll bet this place has a dungeon," I said. We had completed the downstairs tour of the library, den, and Hans's office, and were returning to the central hall.

"No dungeon, but it has one of the finest wine cellars in the country," he answered, gesturing to a doorway under the grand staircase. "I prefer to torture my victims upstairs. Would you like to see where?"

"Of course," I said, as he slipped his arm around my waist and steered me toward the stairway. Jones's researchers had been right. Everything was just as they said. I felt no satisfaction, though, just a bittersweet pain. I leaned against Hans and slipped my arm around him.

My tour of the upstairs never made it beyond the bedroom with its big four-poster bed. In time, I would come to know the upstairs as well as my own New York apartment, but that night Hans and I were only interested in each other, and making up for the years we had lost.

When our passion was spent, I lay quietly in his arms. That's when the tears started, so suddenly that they splashed on his chest before I realized I was crying.

"Darling?" Confused, he raised his hand to stroke my hair, for by then I was sobbing uncontrollably. He held me until my outburst died to a snuffle, then raised my chin so that I was looking into his eyes.

"Did I disappoint you?"

"You know better." I took a deep breath. "You made me feel alive for the first time in months. I feel happy and sad, all at the same time."

If only he knew how sad! The misery welled up inside me. Dammit, I was still in love with him!

"Well, we'll work on the sad part," he said softly, kissing the top of my head. "Let's start by moving you out of that hotel and into my house. I wanted to make love to you last night, but not at the hotel. I was concerned for your reputation."

That drew a laugh from me. "Hans, people will talk if I'm your houseguest!"

"Let them." He covered my mouth with a kiss that ended all discussion for a long time.

It was nearly daylight when he took me back to the hotel. I closed the door of my room, peeled my clothes off, and dropped them into a heap beside me. Hans's roses stood in a vase near my bed. I breathed in their fragrance as I closed my eyes and hoped for sleep. It didn't come.

For three days after, I refused to return his calls. I dropped his notes unanswered on my bedside table. During the day, I conducted clinics with young hopefuls at the Parc des Eaux-Vives near Lake Leman. I wasn't about to disappoint them, though several people said I looked pale. *A touch of flu; it'll pass*, I assured them.

At night, I slept fitfully, wrestling with the urge to get on a plane, fly home and tell Linden to find another spy. My conscience reminded me that he'd said I was the only one who could do what had to be done. If I was doing something for my country, why did I feel like a traitor? And to whom?

It was early morning when I finally picked up the phone and called Hans. "I'm sorry. I needed time to think. It's all happening so fast—"

"Darling, it's all right," he interrupted. "You don't have to explain. I need you, Alice. Come stay with me."

I stared at the case that held my gun, camera, and tools. "I'll pack my bags and be ready after the match tonight."

The butler put my bags down in the large bedroom adjoining Hans's room and excused himself. The room was exquisitely furnished with family heirlooms; double doors opened onto a balcony with a view of a meadow and mountains in the distance.

"Hans, it's beautiful!"

"It's yours, love, but I hope you'll spend most of your time in here." He opened the door that led to his bedroom.

"I'm sure I will."

Laughing, I threw my arms around his neck. He rewarded me with a kiss and a reminder of how pleasurable a visit to his room could be.

Days stretched into a week, then three, and suddenly I had only one more week of tennis scheduled. Leaving the club one afternoon, I turned away from the familiar road leading to the château, and onto the quai Gustav-Ador which took me into Old Town Geneva. It didn't take long to find La Grande Rue and Regenbogen's shop.

Driving slowly past the shop, I could see the goldsmith arranging items in a display window. He probably wondered what the hell I was waiting for. Back in the States, Linden and Jones were no doubt wondering the same thing. Soon.

Realizing I'd sat there longer than I meant to, I made my way back to the route de Chêne and punched the accelerator of the

Jaguar Hans had given me. We were attending a party at the Argentine embassy, and I needed to dress with extra care. Some of the guests were Hans's business associates, and I knew he wanted to show me off.

I was dressed and sitting combing my hair when Hans came to stand behind me.

"You look particularly dashing." I looked at him in the mirror. "Are you sure you want to go out?"

He bent to kiss the back of my neck. "We'll leave early and rush home to make love. Anticipation will make the reality that much sweeter."

I swiveled on the seat to kiss his mouth. "Do you like the dress?" The pale-blue gown had been terribly expensive, but he had insisted on buying it for me because it matched my eyes.

"I was wrong about the dress," he said.

"What!"

"It can't come close to the beauty of your eyes."

"Hans!" I stood and held his face between my hands. "I love you."

"I'm glad. You look gorgeous. Only one thing is lacking."

"What?"

"This." Hans had been holding one hand behind his back. Now he held the velvet box in front of him, snapping the top open to reveal a necklace of diamonds and sapphires, glittering like ice in the sunlight.

"It's beautiful! You shouldn't . . ."

"When will you accept the fact that I'm a very wealthy man, and getting wealthier all the time?" I could feel the weight of the necklace as Hans fastened the clasp at the back of my neck. "I can afford to give you anything—everything—you want. And even some things you don't know you want."

He turned me to face him, and studied the effect of the necklace above the low-cut bosom of the dress. "Now we're ready. You'll see lots of jewelry tonight, but none on a woman as beautiful as you."

He was right about the jewelry. Every vault of every château within fifty miles must have been emptied to decorate the women at the embassy. Dowagers and debutantes sparkled as they moved among the tuxedoed men, dancing to the orchestra or sampling the lavish buffet.

"It's hard to believe there's a war on," I said, tightening my grip on Hans's arm as the receiving line inched nearer to the Argentine ambassador and his wife.

"There is no war here, my dear."

"But there are Germans here." I nodded toward the crowd. The harsh language of Hitler's fatherland was obvious.

"They're neighbors," Hans said.

"Neighbors! Hans, they're killing people."

"And so are the Americans, and the British, and the Russians. We Swiss do not get involved in these periodic European purges."

The man next to Hans nodded his agreement. "We are businessmen, not politicians, eh?"

When I was presented to the Argentine ambassador, he kissed my hand and said, "Miss Marble! I heard you were in Geneva. I'm so glad to meet you. We do hope you'll come to play in Buenos Aires one day soon."

"Thank you," I said. "Perhaps after the war."

"Then we'll hope for a speedy end to it." He winked at Hans.

We moved onto the dance floor, and Hans took me in his arms. I felt the brush of his thigh against mine, and thought that we wouldn't last long if we continued to dance.

"Hans, the place is full of Germans. Why are the Argentines being so hospitable?"

"Business, my dear. The rumor—an exaggeration, no doubt— is that we Swiss hold more than three hundred million German marks in our banks. The Argentines would like to see those millions invested in their country when the war is over."

"Do you have German money in your bank?"

"Of course. I also have money deposited by men fleeing the French Revolution nearly two hundred years ago. Everyone wants a nest egg."

"Doesn't it bother you, dealing with Nazis?"

Hans looked down at me indulgently. "I'm a banker. I don't worry about where the money comes from."

Before I could answer, a lanky red-haired young man tapped Hans on the shoulder, and I was relieved to hear an unmistakable Southern drawl. "Excuse me, sir," he said, "I would kick myself if I passed up a chance to dance with Miss Marble. May I?"

Hans laughed. "You have excellent taste. Just remember to return her to me."

Bob Rawlins,* who worked at the American embassy, introduced himself, and guided me into a waltz. "I'm glad to see another American," he said. "I haven't been here long enough to get used to being nice to Germans. It's tough."

_____
* Fictitious name.

220

"Yes, it is." I knew I would dance with any number of them before the night was over, and that I would have to try not to think about Joe. Any one of them could have shot him out of the sky; they might not literally have done so, but they had in spirit.

"But the war will be over real soon, they say," my partner continued, lowering his voice. "The Nazis will get what's coming to them."

I realized that he was carrying the conversation alone, and hastily changed the subject to tennis.

Soon Bob Rawlins was replaced by another tennis fan, and another, and another. There seemed to be plenty of tennis fans among the men, but most of the women I was introduced to acted as if they had never heard of me—or wished they never had. They only had eyes for Hans, and I quickly realized that he was one of the city's most eligible bachelors. I felt a flash of jealousy, watching him with a lithe blonde in black who danced a bit closer than I felt she needed to.

Jealousy. One minute I was thinking of Joe, the next I was jealous of Hans. It was all so complicated.

I danced again with Hans, even closer than the blonde in black, and had the desired effect on him. We said our goodbyes and sped up the mountain road in Hans's Mercedes.

I changed in my room, then went through the adjoining door into Hans's bedroom. He had been busy. A magnum of champagne stood in a silver ice bucket next to the bed, along with two long-stemmed crystal glasses. Hans leaned against the massive wood headboard, the sheet drawn to his waist, his chest bare. His eyes followed me as I crossed the room and joined him in the bed.

"Champagne?" His eyes were black in the dim light, their pupils wide.

"Not now. I want to find out if the reality *is* as good as the anticipation." I leaned to kiss his chest, and we did what we had both been wanting to do for hours.

The champagne did not go to waste. I sipped at a glassful, and filled Hans's glass every time he emptied it. He had had a few drinks at the embassy, and was soon higher than I had ever seen him. I was still surprised when he said, "You asked me if I had German money in my bank?"

"Yes?"

"I've got better than that. I've got the Nazis by the balls." He grinned and clinked his glass against mine.

"What do you mean?"

"The bastards are stockpiling their fortunes with me, and most of them will never get out of Germany when the end comes. And I've been charging them interest all along, to protect *their* money. Best of all, it's here, not in the bank. You never know what governments will do."

"Here? Is that safe?"

"Yes, my dear, it's safe. The vault is protected by charges. Anybody trying to get in will get blown to hell. One little key . . ." His words were slurred. "One little key hidden in a radiator knob, where nobody would think to look, protects all that Nazi loot." He chuckled and looked at me, his eyes glassy. "I love you, and I'm going to enjoy spoiling you."

"I love you, too," I whispered, taking the glass from his hand. He had fallen asleep.

I slipped out of bed and went to the radiators under the window. The control of the first held firm, but the next gave when I pulled on it, and there, just as Hans had said, was a small key. I left it where it was, replaced the cap, and crawled back into bed. Hans was snoring lightly. I lay watching him, not bothering to wipe away the tears that streamed down my face. I hated myself, hated deceiving him, but now that I knew about the key, I *had* to go through with my spying. With the key, I just might succeed.

33 : THE MISSION

1945

On Friday, I feigned sickness, which was easy enough to do. I felt miserable, and lack of sleep coupled with a strenuous week of clinics had me on the verge of being truly ill.

"Darling, are you sure you don't want me to stay home?" Hans asked as he dressed for the evening. Full of concern, he turned from his reflection in the mirror to look at me propped against the pillows in his bed.

"And miss the biggest party of the year?" I teased. "The ladies will be heartbroken if you're not at the British embassy tonight!" I couldn't look at him directly. Instead, I stared down at my hand, which unconsciously traced the pattern on the eiderdown comforter. "I picked such a rotten time to be sick. I was so looking forward to this evening."

"There'll be many, many parties for us, my love." He sat on the bed beside me. Cupping one hand behind my head, he began to cover my face with soft kisses, his other hand stroking my breast.

"Keep that up and I won't let you leave," I whispered, gently pushing him away.

I concentrated on knotting the bow tie he'd left dangling around his neck, then lifted my eyes to his. "Now, stand up and let me look at you."

He rose obediently and bowed before me. God, he was handsome. His thick, dark hair drooped over his forehead, and curled slightly behind his ears at the nape of his neck. The ski season had left his face with a healthy tan, causing his even teeth to seem all the whiter when he smiled. The tuxedo, white ruffled shirt with tiny diamond studs, and black cummerbund accentuated his broad shoulders and trim body.

"Hans!" I scolded. His eyes were full of passion.

"I can't help it. When you look at me . . ." He shrugged.

"Go. You're late. And *don't* drive fast."

"You're beginning to sound like a wife." A wide smile spread across his face. "Perhaps we can announce our wedding plans at the next party?"

My throat tightened and hot tears burned behind my eyelids. "Hans, I love you. You've made me so happy . . ." My voice broke, and I dropped my eyes. God, I was going to cry. Desperately, I willed myself not to.

"It's just the beginning, Alice." He took both my hands in his. "I'm going to make you happier than you've ever been in your life—for the rest of your life."

He kissed the tips of my fingers and straightened up. "I'll return by midnight. If there's anything at all you need, ring for the servants. If you start to feel worse, call the embassy and I'll bring the doctor home with me."

At the door, he turned to look back. "You'll be all right?"

Numbly, I nodded, watched the door close behind him, and rolled over to bury my face in the pillows. Why me? The question screamed in my head while I cried.

Finally, I raised my head to look at the German-made clock on Hans's massive oak dresser.

"Germans," I muttered, still staring at the clock. The hands came into focus as I remembered my mission, and tried to organize my thoughts. It was seven o'clock. If all went well, I could get into the safe, take the photos, and be back in bed before Hans got home. In the morning, I would leave the house as usual, but instead of going to the tennis club, I would take the film to my contact and head for the airport.

I lay there convincing myself I couldn't do it. I wanted to live the rest of my life with Hans. To have his children. My happiness was at stake. I didn't give a good goddamn about the Germans. The war was almost over. They would all be caught some other way.

I knew in my heart that they wouldn't be caught. They would get away, pigs like the fat man I had encountered at a party who kept breathing in my ear and rubbing against me when we danced. He was one of Hans's "clients." Aryan superiority, indeed. When Hans rescued me, I went to the ladies room and scrubbed my hand where the man's wet lips had touched it.

I imagined them all settling in South America, festering like a sore as they regrouped their heinous Nazi party. Someday the world would end up fighting them again. Maybe I could help keep that from happening. I could at least stop some of them, the ones who had their fortunes with Hans.

"It's important, and only I can do it," I whispered, repeating the words that had convinced me to take the mission in the first place, before I fell in love with Hans again.

I concentrated on the clock ticking loudly in the silence of the room. Inside me, the battle raged. Could I live with the thought that I'd had a chance to act against the Germans, and didn't take it? I wanted to avenge Joe's death. The thought of him made me ache. That's why I was here, to *do something*. But Hans . . .

There was a light tapping at the door. Closing my eyes, I froze. I heard the door open, then after a moment close quietly. There was the sound of footsteps going down the hall. I opened my eyes and exhaled. One of the servants had come to see if I wanted anything. Thinking me asleep, they probably would not check on me again.

I had to move. My eyes dropped to the bedside phone as I swung my feet to the floor. If Hans called . . . I shook off the thought. It was a chance I'd have to take. Going to the radiator next to the wall, I loosened the cap and fished out the key.

In my adjoining room, I quickly dressed in slacks, a loose blouse, and tennis shoes. Reaching into the antique armoire for my jacket, my hand brushed against the smooth silk of the long white dress Hans had bought me for the embassy ball. His eyes had lit up when I modeled it for him. It was a stunning dress. The cabinet was filled with gorgeous clothes, all gifts from Hans. I hesitated, my eyes brimming again.

Pulling a small makeup bag from its hiding place in the back of a dresser drawer, I took out the automatic, strapped on the shoulder holster, and slipped the gun into place under my arm. If the servants discovered me, I would keep them under control with the weapon until I could make my escape. I still didn't know if I could shoot a person, but a gun could be mighty damn threatening.

I slipped on my jacket to conceal the gun. If I was confronted, I could always say I felt better and was going for a walk. Uncertainty stifled me for a moment. Then I shrugged, picked up my bag, and, after listening at the door, stepped out and eased the door shut behind me.

Walking softly down the hall, I strained my ears for some indication of the servants' whereabouts. There were at least two on call every night, the head butler had told me. The youngest servant had a girlfriend in a nearby village. He was probably out. The maid, too: She was young. The cook lived with her husband in a cottage on the estate. That left the head butler and another old family retainer who had quarters in the château. They were probably in the house somewhere.

Creeping down the wide staircase, I jumped and cursed silently when my sweaty hand squeaked on the polished wood banister. I had to get hold of myself. I took a deep breath and eased down another step.

When I reached the central hall with its massive carved door opening onto the front portico, I slipped into a dark place under the stairway and listened. Nothing. On tiptoe, I approached the door to the cellar.

The sound of laughter made me freeze in my tracks. Then my knees went weak with relief. It was coming from the kitchen. Now I knew where the servants were. The cellar door opened easily, without a sound. I darted through, closed it behind me and leaned against it, grateful for the cool, damp air. I was perspiring.

Descending the stone steps, I switched on my flashlight and hurried along a passageway to the wine cellar. Hans was right; the collection was impressive for sheer volume alone, rack after rack of ornately labeled bottles.

I glanced around for a door. Dead end. Starting back the way I'd come, I noticed something I'd missed before. Recessed into the stone wall of the passageway was a heavy wooden door, a small lock in its rough surface. I stuck the key in the lock and turned it, tensing as I did. When nothing happened, I pushed gently and the door swung open, revealing the safe.

I had learned during training that explosives were usually set up to kill an intruder without disturbing the safe or its contents. My greatest risk, the instructor had said, would be in trying to disarm such an explosive device. After he'd shown me everything he knew about them, he said quietly that he'd be praying I didn't encounter one.

He was right, I realized, examining the wires that led from the door to twin canisters on either side of the safe door. It was doubtful that I could have picked that tiny lock without triggering an explosion. Thank God Hans had told me about the key.

Stepping back into the passageway, I glanced up. The door at the top of the stairway was clearly visible to me, but anyone looking down from there would not be able to tell that the door to the vault was open. And I thought I would hear it if anyone entered the cellar. Satisfied, I hurried back inside and turned on the overhead light.

226

Glancing around, I saw that a shaft of light was cast into the passageway.

"Damn," I said, jumping at the sound of my own voice. The light was a dead giveaway to anyone who opened the cellar door above. I turned it off and dug into my bag for the headband with its battery-powered light.

34 : ESCAPE

1945

I rose from my kneeling position in front of the safe, wincing at the cramps in my legs. The safe was remarkably similar to one I had practiced on, but nervousness had made me clumsy. Finally, the tumblers in the locking mechanism clicked into place. The safe was open.

Taking a second to stretch, I glanced at my watch, then looked again, incredulously. It was nearly eleven o'clock, four hours since I'd been upstairs. If Hans had called to check on me, the servants could be searching for me at that moment.

He said he'd be home by midnight. I imagined the silver Mercedes, Hans driving with one hand, loosening his tie with the other as he rushed home to me. I shook off the thought, grasped the handle of the safe, and pulled.

The big door swung open, and I walked inside the vault. Several large, rectangular packages wrapped in heavy brown paper stood leaning against one wall: paintings. Another wall was lined with row after row of gold bars, too many for me to count, each with the unmistakable imprint of the Third Reich, the swastika. The very sight of the symbol made my anger flare.

On the third wall was a neatly numbered box. Thinking once more about booby traps, I slowly lifted the lid. Inside was a vast quantity of glittering jewelry—rings, bracelets, necklaces, tie tacks, buttons, studs. I lifted one necklace, stared at the Star of David at the end of the heavy gold chain, and dropped it back in the box. My anger turned to nausea.

I pushed the box back into line with the others, row after row on shelves reaching to the ceiling, and continued to search. There was a fortune in things inside the vault, but from what Colonel

Linden had told me it was just icing on the cake. The real treasure lay in the currency flowing from the Nazis, through Hans, to his bank. Somewhere in this room was the answer, a record of those millions.

A moment later I saw the leather-bound ledger lying in plain sight on a shelf. I opened it and trained the light of my headlamp on the page. German names and columns of figures told the story of Hans's enterprise, line by line, in his bold, precise handwriting.

In addition to records of deposits—no withdrawals—the ledger contained detailed lists of valuables, probably those around me. I lost sight of my mission for a moment, contemplating the room. How many stolen family heirlooms were in the boxes and packages around me? What had been the fate of those families?

I shook my head to reorder my thoughts. I carried the book out to the safe anteroom, opened it on the floor, and switched on the overhead light. I'd have to chance the light being seen. Grabbing my camera, I clicked the shutter, column after column, page after page. My heart raced. It was taking so long! With every passing minute, my awareness of the potential consequences heightened. If I were discovered now, what would I say? That I was trying to rob Hans? No one would believe that. What happened to spies here? Switzerland was a neutral country, but the Nazis were so powerful. What would Hans do?

Choking back my panic, I concentrated on stopping the trembling in my hands. I had to stop thinking and keep shooting, as if my camera were a gun and my very survival was at stake. I continued turning pages and clicking the shutter until finally I reached the end. About twenty pages were captured on film, enough evidence to nail a lot of Nazi thieves.

The tomblike stillness of the cellar was maddening. After a quick check on the servants, I would replace everything as I had found it, and make my way back up to my bedroom. I ran up the steps and pressed my ear to the door. All hell was breaking loose—there was the sound of loud voices and hurrying feet on the hardwood floors. I had no idea how to get out of the cellar unnoticed.

Easing the door open, I heard the servants calling in their Swiss accents, "Miss Marble? Miss Marble?" from both ends of the downstairs hall. I stepped out, closed the door behind me and quickly slipped into a dark recess under the stairway. If I could make it upstairs, maybe I could pull it off. I could say I was in the bath. No, they would have checked there. . . . Why were they looking for me, anyway? And then I knew.

"Alice, where are you?" Hans called. At the sound of his voice,

I wanted to call his name, to run into his arms and tell him . . . tell him what? I pressed my back against the wall, motionless with fear and indecision.

Then I heard the cellar door open. "Herr Steinmetz, come quickly!" shouted the head butler. Cursing my stupidity, I realized that I'd left the light on in the safe anteroom, and it was shining out into the passageway. In seconds they would know where I'd been.

Running footsteps sounded on the hardwood floor of the up-stairs hall. I couldn't let them catch me. Bolting from my hiding place, I ran straight into the soft belly of the head butler. Thrown off balance, he let out a short grunt, his eyes widening in surprise. Before he could recover, I shoved him away from me and darted for the front door. Heaving it open, I ran outside.

Like an offering from heaven, Hans's Mercedes sat in the glow of the porch lamps. The keys would be in it; they always were, so the servants could drive it to the garage. Praying that Hans hadn't changed his pattern, I ran down the steps toward the car, ignoring the hubbub of voices behind me. I reached the driver's door and yanked it open.

"Alice! Wait!" Hans's voice boomed across the portico, full of hurt and confusion, the voice of a man betrayed. I looked back, knowing I shouldn't, and our eyes met.

"I'm sorry," I cried, but the words came out in a strangled whisper. He couldn't have heard me.

He started down the steps, the servants trailing behind him. Knowing nothing else to do, I jumped into the car and threw the camera on the seat beside me. Fumbling in the dark for the ignition, I felt Hans's keychain with the heavy gold medallion, and turned the key. The engine started up without a pause. I floored the ac-celerator and, in a spray of gravel, the car careened away from the house, its back end slipping like a fat man on ice. Going faster than I'd ever driven, I was through the open gates at the end of the driveway in a flash, then on the highway that led to Geneva.

Almost numb with shock, I hardly knew what I was doing as the silver coupe shot into the night, its headlights stabbing the blackness of the narrow mountain road. On my right, the mountain rose in a sheer rock face; on the left, the roadside dropped into a still abyss. I remembered Panama and shuddered. I'd been lucky there.

I knew this road, knew there was no margin for error. The narrow shoulders made me squeamish in broad daylight, and I knew I would need wings to survive if I let the car stray. Curve after curve

230

leaped at me from the darkness. The tires shrieked their protest as I whipped the wheel left, then right, leaning my body into each turn as if that would help the car hold the road.

"Goddammit!" The sound of my own voice nearly caused me to miss a curve. "Everything's gone wrong! I'm a *tennis player*, not a spy."

The handgun under my jacket nudged against my ribs. I jerked it out when I was on a straightaway, threw it on the seat beside the camera, and convulsively gripped the steering wheel. A gun, a camera, and a stolen car. I was definitely a spy—not a good one, but a spy nevertheless. And a liar.

The tears started then. I wiped them away as best I could, lest they blur my vision. I flashed on Hans standing in front of his picture-book château, the bewilderment on his face.

"Hans, I'm sorry. I'm so sorry," I whispered into the darkness. "I love you so much. We could have been so happy."

I should have left war to the warriors.

A pinpoint of light flickered in the rearview mirror, interrupting my thoughts. I raced through a short straightaway, perspiring even more as my fear redoubled. After another long, sweeping turn, the lights in the mirror disappeared. A moment later, they were there again, and gaining on me.

I wanted to believe it was a coincidence that there was another car on the road at that hour, but I knew better. Its driver, like me, had to have a damn good reason for tearing full tilt through the dark Swiss mountains. Was it Hans? The Russians? I prayed that it was the army, or the police, or the goddamn Marines, anybody who meant me no harm. Please let it be one of the good guys!

Time had slowed to a crawl, in sharp contrast to the passing blur of trees and landmarks outside. At last, a sign reflected the beam of the headlights: GENEVA 10K. Six miles. Maybe I could make it, but what should I do when I got there? Suppose I got to the shop on La Grand Rue and Regenbogen wasn't there? If he was, would he be quick enough to save me?

I had my gun. I would use it if I had to . . . unless it was Hans following me. Dear God, don't let it be Hans. I pushed the thought from my mind and tried to concentrate on my driving. It would be a miracle if I didn't die at my own hands.

I threw the car through turn after turn, one foot on the gas, the other on the brake. When the road straightened. I floored the gas, feeling the powerful surge of the engine. But nothing slowed the advance of my pursuer, and I could feel the perspiration on my forehead, and between my shoulder blades. I shivered, fighting off the terror. Giving in to panic would only send me over the edge to certain death. Better the devil I *didn't* know than the one I did.

The mirrored headlights were blinding now and I squinted to see the road ahead. The car behind me closed the gap, then moved over into the other lane. My heart pounded faster. What did its driver intend to do? Shoot me? Edge me over the side of the mountain? I steeled myself against whatever was to come and drove as fast as I dared. The other car came alongside, and we rocketed in deadly tandem through another turn.

Like a cornered animal facing its executioner, I risked a glance—and almost fainted with relief when I saw the man in the car alongside. Al Jones, my army contact, was gesturing to me, telling me to pull over. I took my trembling foot off the accelerator, leaned back in the seat, and let the Mercedes drift to the side of the road. Involuntarily, I glanced at the rearview mirror. There was another car approaching in the distance. I stiffened, then relaxed. I was no longer alone. Jones would take care of me now.

Opening the car door, I flew into his arms. "Al, thank God it's you. I was frightened to death. I have the film!" I waved the camera at him.

"Wonderful," he answered with a tight-lipped smile.

"Let's get to Geneva! Hans or the Russians or God knows who is following us. We can leave Hans's car; he'll find it."

"There's been a change in plans," Jones said, taking my arm. "Let me have the film *now!*"

Something in his voice made me grip the small camera tighter. "No. When we get to Geneva, as planned."

"Stop wasting time on that bitch," a guttural voice shouted from the driver's seat of Jones's car. "Get the film! Someone's coming!"

I looked at Jones's face, stunned. A double agent. The reality was just sinking in when he tried to tear the camera from my hands. He was a big man and on the edge of panic, but it wasn't easy to break my grip. We struggled, and the camera slipped between us and fell to the gravel. Frantically, Jones reached in his jacket and jerked out a handgun, its barrel gleaming in the lights of the oncoming car.

"C'mon, fool! Kill her! Hurry!" his partner screamed, throwing the car into gear.

I reached for my gun, but the holster was empty. I'd forgotten: I'd taken it out while I was driving. I stared at the weapon trained on me; the opening in the barrel was like a cannon, like the eye of death. If I tried to jump him, he would pull the trigger. Jones stooped

232

to grab the camera and, obeying my animal instincts, I turned and ran like hell.

The hairs rose on my neck as I sprinted, expecting a bullet in my back. My adrenaline surged and the sounds behind me became remarkably clear—the squeal of the car's brakes on the road surface, doors flung open, shouts, and gunfire. Then it came—the white-hot pain of a bullet finding its mark.

My vision blurred, and the ground rose up to meet me.

I opened my eyes to a familiar, yet unfamiliar sight. White walls, white sheets, white metal bedframe: another hospital room, but where? What'd happened this time?

It started coming back, a kaleidoscope of gold bars with swastikas, Hans's face, the white line of the road, Jones. . . .

"Welcome back."

I jumped at the sound, wincing in pain when I turned my head. Most of my upper body seemed to be bandaged, and it hurt like hell when I moved.

"Colonel Linden! What are you doing here?"

"I came to rescue you, but I was a bit late."

"What happened? I remember running. Was I shot?"

"Yes, in the back. But you're going to be all right. You'll be a little stiff for a while, but the doctors say you'll recover completely."

I tried to sit up, flinched, and decided against moving again. "Did you catch Jones? He was a double agent, wasn't he?"

"He was working for the Russians, and yes, we got him. I couldn't tell you in advance, but we had men watching the roads from the château, in case you made it that far. They followed you, and killed Jones and his partner, but not before Jones fired at you." Linden shook his head. "I've gone over it in my mind a hundred times. I worked with the man for over two years, and never suspected, not until last week.

"He kept saying you were taking too long, and finally insisted on coming over, so I let him. After he left, I began to worry that he would push you into something you weren't ready for. Something didn't smell right, so I came to Geneva on the next plane, prepared to scrap the mission and pull you out, if I had to."

"I'm glad you didn't. I love Hans, but he *is* hoarding the Nazi treasure, and I would have hated myself if I hadn't done something about it."

Linden looked away, and the lines in his face seemed deeper, as if he had suddenly grown very tired. "Alice, I wish I could tell you that your mission was successful, but I can't."

"What do you mean?" I sat up, feeling dizzy with pain. "I took photos. Didn't you get the camera?"

"The last thing Jones did before he died was open the camera and expose the film. I suppose he hated us. If the Russians couldn't have the information, he didn't want us to have it. As long as we don't know for sure what Hans is holding, they still have a chance. Not much of one, but still. . . ." His voice trailed off.

I sank back on my pillows and closed my eyes. Linden was quiet.

"Colonel, I think I can still help you."

"You've done enough. You're a hero for risking your life, and should get a Purple Heart like any soldier wounded in battle, but it doesn't work that way in our business. You won't ever be able to talk about it. I'm just sorry you got hurt."

"I can help you with the records."

Linden looked blank.

"I had to look at all the pages I photographed. When I close my eyes, I can see them. I think I can give you a lot of the information."

"What?" Linden looked incredulous.

"Remember? My memory?"

"I'll get a stenographer in here!"

35 : MISSION ACCOMPLISHED

I was able to recall a great deal of what I had seen in the basement vault of Hans's château. When I closed my eyes, I could see name after name listed in the ledger I had photographed; before I left the hospital those names were on paper. One of Colonel Linden's operatives sat by my bed taking notes until I had exhausted my memory.

The colonel came to visit me, a typed transcript in hand. He asked me several questions, jotting notes in the margins as I spoke, then closed the folder and looked at me.

"You've done an amazing piece of work, Alice. The war will end any day now, and many of the Nazis will not get away. We know who they are, thanks to the work of people like you. They'll be tried as war criminals and put out of circulation for a long, long time."

"What about Hans?" I asked. "What will happen to him?"

Linden hesitated. "Probably nothing. Confronted with this," he hefted the folder, "he'll probably be willing to cooperate and turn over the holdings in his vault. But of course, our records are incomplete and he is a clever man. I'm sure he devised a way to protect himself when he knew what you had done. He's wealthy already, and after this, he will only be wealthier. '

My relief must have shown. "You really care for him, don't you?" Linden said, his expression softening.

I nodded, wanting to cry. "This has been one of the hardest things I've ever done. He offered me a wonderful life, a family, and the kind of love . . ."

"I'm sorry," Linden said. "I know you're hurting now, but you did the right thing. You know that, don't you?"

"Yes."

"You'll be safe from retaliation once we get you back to the States," Linden went on. "The Nazis have enough to keep them busy. Still, be cautious; don't go anyplace alone, and be wary of strangers. And remember, don't discuss anything that has happened with anyone. This is a matter of national security, Alice. Revealing anything about your mission is against the law."

"I understand. Do I report in when I get back?"

"No, your mission is over. Forget it ever happened." We smiled at each other, the irony of his words all too obvious.

"I'm flying to Washington today and won't see you again, Alice, but thank you. Your country is grateful too, and one day, I hope, will be able to show you properly."

During this hospital stay, there were no flowers, cards, or visitors, because no one knew I was there. Linden had made all the arrangements. The hospital was on an army base, and the doctors and nurses who cared for me were under strict orders to keep quiet. The Swiss tennis people were told that I had to leave unexpectedly because of an emergency at home, and Teach got a wire saying my return was delayed because I was having an inflamed cyst removed from my back.

I slipped quietly into New York on an army transport on May seventh, my arrival overshadowed by another celebration: The war in Europe was over.

On November twentieth, the International Military Tribunal convened at Nuremberg, to continue for almost a year. More than two hundred Germans stood trial for everything from the concentration-camp atrocities to stealing Germany's wealth. Among the names of the accused were some I recognized from Hans's ledger. By helping to bring them to justice, I had, in a small way, avenged Joe's death.

Also at the end of the war came the discovery of the Kaiseroda salt mine near Eisenbach, Germany, where billions in money, art, and valuables taken from concentration-camp victims had been stored by the Nazis. The news made me wonder if the treasures in Hans's safe were ever recovered. I'll never know, just as I'll never know what happened to Hans.

Forget everything, Colonel Linden had told me. How I wished I could. I went home to New York, to Teach and Brownie, with a healing bullet hole in my back, and a deeper wound in my heart. I badly wanted to tell Brownie about Hans, to draw some comfort from her, but instead I talked about tennis and the sights of Geneva.

"Either your trip was very dull, or you're leaving something

236

out," she said when I parried her questions, "and I think it's the latter. I don't believe you spent all that time away from Teach, and acted like a saint!"

Will du Pont gave me a new black Buick on September twenty-eighth, my thirty-second birthday, asked me to marry him, and accepted my refusal in his usual phlegmatic way.

"What will you do now?" he asked, "go on another pro tour?"

"Not right away." I wouldn't be fit for strenuous tennis for several months, yet I needed to make money.

Will had invested the money from my first pro tour, and had put a hundred thousand dollars in a joint account for Teach and me, but I didn't want to touch it. I arranged a forty-stop lecture tour, which assured me of income, but I had a bigger problem—Teach.

When Brownie returned to Ohio, Teach became a tyrant, trying to run my life as she had always done, but I was no longer a willing, malleable Eliza Doolittle. Too much had happened. I knew I owed Teach a debt of gratitude, but I reasoned that part of that debt had been repaid. During my career, Teach had become as famous as I was, and her status as a teacher was secure now, with or without me. It was time for her to leave me and find another champion.

But it wasn't that simple. Teach had become as dependent on me as I was on her. The woman to whom affection meant a pat on the head rather than a kiss finally realized that she loved me, and her desire to hold onto me ultimately destroyed our relationship.

When she was drinking—and she was doing more of that—Teach humiliated me in front of my friends, only to brush such incidents off the next day, without apology, as "yesterday's news." She became increasingly jealous, wildly accusing me of affairs with anyone who came close, man or woman. When I refused to yield to her domination, she threatened to kill me or to kill herself. I dreaded going home to the hotel suite we shared, knowing she would hear my key in the lock and be half out of the eleventh-story window when I opened the door. This became an insidious game. I would beg her not to jump, and under those circumstances she would extract promises from me that she knew I didn't intend to keep.

Finally, in exasperation, I said, "Teach, give it up. If we had been lovers, it would be easier to understand, but . . ."

"I was always young enough to be with you, wasn't I?" She glared at me.

"You're still young! Age has nothing to do with it."

"Then why do you need these other people?"

"Because I *need* other people! I've lived my whole life in one dimension, the tennis court, and it's not enough anymore. I'm a person, not a trophy for you to show off. You have to give me some freedom!"

We were talking, trying to work things out, and I was hopeful of a compromise until I came home one day and found my car gone. Teach had left in it with some suitcases, the doorman said. Before I had time to react, Will du Pont called.

"Teach is at the bank trying to withdraw all the money in your joint account. The bank called me for approval."

"She's got my car, too," I said. "Half the money's hers, Will. You know how much Teach did for me. Let her have it."

"She's a thief!" Will was hurt; he cared for Teach, too.

"Don't say that! She's just upset. Give her the money." Will released ten thousand dollars. Two days later, Teach returned to the hotel where we lived.

"Nice weekend?" I asked, trying to be calm.

"Very nice, thank you," Teach said.

In moments we were arguing again.

"I can't live this way," I said. "I'll move out."

"You don't have to," she snapped back. "I'm going back to California. I came to get the rest of my clothes and the money I have coming."

I had wanted my freedom, but now that it was to be a reality, I was stunned. I didn't want it to end this way, after all we'd shared.

"Teach, I'll miss you." I put my arms out to hug her, and she shoved me so hard I fell back on the couch. I was still there when she went to the bedroom and started packing.

Pauline, the maid, came through the door at that moment and stood, assessing the situation.

"Miss Marble, I want you to go down to the deli, get one of those big sandwiches you like, and sit in the park and eat it. Don't come back for a couple of hours."

Numbly, I did as she said, though I hadn't the slightest interest in food.

I found a shady bench in Central Park and sat watching children playing jacks.

"Alice! What a surprise!"

I looked up to see Marlene Dietrich pushing a baby buggy. "I'm showing off my grandchild!" She gestured to the baby inside, and dropped on the bench beside me.

I handed her half my sandwich. "Do you remember the time that soldier said my legs were better than yours?" I asked.

238

"Yes! And we both stood on chairs and pulled up our skirts so that everyone could judge for themselves."

We laughed, and I momentarily forgot my misery as we chatted about our experiences on tour.

When the baby started to cry, Marlene left. and once more my thoughts reeled back to Teach. It was over. We had been together all my adult life, and now she was gone. I couldn't imagine being without her.

Almost three hours later, I walked back to the hotel, heavy-hearted. I opened the door with my key, and stood dumbfounded. At first I thought I was in the wrong suite; then I realized that the furniture had been rearranged, and there was a new couch in the sitting room. Pauline came out of the bedroom looking smug. Everything in there had been changed too.

"You did all this?"

"With a little help." No one in the hotel said no to Pauline, and I could imagine the activity that had gone on while I was in the park.

She smiled, and patted my back when I put my arms around her and sobbed. The effect was as she intended, though. The familiar setting Teach and I had shared was gone. Nothing would keep me from missing her, but it would be easier for me to start over in fresh surroundings.

Starting over—again.

EPILOGUE

I threw myself into lecturing, tennis, and night classes at NYU and Columbia, studying anything that interested me. In the absence of a pro tour, I played mostly exhibition matches. There was no word from Teach in California, and people stopped asking me about her.

My circle of friends grew, and I became involved with a handsome, moody artist who liked to paint Christ with his head on crooked. Frederick Puma was dark like Hans, and a wonderful lover. He used to dance for me wearing his top hat and carrying a cane, but with no pants on. Delightful as it was to have the attention of a man, he was a brooding, selfish soul, and rude to all my friends. I broke off our affair before the year was out. Soon after, Puma left for Europe. His modern art had been poorly regarded in the States, but he found a kindred spirit in Matisse, and became quite famous on the Continent. He was still a young man when I got word that he had died of leukemia.

Through mutual friends, I met Rod Serling, writer of the television series *The Twilight Zone*. He was married, but we were drawn to each other, and began an affair that lasted for years, until his show moved to Hollywood. Ulcers made him perpetually grim-faced, and like Puma, Rod would sometimes sit all evening at a party and not say a word. Yet he loved the theater with a passion, and the crew on his show thought highly of him. So did I. He had a marvelous mind, and we got along well. I often typed his scripts for him, and if I changed one comma he would notice, and tell me he didn't need an editor.

The one man who remained a constant in my life was Will du Pont, who valued loyalty and friendship over all the money in the

240

world. Every week, we played tennis, attended the theater, and went out to dinner.

One evening I was entertaining some friends at my apartment when a huge crate arrived from San Francisco. The shipping label had Will's name on it, but I was mystified.

The building custodian goodnaturedly came with his tools and pried the crate open. Inside was the portrait of me painted by Dorothy Bijachai in London in 1938. A lifetime ago. I stared at the painting, oblivious to the comments of my guests. my gaze lingering on the Teach Tennant signature racquet, then moving to the face in the portrait. That girl was a stranger to me now, an eager young player with all the world before her. So much had happened. . . .

It was a wonderful gesture, and I called Will immediately to thank him. He'd heard the painting was in a San Francisco museum, he said, and just had to buy it for me.

In 1947, Will came to see me with Billy Tallent, a former doubles player who became the head of the USLTA and the Tennis Hall of Fame. I had been in bed with the flu for weeks, but I could tell this was not just a call on a sick friend. Will was nervous, and as usual got right to the point. He was thinking of asking Margaret Osborne to marry him, and asked my opinion.

His question surprised me. Will and Margaret? She was twenty years younger than Will, who was now forty-seven, but she liked all the things he liked. She rode horses and played pool, and had the easygoing temperament it would take to live with Will's idiosyncrasies. At last Will would have a tennis player for a wife, a top player whose career was in full swing. I told him I thought Margaret would make him a wonderful wife.

Margaret did marry Will. The four-hundred-acre Bellevue Hall in Wilmington became her home, and even more of a haven for tennis players. Every Sunday, players from Philadelphia came to the estate to play on Will's courts, which were the finest around. The only thing he asked in return was that the group walk his mile-long exercise track, throwing out rocks that might hurt his horses' hooves.

Bellevue Hall also became a second home to Louise Brough, to whom Margaret had been linked since 1941. When Margaret's doubles partner, Sarah Palfrey, became pregnant, she had, at Will's suggestion, taken nineteen-year-old Louise as a partner. The combo was magic, and the two were inseparable for the rest of their careers. "Ozzie" and "Broughie" won twenty of twenty-four Grand Slam (Australian, French, United States, and Wimbledon Championships) finals, losing no more than eight matches in their time together.

I was happy to see Will with Margaret, though I knew the marriage was sometimes trying for her. Will was the master of his household. That meant that he and his wife never stayed to celebrate after tournaments, catching the train home to Wilmington instead, so Will would be there for business the next day. It also meant that, rather than playing in the Australian Open, Margaret went to California with Will in the winter, when the Delaware dampness and cold aggravated his respiratory problems. And she became pregnant in the middle of her tennis career. But Margaret had lived as so many of us on the circuit did, never having a penny to our names. The life-style Will provided was worth some sacrifice.

Will went west for the dry warm air, but in New York I found no escape from frequent bouts with pneumonia. The right lobe of my lung became terribly infected, beyond treatment, the doctors said. I had two choices: the life of an invalid, which was no choice at all, or having the lung removed. There was a fifty–fifty chance of my surviving the surgery. I'd faced worse odds.

I went into the hospital for three days of injections before surgery, and found that crude penicillin was no less painful than the crude iron shots of my anemic days. My rear felt like a pincushion.

I awoke after the operation minus two ribs and one lobe of my lung, and with a twelve-inch scar under my right breast. I promised to sue my doctor if my bosom was lopsided, and he was thrilled at my show of spirit.

It was a shock to me when Walter Winchell announced on the radio that I was "at death's door" after the surgery. I quickly contacted my family to tell them it wasn't true, and had retractions printed, but the damage was done. A lecture tour I had scheduled was canceled, costing me a great deal of money.

Six weeks after surgery, my doctor told me to start playing tennis to stretch the muscles that had been sutured. I was dubious: The incisions were healing, but it was still hard to raise my arms.

Obediently, I called up Jack McDermott, who scheduled a match with Gladys Heldman, founder of the Virginia Slims tournaments and *World Tennis* magazine, and Elizabeth "Bunny" Ryan, who was older than Brownie (she won Wimbledon with Brownie in 1926) but still had the skills that had won her a dozen Wimbledon doubles championships through 1934.

It felt good to be in a locker room again, and I was looking forward to a friendly match when I overheard Bunny and Gladys. They knew I would have trouble handling overheads, and were planning to lob me out of the court.

242

I wanted to confront them, but I held my tongue. When they left, I joined Jack on the court, and told him what I had heard. As burned as I was, he assured me that he would handle the lobs.

I thought about something Bill Tilden used to say. "If you can walk onto the court like a champion, you *are* a champion." I also thought about winning Wimbledon with a torn stomach muscle. When I walked onto the court with Jack, my head was held high, and all my competitive juices were surging. We would beat these two broads, even if it killed me.

Jack took all the overheads, I used all the spins I could muster, and we badly defeated the two ex-champions, who looked properly downcast when they offered their congratulations.

"It's so marvelous to be back on the court," I said in my sweetest voice. "Thank you for the exercise."

I walked toward the locker room, fighting the urge to hold my side, and was glad that winning had never meant as much to me as it obviously did to our two opponents.

I healed quickly, and Jack and I played indoors all winter.

The tennis world was beginning to buzz with news of Teach's new protégée, Maureen "Little Mo" Connolly. When I heard that they were coming east, I got in touch with Teach. I wanted to see her, and hoped that her resentment had cooled. It hadn't.

After an embarrassing evening of hearing how much better Maureen was than I, it was with great curiosity that I went to see the new superstar play at Forest Hills. Maureen *was* good. I wish I'd had her ground strokes, but her serve was her greatest weakness, whereas it had been my strength. Maureen double-faulted constantly, and I could see Teach's frustration from where I sat in the row behind her. Nevertheless, she bragged on her pupil until the man beside her finally said, "Teach, she's some player for sixteen, but she can't hold a candle to Alice."

I thought Teach would hit him; she hadn't changed.

Soon I was traveling again. The surgery had ended my days of competitive tennis, but I gave clinics in schools and lectured to various groups on the will to win, the art of living, and other topics—seven speeches sharpened by my old friend Amy Scherer, Eleanor Roosevelt's speech coach.

At a high school someplace in Texas, I stumbled going up the steps, running my stockings. I began to speak, but I could sense that the students' eyes were on my stockings; several in the front row were counting the runs.

I finally stopped speaking, reached down, and pulled off both stockings.

"Now, do you feel better?" I laughed with them, and went on with my speech.

After I had done more than fifteen hundred lectures and clinics across the country, I realized I couldn't stand it anymore. Since before the war, I had been on the road for most of every year, a blur of one-night stands, driving three hundred miles a day and forgetting what town I was in. I couldn't face too many more suitcases. In 1951, I packed once more, this time to return to California.

When Teach heard I was coming, she asked me to work with Maureen on her serve. I knew how difficult it was for Teach to come to me, so I agreed, willing to do anything to heal the wounds between us. I spent several weeks in La Jolla with Maureen, who was willful, cocky, and difficult to teach. I had a San Diego pitcher teach her how to throw a curveball, so she would have a slice, and then refined her serve. I was glad when the work was over, but satisfied when I saw the change in Maureen's game.

That year Maureen became, at sixteen, the youngest national champion, a record that stood for nearly forty years. The next year she won Wimbledon, and the next, the Grand Slam. Teach had her champion until 1954, when a riding accident ended Maureen's career. She died of cancer at thirty-four, leaving a husband and twin daughters.

As I had hoped, my work with Maureen mended the rift between my old coach and me. In 1952, we were asked to work on the movie *Pat and Mike*, with Katharine Hepburn as an athlete being promoted by Spencer Tracy. Teach was the tennis technical advisor, and Don Budge, Babe Zaharias, Gussie Moran, Frank Parker (one of America's top ten players at the time), and I had small roles as ourselves.

Teach coordinated the tennis scenes as she had done in several other movies, setting up a sequence with the camera showing one side of the net at a time. Budge would hit, I would volley, and then the camera was on Hepburn. Teach tossed her a ball at just the right spot for her smash. The only trouble was, the star had tennis elbow, and could hardly hold a paper cup of coffee between scenes. I saw the tears in her eyes every time she hit the ball, and admired her courage.

I had been in California a few months when I met with Joe Bixler, the head of Wilson Sporting Goods, at the Los Angeles Tennis Club. Joe was married to Ruby Bishop, who had defeated me in my first National Junior finals and had been my friend since I first started working for Wilson Sporting Goods. I told Joe I needed a change from tennis and asked his advice.

Joe pointed out that I'd been around doctors all my life; why didn't I go to work for one? He suggested Dr. Joan Bach, a gynecologist with whom I had played.

Dr. Bach was more than willing to hire me; after taking courses at Hollywood High School, I became his practical nurse and receptionist. At first I commuted from Los Angeles to his office in the San Fernando Valley, but when I realized how much I liked the job, I bought a small house in Tarzana, near work.

For eight years I worked for the doctor, content to play social tennis. Then Joe Bixler called me. There was a player he wanted me to see, a very promising youngster.

Liking what I saw in Darlene Hard, an aggressive, tomboyish player, I agreed to teach her. She went on to win twenty-two international titles, and was twice national champion, in 1960 and 1961.

Then Joe brought me another student, one he said was a replica of me. I shuddered at the thought!

I could tell Joe was excited about this one, despite all the players he had seen in his life; when I met her, I understood why. Billie Jean Moffitt (later King) was short, fat, and aggressive. At five feet seven inches I had weighed 150 pounds; Billie Jean weighed the same, but she was five three then.

I made her weigh in every day on the doctor's scale. She was fast, but I was worried about her stamina with the extra pounds, as Teach had been about mine.

Billie Jean was all serve-and-volley, with no ground strokes to speak of, but she loved tennis and at fifteen was remarkably earnest about improving her skills. She had "champion" written all over her. Her father, a fireman, had taken a second job to finance lessons, and I began working with her on weekdays from one to five and all day on Sunday.

I had been teaching Billie Jean for about eight months when I got pneumonia and pleurisy. When I called to tell her I was ill, she showed no concern for me, only for her missed lesson. I was bedridden and miserable, and stunned at her insensitivity. When her parents called to apologize for her, I told them to find a new coach.

Billie Jean's singleminded ambition took her to the pinnacle of the sport, where she became one of the most influential—and controversial—women players of all time.

At Wimbledon in 1984, I was sitting with the Duchess of Kent when Billie Jean came in from the broadcast booth when she was commentating. She curtsied to the duchess and hugged me.

"Do you know Alice?" the duchess asked.

"Know her? She taught me!"

It was the first acknowledgment I had ever gotten from Billie Jean, and it made me feel good.

After Billie Jean, teaching became as addictive as playing had once been, and I soon had twenty-four students. When the doctor told me to make a choice between my job or tennis, I made the predictable decision, and tennis became my life again.

I started teaching at the new Deauville Tennis Club in Tarzana, where I quickly had a following of two hundred students, then later at the Lake Encino Racquet Club, where in 1963 I set up the first Motion Picture Tournament in twenty-five years, with stars like Charlton Heston, Gilbert Roland, Robert Stack, and Efrem Zimbalist, Jr. Mary Pickford was my honorary chairman.

Nine-year-old Sally Ride, who would grow up to be an astronaut, came to me for lessons. For two weeks I stood at the net, tossing her balls to volley, and for two weeks she tried to hit me in the face. I told her parents to find another target. She went on to be a decent junior player, and I often thought how Teach would have loved the fight in her.

Teach and I were rivals for a few years, until arthritis and failed eyesight put an end to her teaching. We became friends again, and corresponded until she died in 1963. Her letters were written in a very bold hand, as if she was positive about everything. Come to think of it, she was.

Will du Pont bought land near Palm Desert, and began building an estate. Since he spent only three months a year in California, he asked me to take photos periodically so that he could see the progress of the building and planting. I agreed, making monthly trips to the ranch for three years and finding that I liked the desert. When I went east to be inducted into the Tennis Hall of Fame in 1964, I told Will I was going to move to Palm Desert Country Club. He insisted on building me a house on the ranch instead.

Margaret had just divorced Will to live with one of her doubles partners, Margaret Varner Bloss, who trained racehorses in El Paso, Texas. At sixty-four, Will was once more a lonely man. He was delighted when I agreed to move to the ranch with Brownie.

Brownie, in her seventies, spent most of her time playing golf and painting, both of which she did beautifully—and naturally. Back in 1924, two weeks after losing a close match to Helen Wills Moody in the semifinal round of the nationals (a match which earned her the number two ranking nationally), Brownie was runner-up in the women's national *golf* championship, beating Glenna Vare, then losing in the final. She never figured in national golf again, mostly because she didn't try, but she was a scratch golfer the rest of her life.

We moved into a guest house on the ranch, and watched as construction began on a beautiful little house for us with a pool, a studio for Brownie, and a tennis court. On December 29, 1965, we spent our first night in the new house. Will died of a brain tumor two days later.

I was devastated by Will's death, and shocked by what followed. His daughter, Jean, inherited the ranch and, still bearing her lifelong grudge against me, demanded that Brownie and I leave at once. Will's own attorney pleaded with me to contest her action, but I refused. How could I sue the estate of a man who had done so much for me?

Brownie and I lived together at the Palm Desert Country Club for two delightful years after we left the ranch. We competed ferociously on the golf course (we had the two lowest handicaps in the club), had pillow fights, and generally cavorted like two happy children.

Then Brownie moved to Santa Fe to paint portraits. One weekend in 1971, I was expecting her for golf and bridge when I got word that she had suffered a massive stroke. She died shortly after, and I felt more alone than I had for a long time. I had one more real link with my past, other than my family: Tica.

In 1981, I was diagnosed as having cancer of the colon. After three surgeries at the Eisenhower Medical Center in Palm Springs, I emerged dependent on a colostomy bag (the next year I had two operations which successfully resectioned my bowel) and on morphine. Despite my high threshold of pain, the doctors had kept me drugged most of the time I was in the hospital. As soon as I was home, I stopped taking the stuff, and suffered through an unpleasant withdrawal.

It was during that time that Tica called from New York. She had sensed something was wrong with me. After that, we talked every weekend, and she soon told me she was dying of throat cancer. One weekend she didn't call, and I couldn't get an answer at her number. On Monday, a package arrived from New York. In it was a cigarette case I'd had made for her with one of my championship medals inset in the top, and ten of her language books, inscribed to me. I'd lost her, too.

I found solace where I always have—in tennis—and I'd like to think I've put something back into the sport through the students I've taught and the players I've helped, like Althea Gibson when she ran up against a racial barrier. Despite the fact that she was recognized as a leading player, the national championship organizers at Forest Hills failed to invite her to play. After I wrote an open letter to the USLTA in *World Tennis* magazine, the barrier fell, and in 1951, she became the first Negro to play at Forest Hills. In 1957, she became the first black woman to win Wimbledon. She took the U.S. Open that year, and repeated the feat in both championships the following year before turning pro.

I'm seventy-seven now, still living at Palm Desert Country Club on a trust fund Will du Pont established for me in 1964; though I stopped teaching a few years ago, I still attend the major California matches, and the U.S. Open and Wimbledon as often as I can. I love the opportunity to compare notes with players like Graf, Navratilova, Garrison, and Sabatini—they're all good friends of mine, and kind enough to say that I would be a challenge to them if I were competitive today.

Their respect for my game is gratifying, but it makes me wonder how my contemporaries and I *would* fare if we were playing today. Players today *really* train. People ask me how I'd do against Martina Navratilova. She would have wiped me out, and that's not modesty. Just look at her. Not only is she stronger than I ever was, she's fitter. In my time, training didn't exist in any real sense. I thought I was doing great to run a little to build my wind.

Training also gives today's players more endurance. Look at the three-hour-and-forty-five-minute match Monica Seles and Gabriela Sabatini played in the Virginia Slims Championship final at Madison Square Garden in November 1990, the first time women have gone to five sets since 1901. They were hitting as hard at the end as they were in the beginning.

Coaching has made a world of difference. I was the first woman to travel with a full-time coach and, usually, a male practice partner. Some of today's players go way beyond that; they have support staffs—coaches, practice partners, sports psychologists, physical therapists and a groupie or two.

Don't forget modern equipment—all those oversized graphite racquets strung to perfection. They're light-years ahead of our old wooden Wilsons. The new racquets give today's player better control and more power, and lessen wear and tear on the hitting arm. There's less "touch" to the game than before. Compare the artful play of John McEnroe—he's the last of the breed—in the 1990 U.S. Open to the way Pete Sampras whacked the heck out of the ball in the final.

Court surfaces have improved (grass, of course, will always be a deceitful surface). Tennis footwear is now wonderfully correct, a far cry from when I wore woolen socks over my shoes to keep from slipping on grass.

The technological changes followed the biggest change of all. Tennis has become a money game, and I admit to mixed feelings about that, despite the fact that I turned professional at a time when public sentiment was against it. My first tour earned me about $100,000; today's players make that in one tournament. There's so much at stake, I wonder if it's still fun. It concerns me to see purses and endorsements becoming the measure of success, and young players aging faster than they should under financial pressure.

Splendid as it all seems, the high-tech gear and the endorsements can't make a champion. That still comes from inside, just as it did in my day. Every player will still have strengths and weaknesses, good days and bad. The "unbeatables" will keep on getting beat.

About thirty years ago, I created a composite "perfect player" for one of the tennis magazines. Attempting the same thing now sparks a flood of memories—and comparisons:

Polish champion Jadwiga "JaJa" Jedrzejowska, who was killed in World War II, had a forehand like a rocket. With little else but that forehand she was twice runner-up at Wimbledon and once in the U.S. Open. Like JaJa, Steffi Graf can hit anything off the forehand; unlike JaJa, she can hit *anything*.

On the backhand, Pauline Betz and Chris Evert have my vote. I was awed by Helen Wills Moody's backhand until I played Betz. Her one-handed swing was deceptively quick and very smooth, like Evert's two-hander.

Bunny Ryan was a killer at the net—the best volleyer the game has ever known—until Navratilova came along. With both, the volley is an offensive move used with great finesse.

Navratilova takes second place in drop shots to the 1937 U.S. Open champion Anita Lizana, who had the most frustrating, beautifully disguised shot I've ever seen.

My smash was considered revolutionary in women's tennis, but Althea Gibson elevated the stroke to a new level with her combination of power and ease. Navratilova goes Gibson one step better in that her placement can be almost faultless.

I'm glad I don't have to face Graf's serve. She's the first woman I've seen who could ace them all. Moody had a wicked, wide-breaking slice serve that drew you so far out of the court you really had to scramble to make the next return. Louise Brough gets credit for perfecting the American Twist that I liked so much. A difficult serve, it went out of style but now seems to be in vogue again.

I only saw Suzanne Lenglen play twice, but she deserved the "Pavlova of the courts" accolade of the sportswriters for her footwork. Perhaps all players should spend some time training for the ballet, as she did. Evonne Goolagong Cawley was the second most graceful player I've seen. Navratilova, Graf, Evert, Sabatini, Seles —all of these modern players cover the court beautifully, and I'm sure fitness contributes greatly to their mastery.

Tennis is as mental as it is physical—that hasn't changed. I slumped in 1937 when I was ranked number one; Graf did the same in 1990. Concentration and fighting spirit are as vital as any of the strokes. Helen Jacobs, my longtime friend and opponent, had no strokes that one could hold up as an example to future generations, but she had something else—drive, guts, and the will to win. Was she willful! Despite her many injuries, she never gave up, and that determination earned her four U.S. Open titles and one Wimbledon championship. My onetime student Billie Jean King comes close in toughness and, in an entirely different way, so does Chris Evert.

I used to play with Evert's father, Jimmy, in Florida, and when I first met Chris, she said, "I was raised on you." She's been a wonderful champion, a credit to the sport, and a lady. She would have fit nicely into the tennis of Helen Moody's time, or mine, or probably anytime. She's a classic. My desire to see her show more passion finally was satisfied when she played her last Wimbledon, and at last we saw how deeply she cared about the game.

Martina Navratilova and I met at Wimbledon in 1978, when she was the new champion, shy and overweight, which reminded me of myself. We had lunch together and I realized what courage it had taken for her to defect to America. The next time she played in Palm Desert, Martina had a chair placed on the sideline for me, so I could watch her play closeup. Her love of tennis is always written all over her face and, seeing her weep after a win or loss, I've often cried with her.

When you've lived as long as I have, the sheer joy of having played the game comes to matter more than the victories, the records, the memories.

The memories. I'm grateful for the wonderful mosaic of memories—of tennis, of being famous, of serving my country, of loving and being loved. Every night, I end my prayers with one my mother taught me: "God bless and angels keep. . . ."

My prayer has been answered many, many times in my life.

INDEX

251